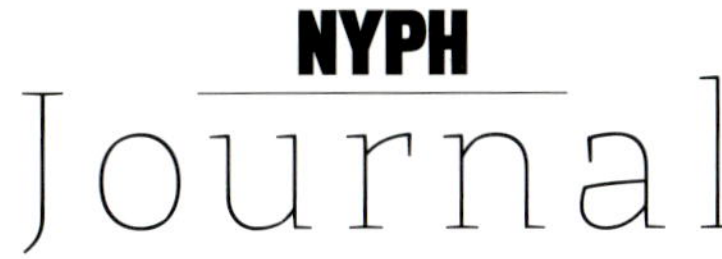

Welcome:

Welcome to the very first volume of *NYPH Journal*, a very select grouping of the best new photographic work being produced around the globe at this very moment, deemed so by our internationally renowned board of judges, selected from thousands of submissions to the 2012 edition of The New York Photo Awards. The photographic work herein showcases a phenomenal breadth of clarity and vision, and points to remarkable trends developing in this always-captivating artistic and journalistic medium. Congratulations to each photographer showcased in this volume; your achievement is celebrated permanently in this new publishing initiative. Look for subsequent volumes to continue this unfolding journey towards the future of contemporary photography.

Daniel Power
cofounder

Jacob Pastrovich
director

New York Photo Festival

The Future of Contemporary Photography

NYPH
Journal

Contents:

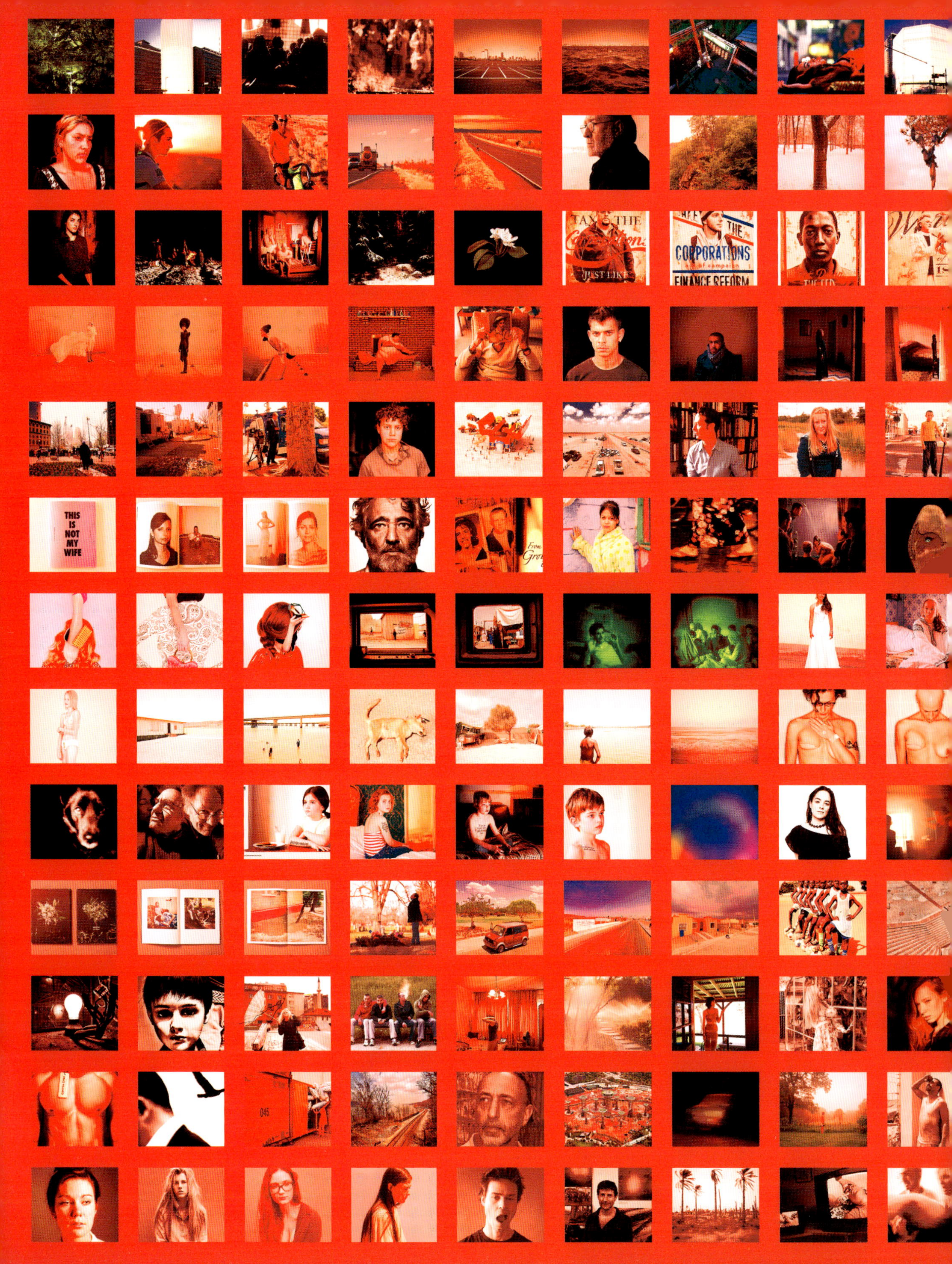
THIS IS NOT MY WIFE
CORPORATIONS
FINANCE REFORM
JUST LIKE

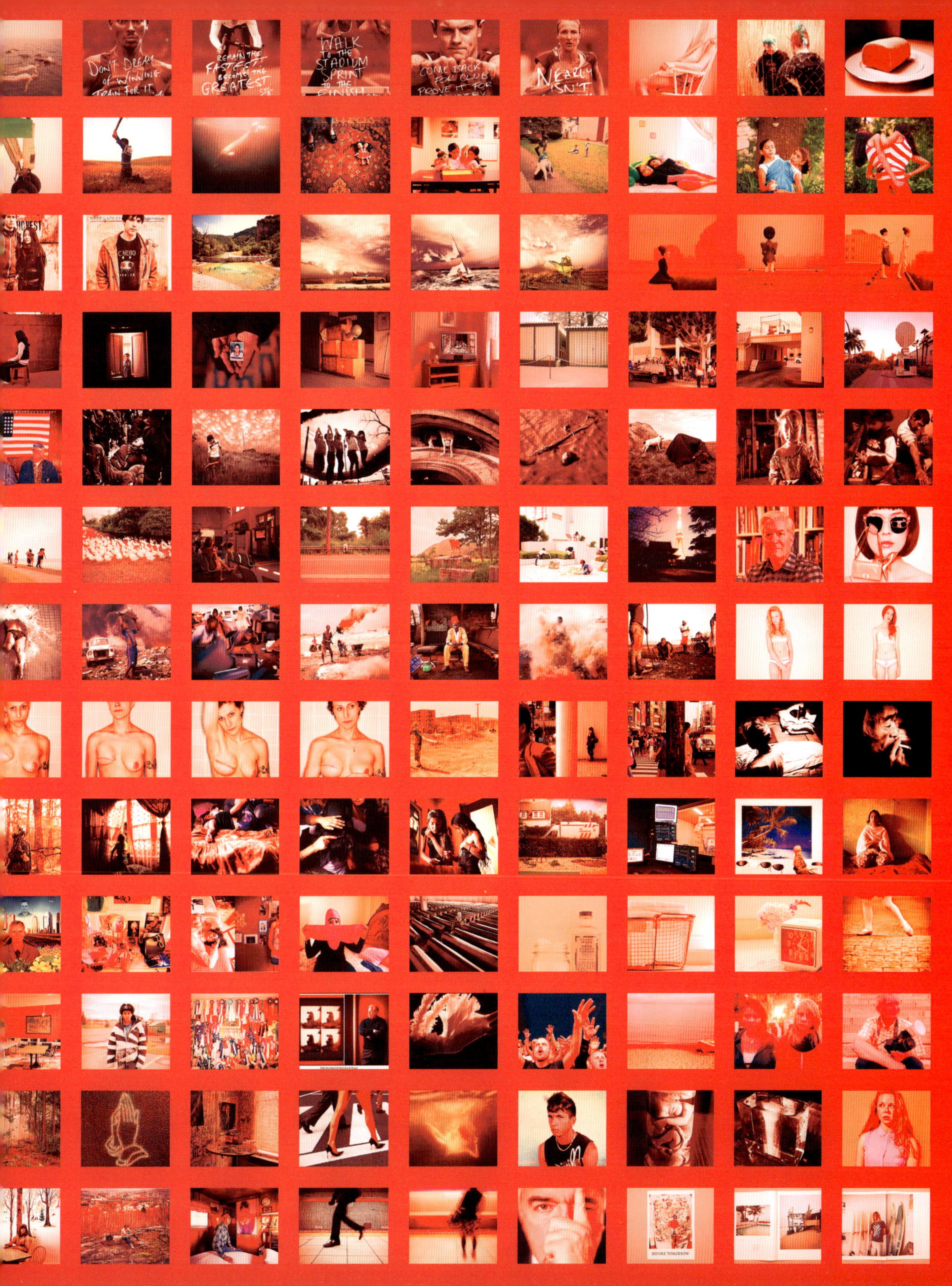

DON'T DREAM of WINNING TRAIN FOR IT.
REMAIN THE FASTEST. BECOME THE GREATEST.
WALK TO THE STADIUM SPRINT TO THE FINISH
COME BACK FOR CLUB. PROVE IT FOR
NEARLY ISN'T

Raul Krebs
Cintia Gym

WINNER
ADVERTISING

Raul Krebs is a Brazilian photographer with an eclectic body of images that represents a wide range of aesthetics. His awards in advertising photography include: Honorable Mention, The New York Photo Awards, 2010, Advertising Series; Nominee, Campaign Photo Awards, 2009, Health & Pharmaceutical; Nominee at Fundação Conrado Wessel Awards, 2005 and 2006, Brazilian Advertising Photography. Krebs' most recent solo exhibitions include: *Mask* (Urban Arts Gallery, Porto Alegre, Brazil, June 2013), *To Die For* (Canela Foto Festival, Brazil, April 2013), and *Traum* (Lunara Gallery, Porto Alegre/Brazil, May, 2012). As a fine art photographer, Krebs develops projects using various techniques, such as pinhole, polaroid, lomography, and digital photography to shoot portraits, street photography, and the human figure. Krebs also works at Alfaiate Filmes as a fashion film creator and director.

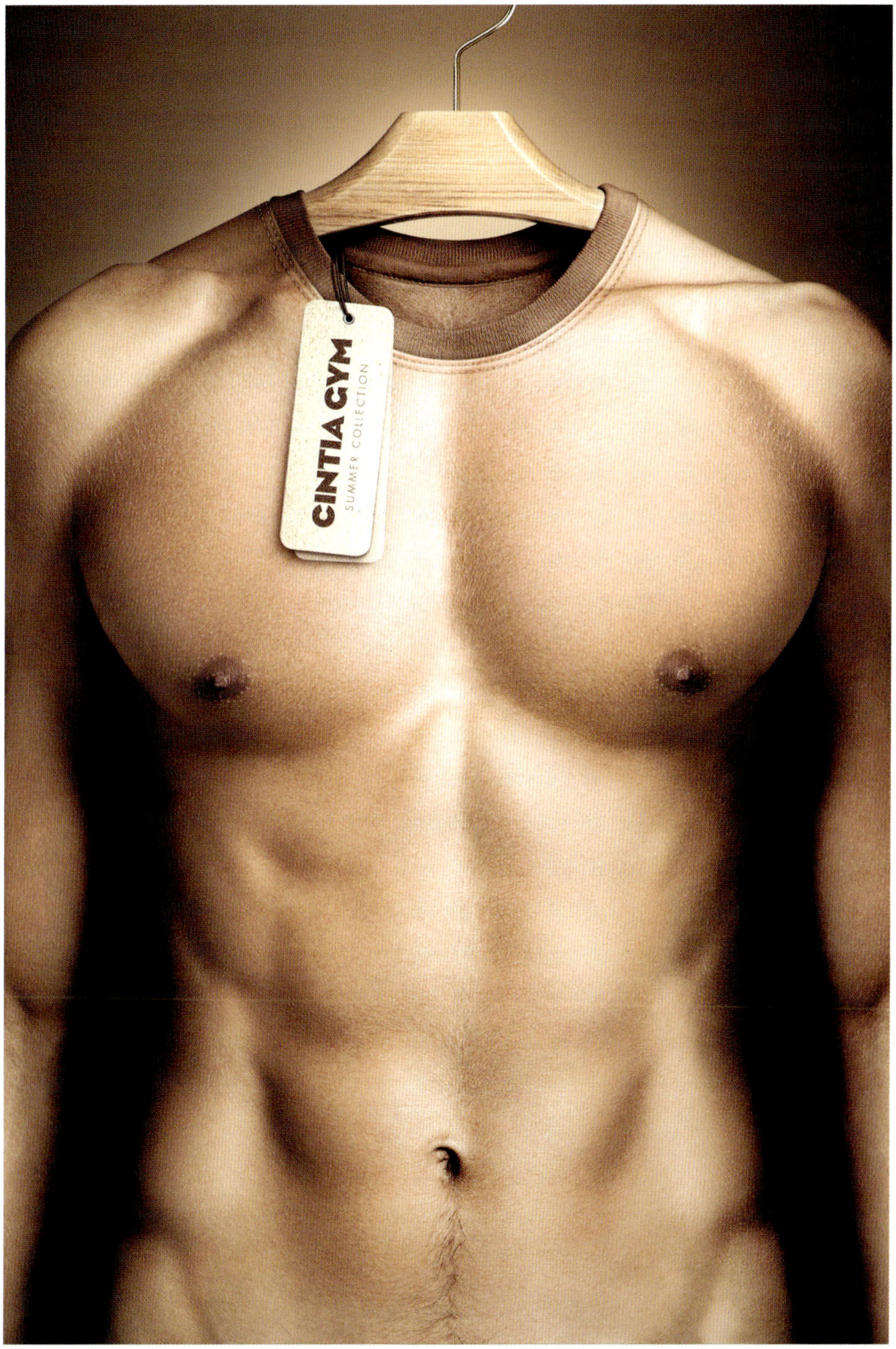

CINTIA GYM
SUMMER COLLECTION

1. Luca Sage
2. Claudio Meneghetti
3. Simon Harsent

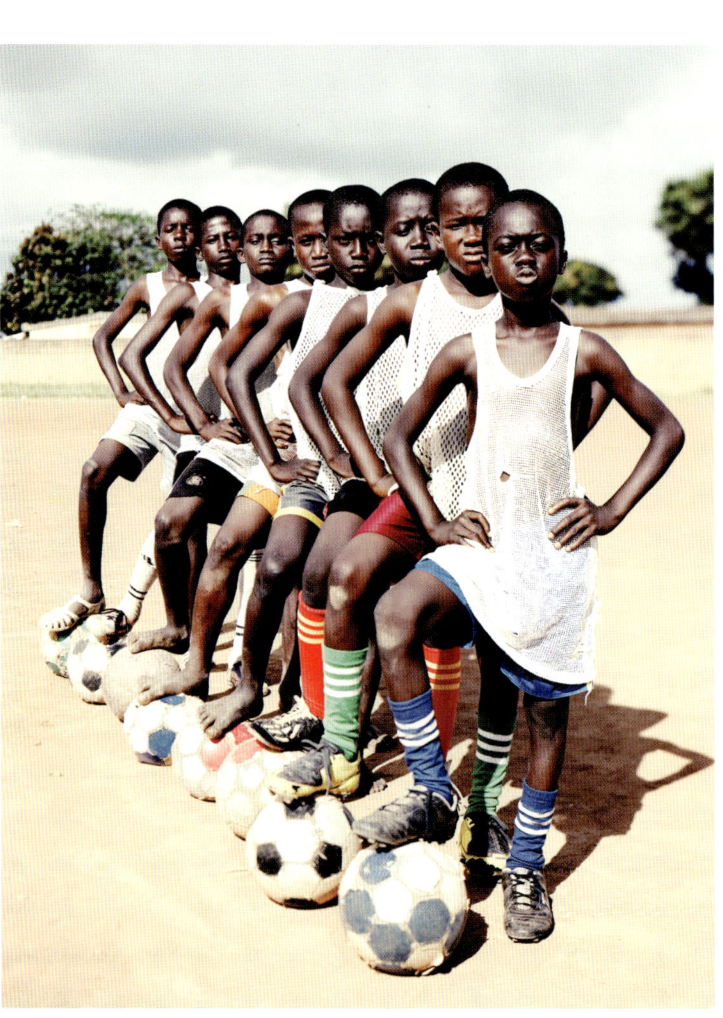

1

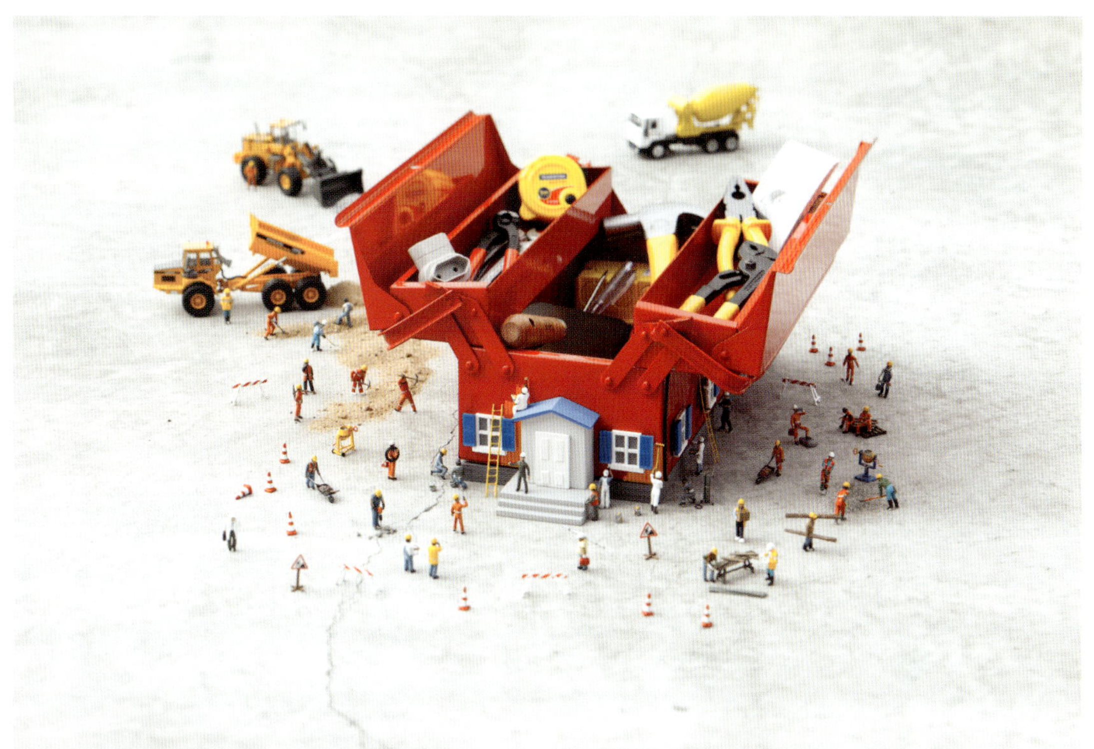

❷

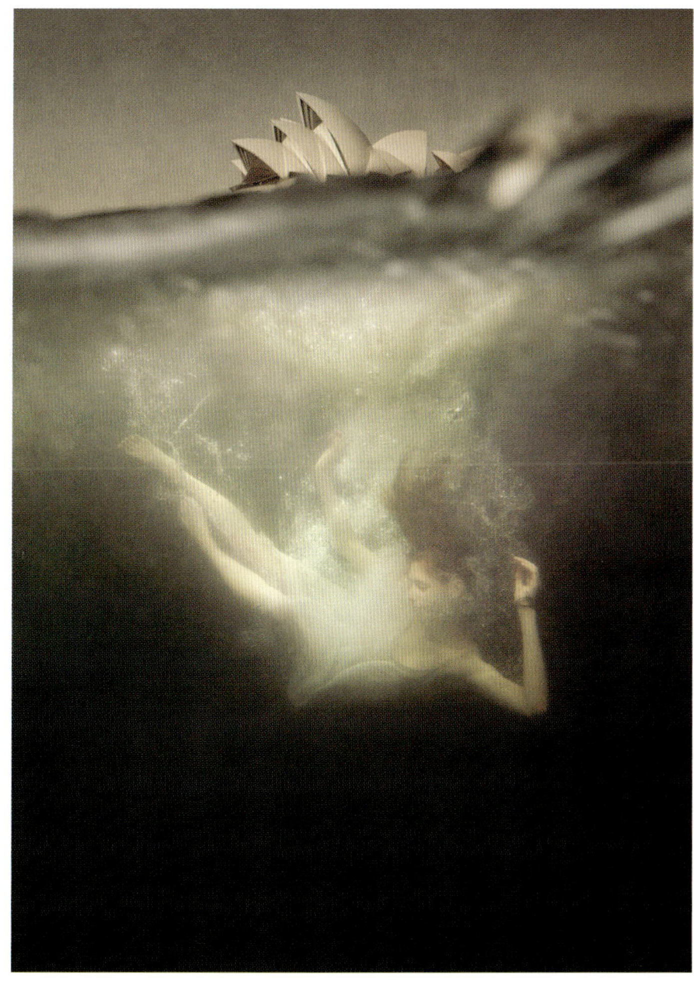

❸

Bénédicte Desrus
Globesity

Bénédicte Desrus is a documentary photographer from France. She is represented by Sipa Press and covers breaking news for Reuters. Her photography explores the lives of people ostracized by society, and the communities they form to survive and to find respect. Recent stories explored the lives of elderly sex workers living in a shelter in Mexico City and the persecution of homosexuals in Uganda.

Her work has appeared in *Harper's*, *Courrier International*, *Le Monde*, *Marie Claire*, *Internazionale*, *Neon*, and *The Sunday Times Magazine*, among others.

Desrus' awards and distinctions include the REVELA 2013. II International Photography Award for the Social Rights Holders, the Mexico Contemporary Photography Contest of the Mexican Foundation of Cinema and Arts, the NPPA Best of Photojournalism, the OPENPhoto of the Open Society Initiative of Southern Africa, the PDN Photo Annual, the Kuala Lumpur International Photoawards, the Pride Photo Award, the Humanity Photo Awards, and the Open Society Institute's Moving Walls 18, among others.

WINNER
DOCUMENTARY

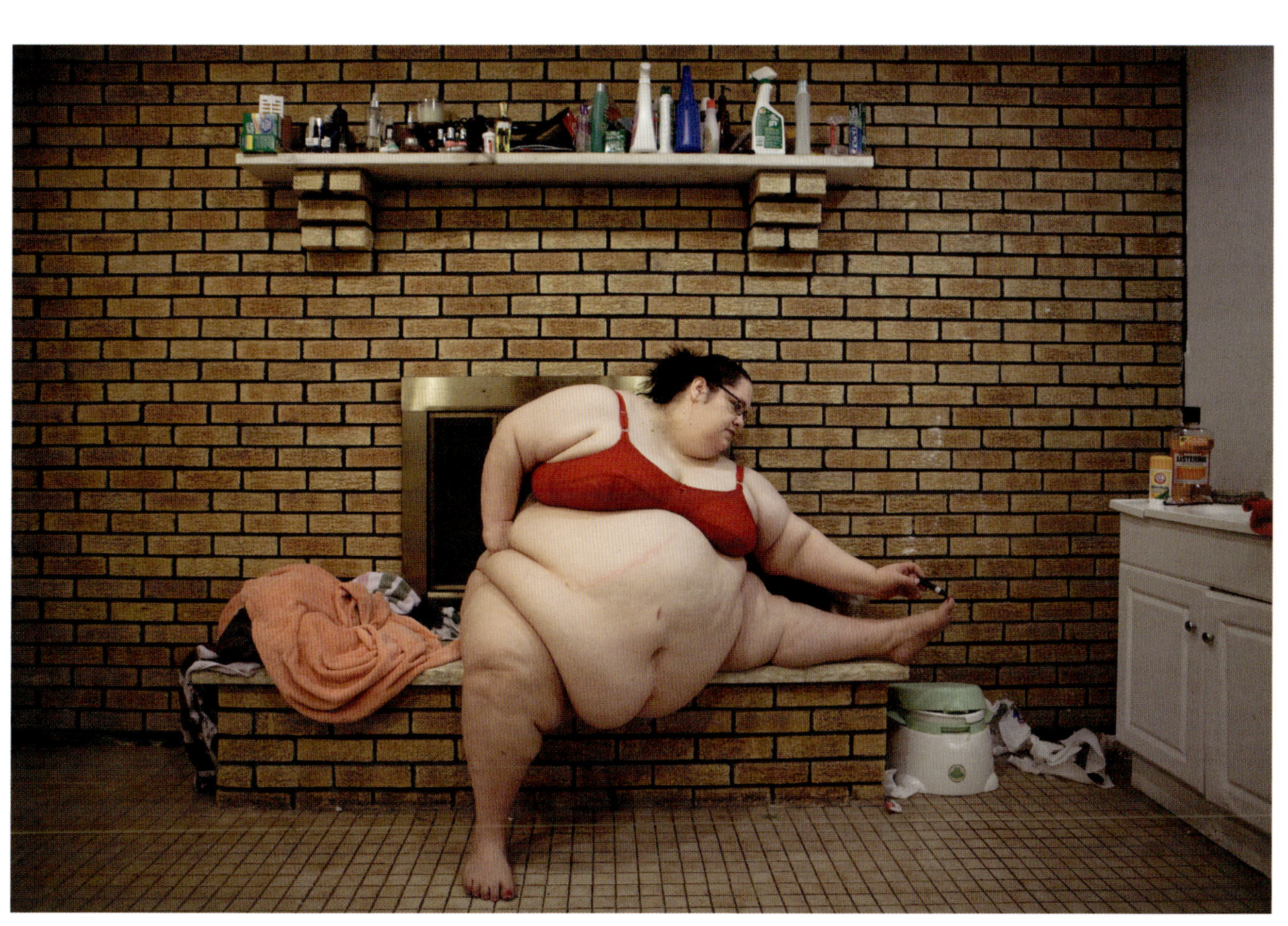

1. Jan Cága
2. Mattia Vacca
3. Yusuke Harada
4. Enrico Fabian

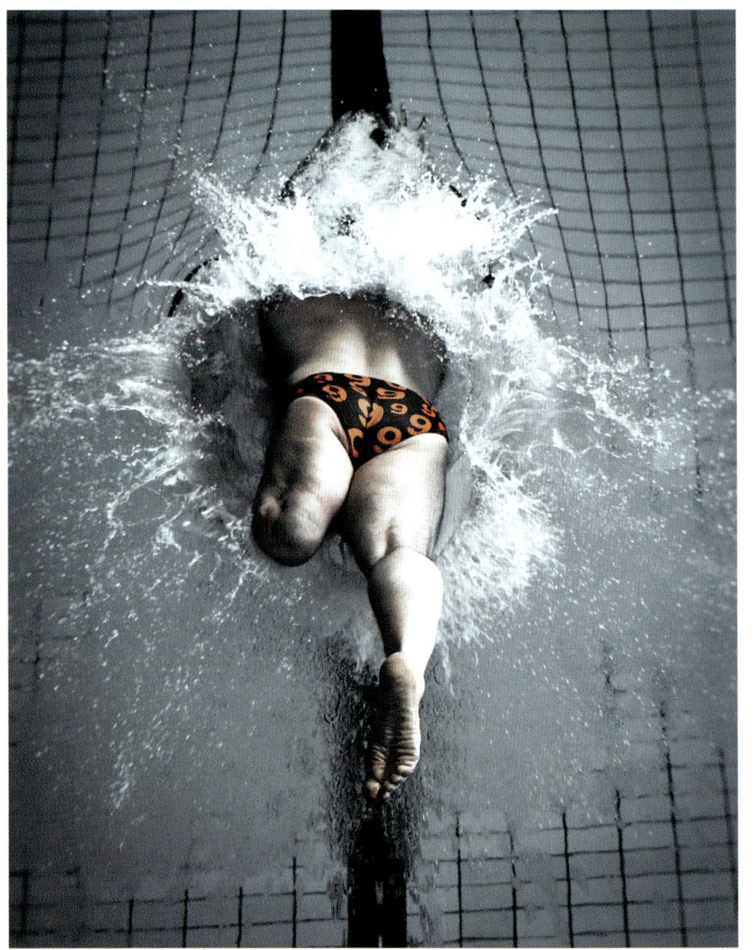

1

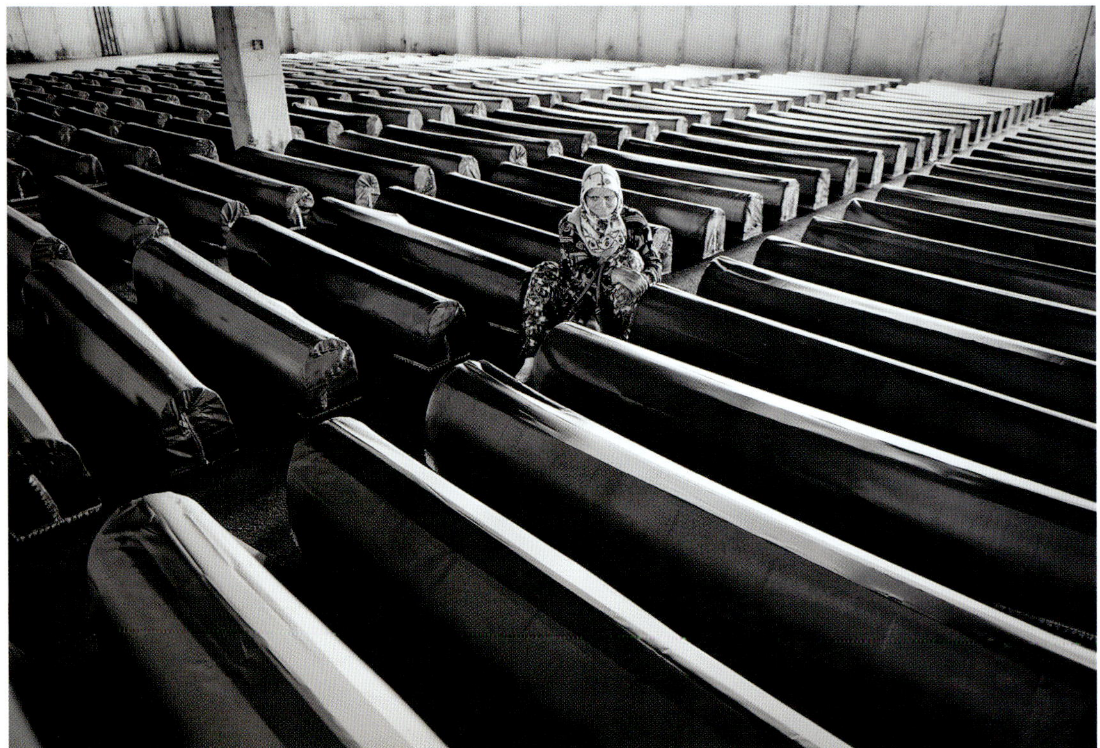

2

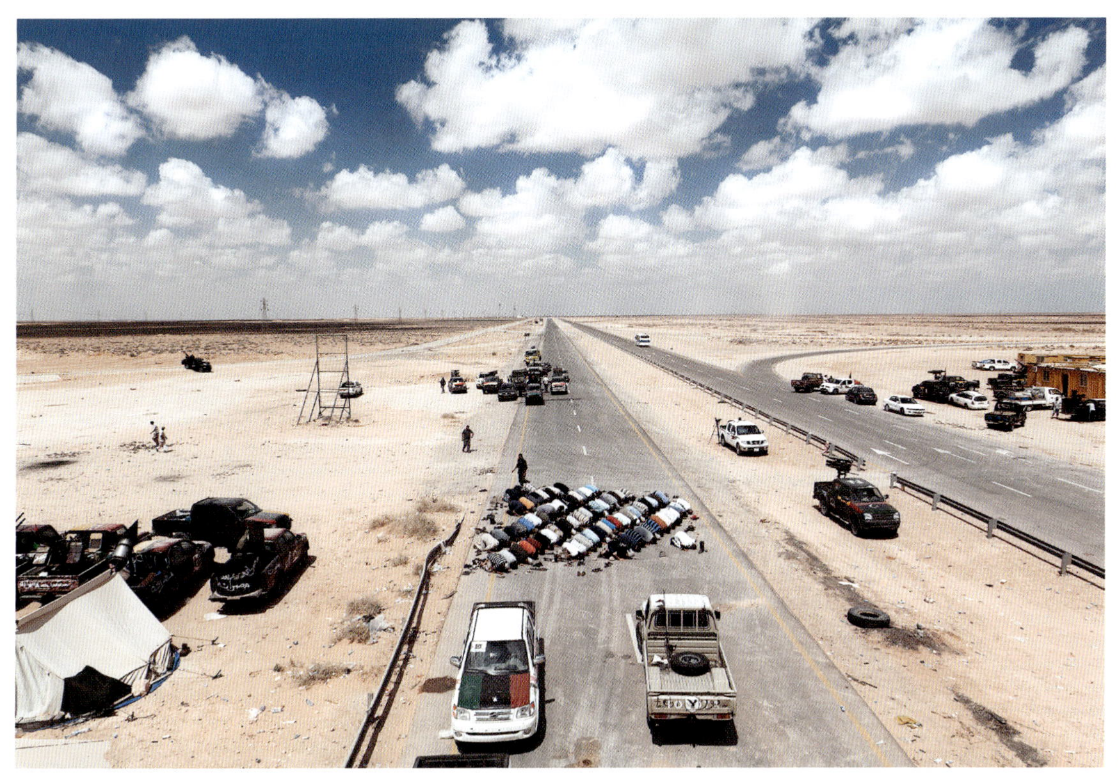

❸

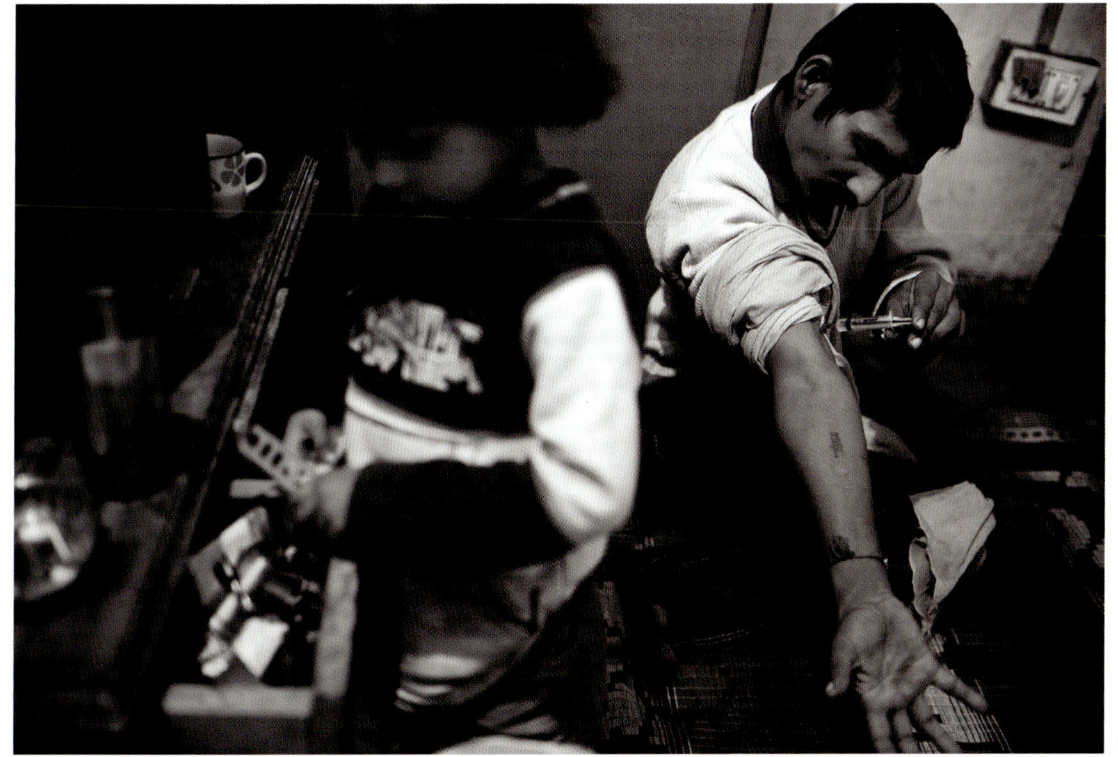

❹

Robert Rutoed
Right Time Right Place

WINNER
FINE ART

Robert Rutoed is an Austrian-based photographer and filmmaker. He has made numerous short feature films that have been screened worldwide. His photographic work has been exhibited throughout Europe, the United States, and Asia. His books include: *Less Is More* (2009), *grayscales. early b&w photographs* (2010), *Right Time Right Place* (2012), and *Milky Way* (2013).

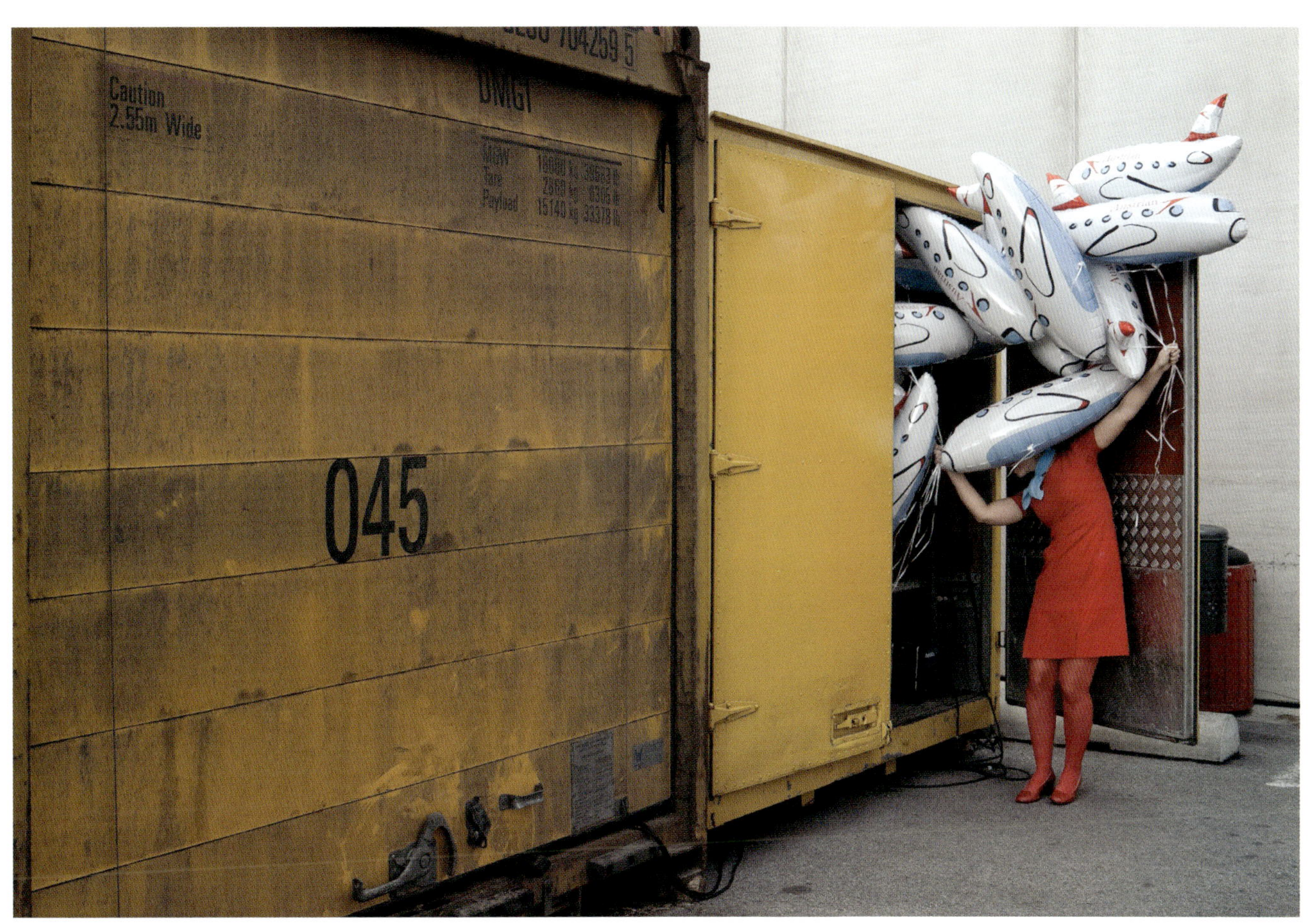
Caution
2.55m Wide
DMGT
045

1. Arnaud De Wolf
2. Marcus Laranjeira

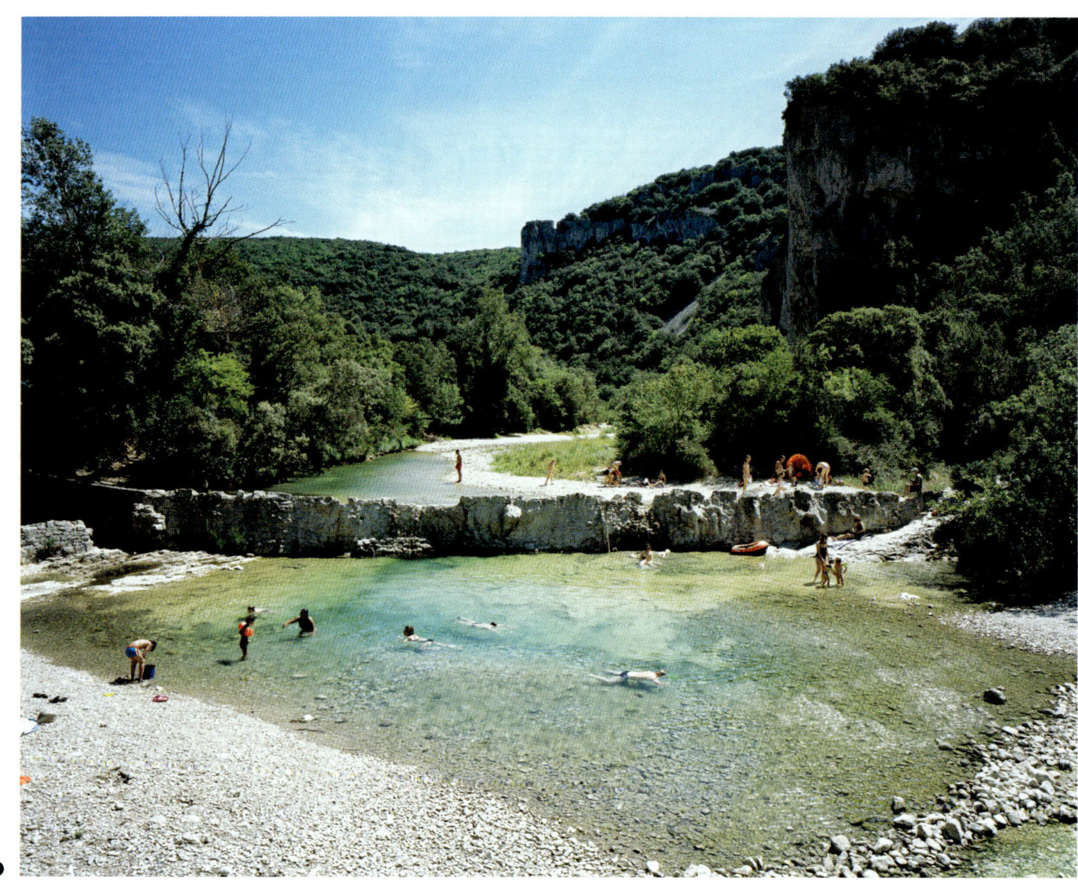

1

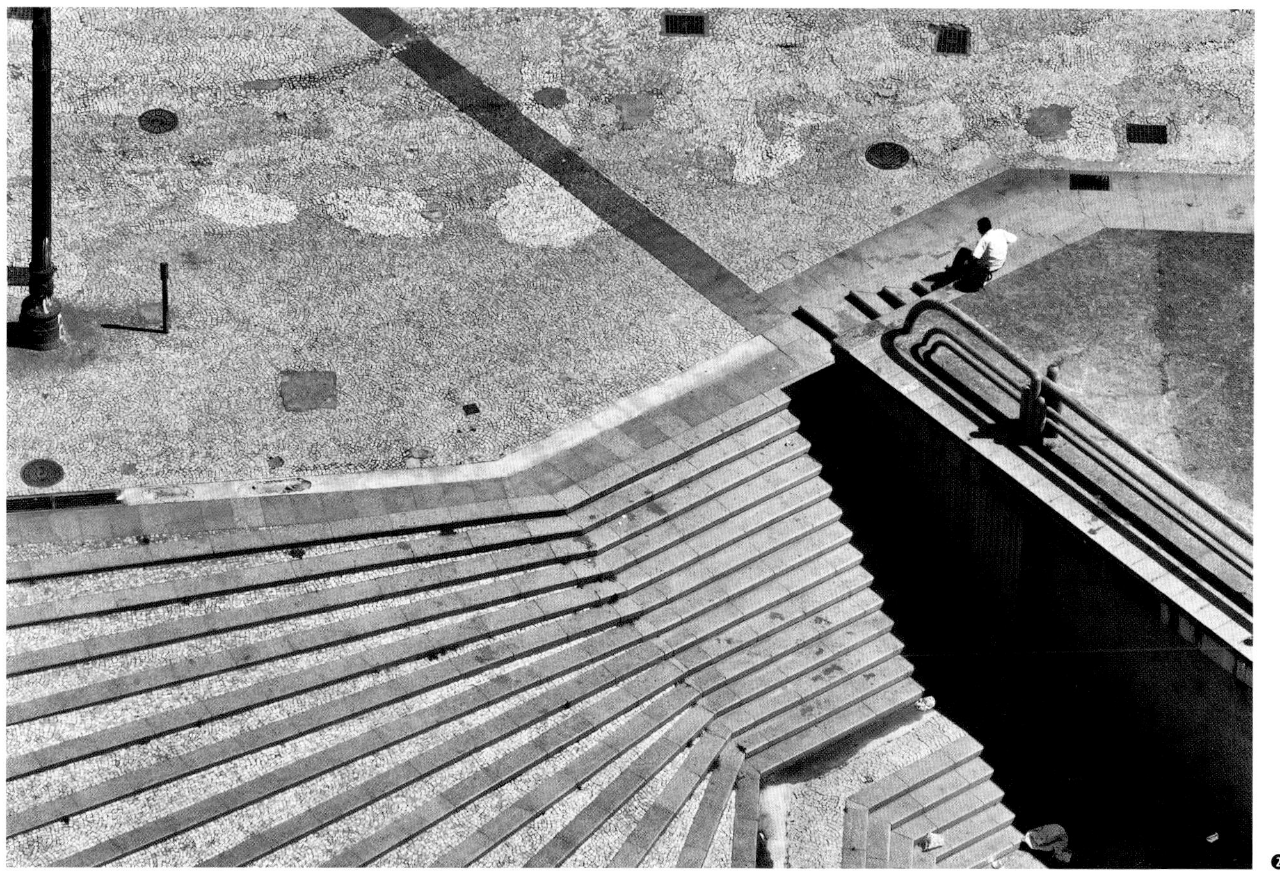

❷

Rami Hanafi
Martin Parr—Making of
Think of Finland

WINNER
MULTIMEDIA

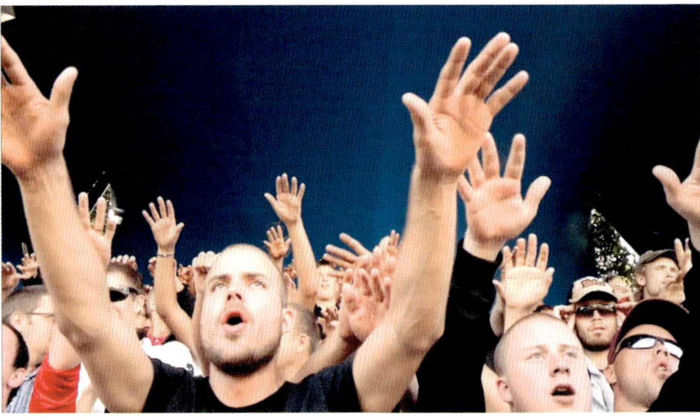

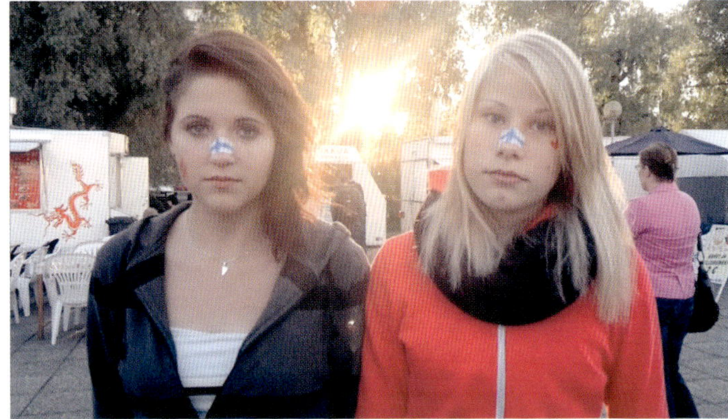

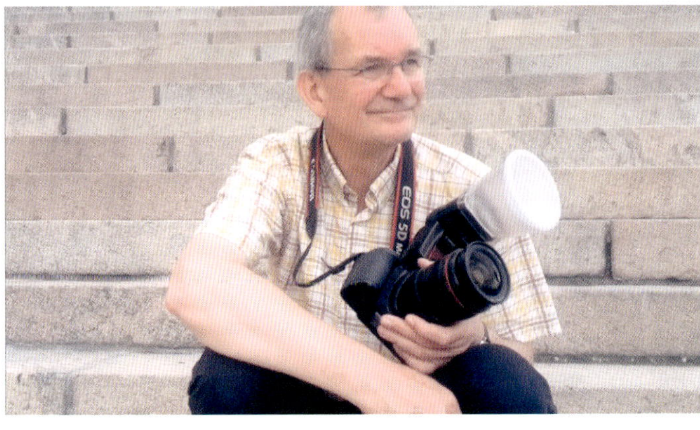

Rami Hanafi is a Finnish photographer who switched from a career in snowboarding to photography in 2002. Following his studies in photojournalism, he started working for a Finnish newspaper shooting personal and commercial projects on the side.

In 2008 he was nominated for the Fotofinlandia award. His work has been exhibited in galleries and photo festivals worldwide. Since 2010 Hanafi has been concentrating on personal and commercial projects for clients such as Nokia and Finnair to name a few, but still enjoys the world of snowboarding through the lens.

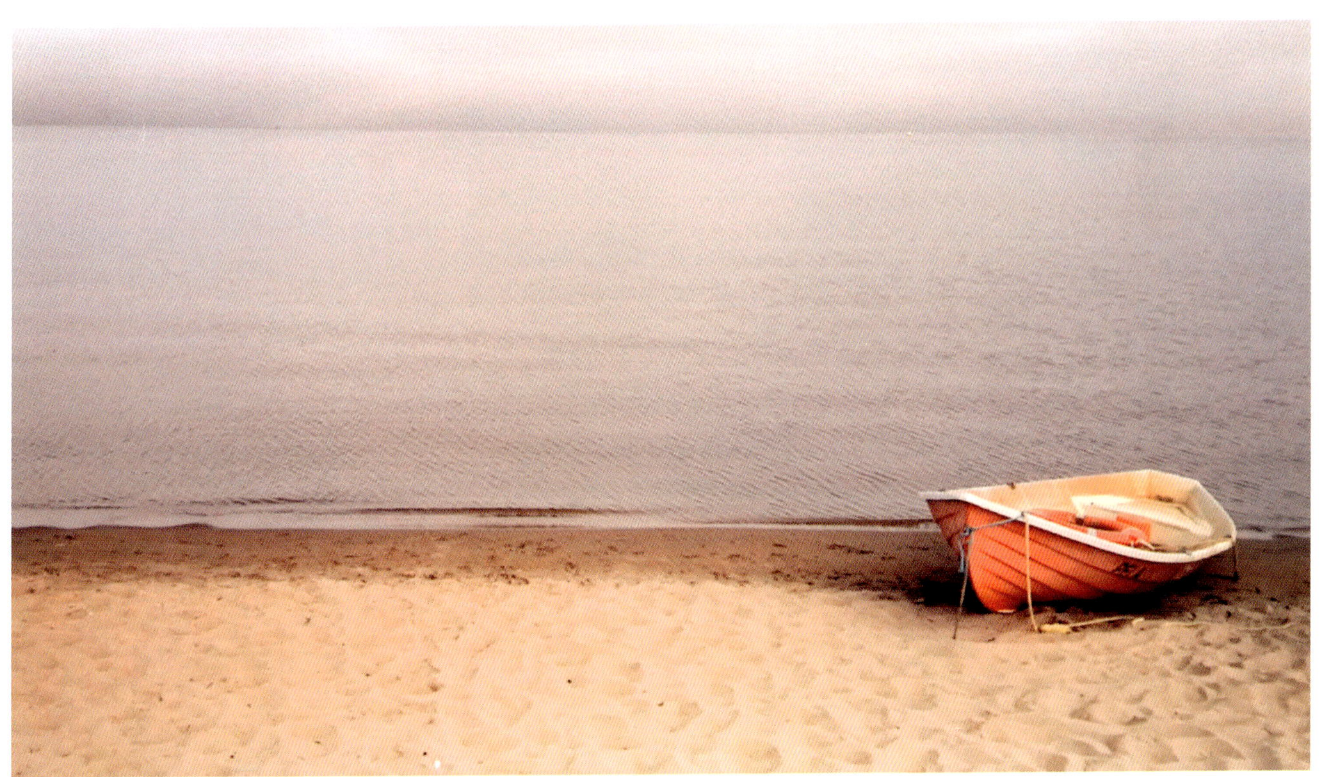

1. Robert Knoth, Antoinette de Jong, Peter Claassen
2. Romain Blanquart, Kathy Kieliszewski, Suzette Hackney
3. Samm Blake
4. Zoltan Tombor

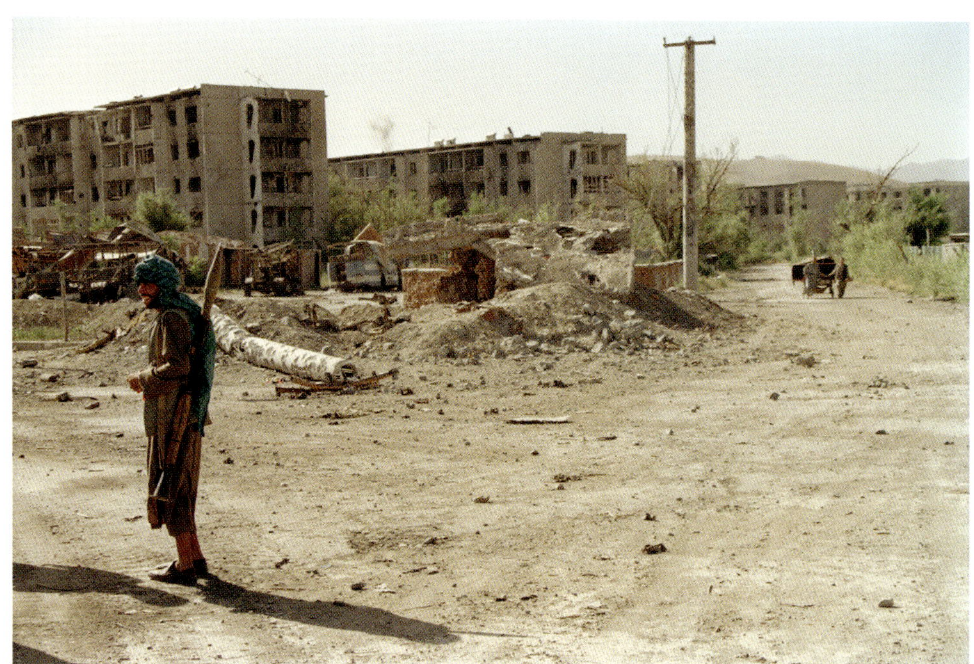

1

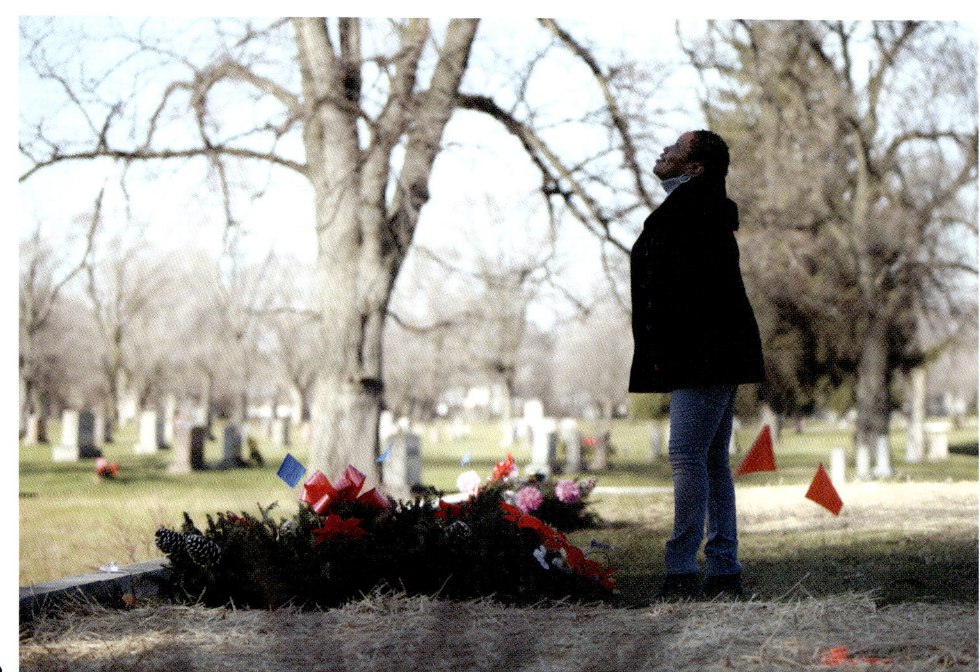

2

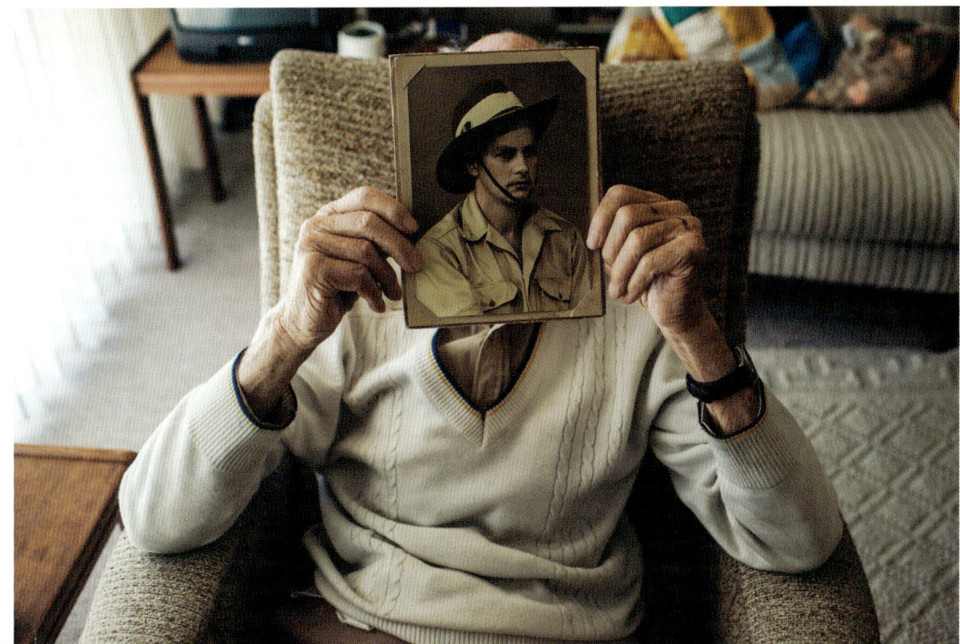

3

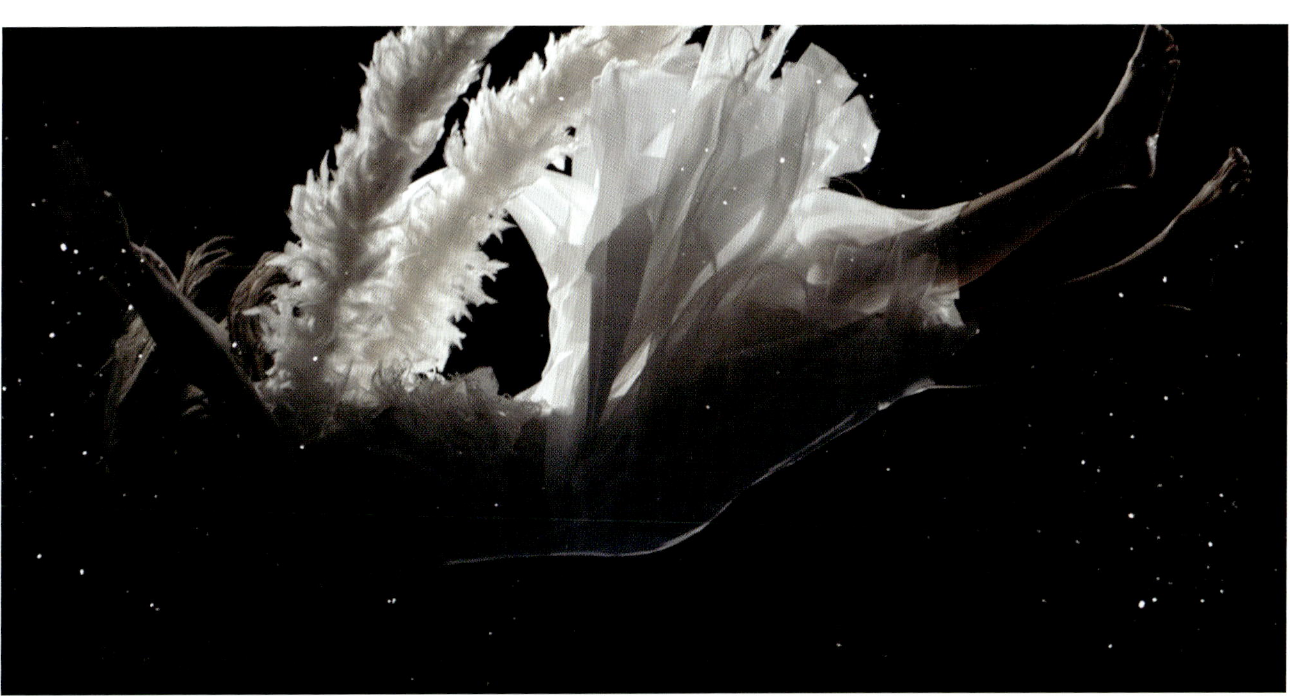

4

Ryan Koopmans
Supertrees

WINNER
STUDENT DOCUMENTARY

Ryan Koopmans is a Dutch-Canadian photographer based in New York City. His project *Paradise Now* explores how urban fantasies and construction function as expressions of nationalistic ambition, blurring the line between the natural and artificial within the hypermodern city.

Upon graduating in 2009 with a BA in interdisciplinary studies: geography, art history, and psychology from The University of British Columbia, Canada, Koopmans completed an MFA in photography, video, and related media at the School of Visual Arts, New York. He continues to work both nationally and internationally on assignments for a wide range of clients.

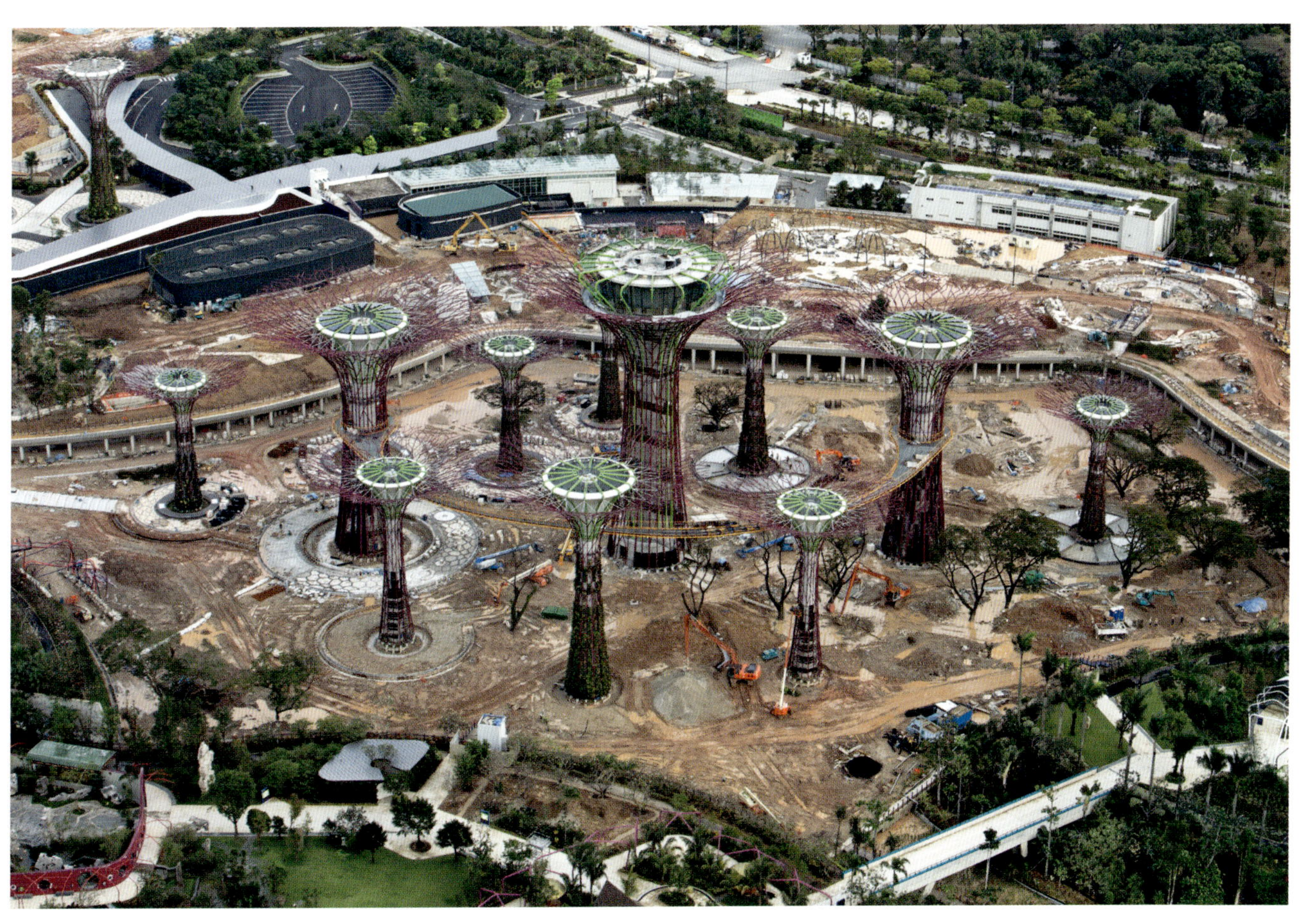

I. Duy Ta

FINALIST
STUDENT DOCUMENTARY

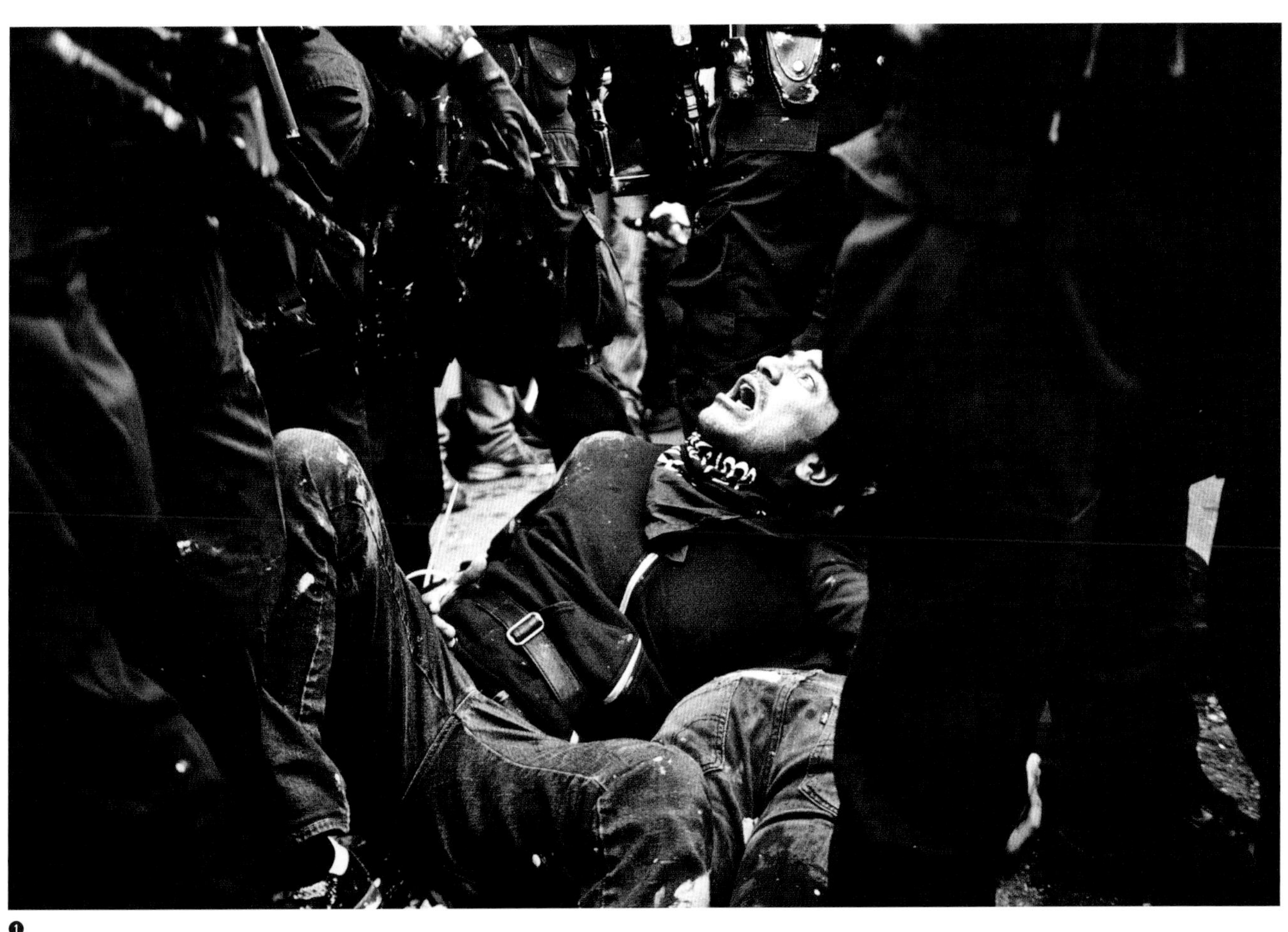

❶

Acacia Johnson
Untitled

WINNER
STUDENT FINE ART

Acacia Johnson is a fine-art photographer whose work deals with mythical aspects of the far northern landscape, and the way that those environments impart a heightened sense of being alive. Greatly influenced by her experiences growing up in Alaska and Norway, she maintains the pursuit of immersive journeys to the far north as an integral part of her creative process.

Her work has been exhibited in Alaska, Rhode Island, New York, and Pennsylvania, and is held in collections at the Rhode Island School of Design Museum of Art and the Smithsonian Museum of American History. She currently resides in Providence, Rhode Island, where she is a senior in the photography department at Rhode Island School of Design.

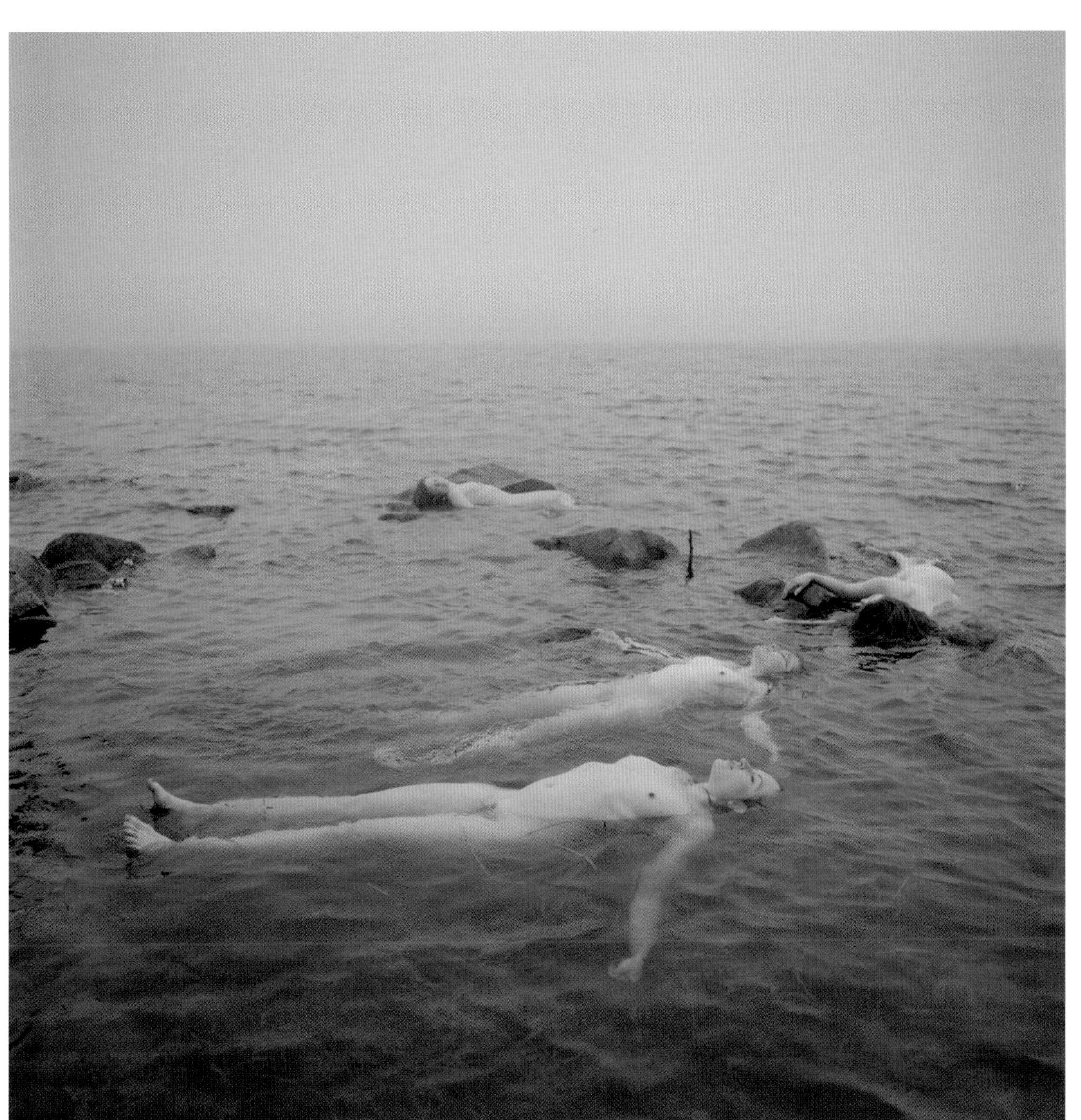

1. Roger Generazzo
2. Hannah Gopa

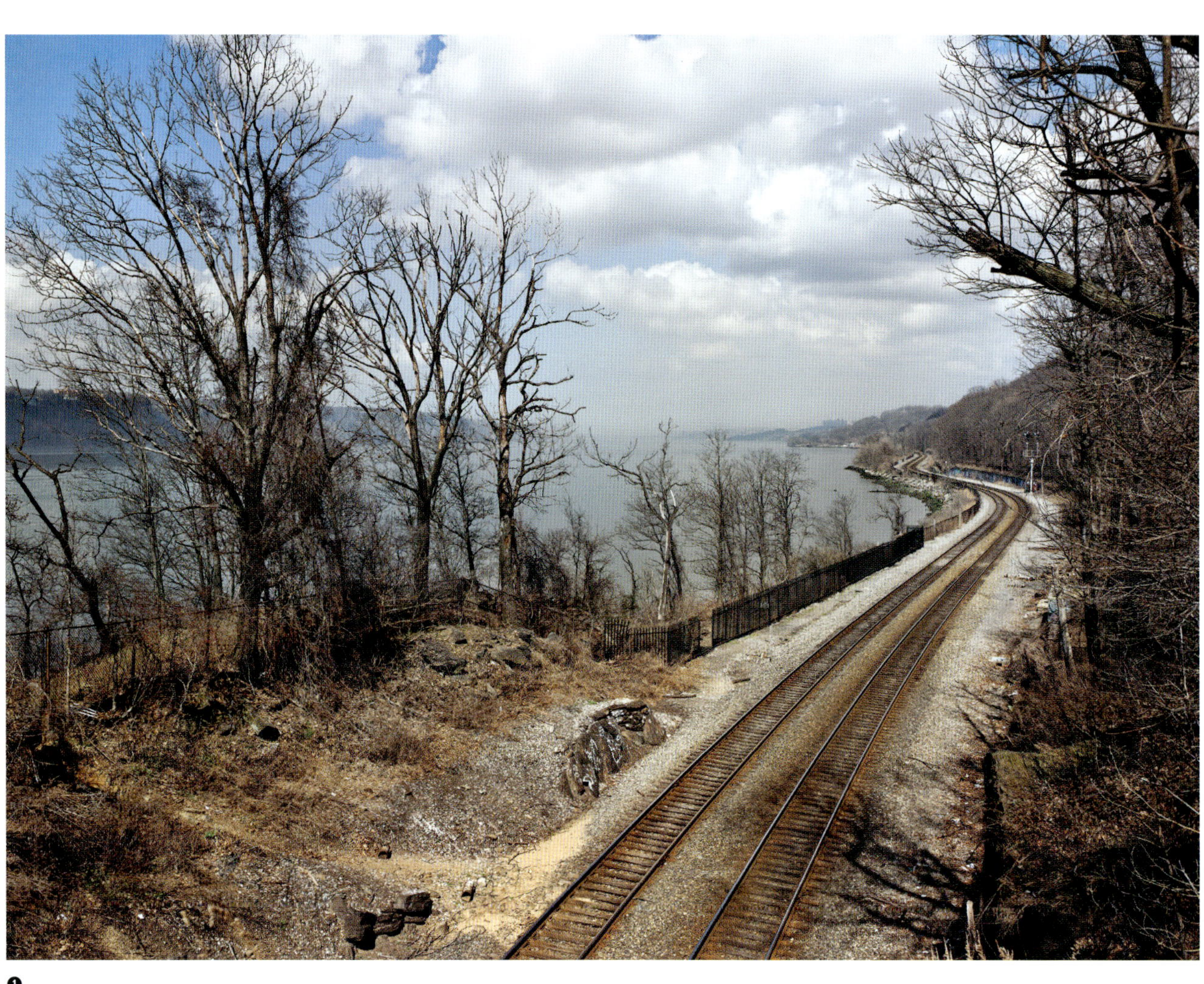

❶

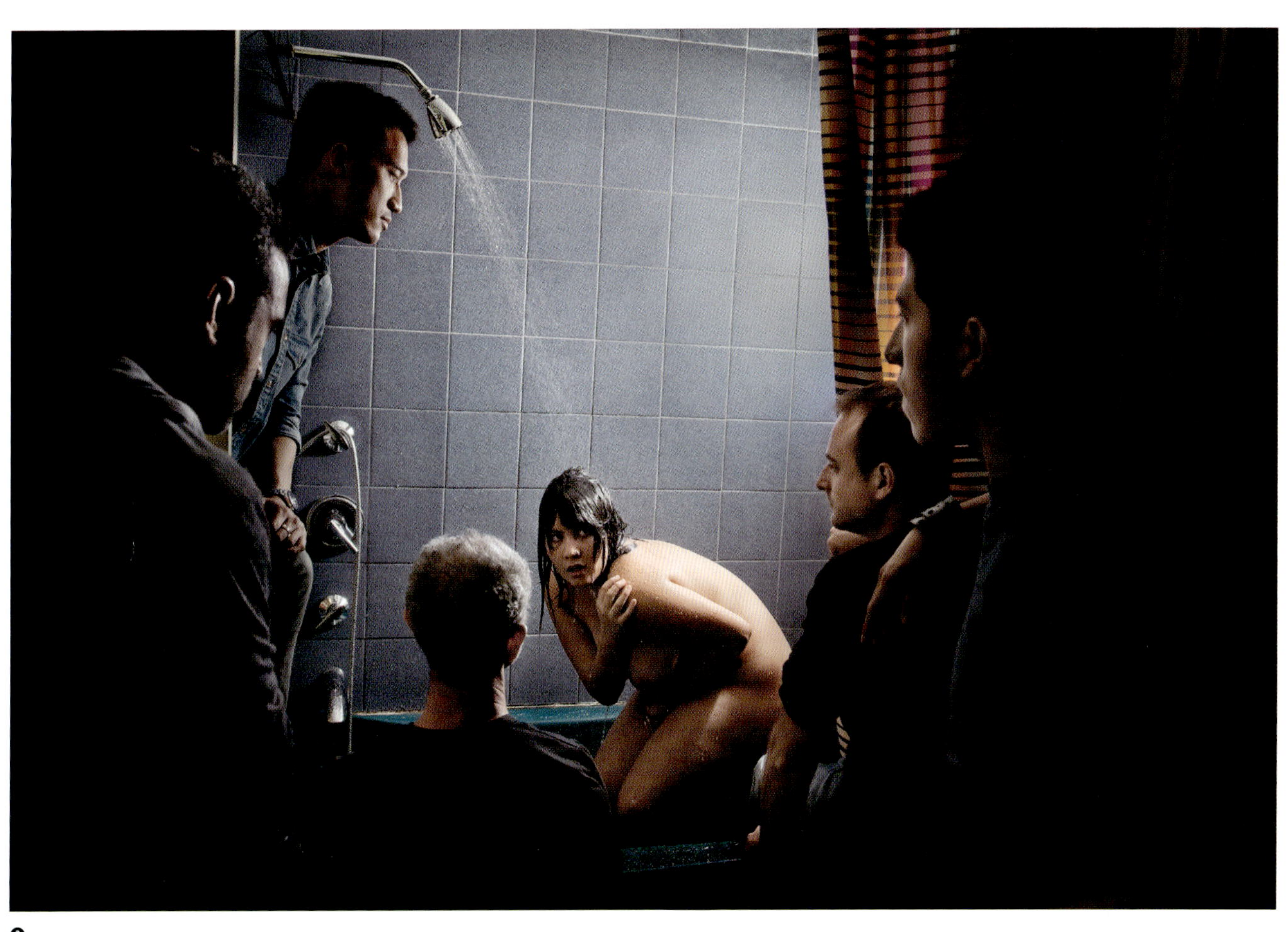

❷

Alexander Kreher
Street Dreams

WINNER
STUDENT MULTIMEDIA

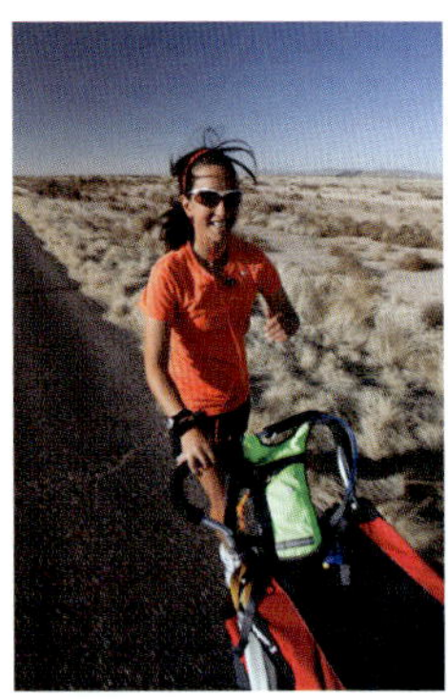

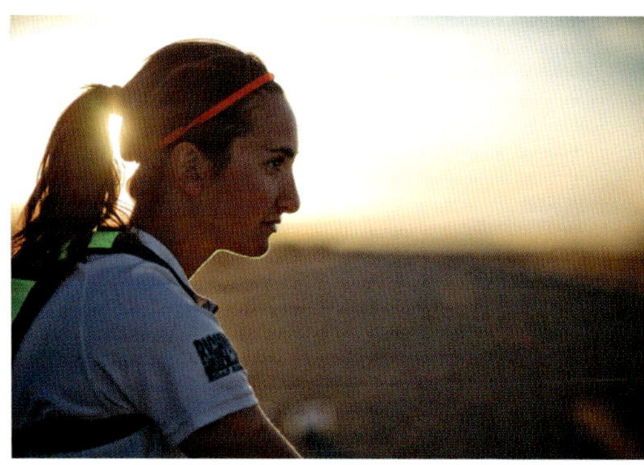

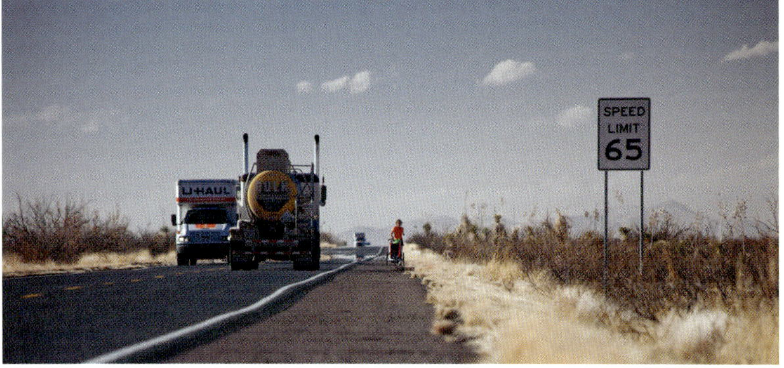

Alexander Kreher, a native of Germany, is a photographer and filmmaker who currently lives in Richmond, Virginia. He works primarily in documentary photography and film, and delves deeply into his subjects' lives by developing a style that seeks to understand eccentric personalities holistically, rather than displaying them one-dimensionally.

He studied digital media and print design in Germany, won a scholarship to study at the renowned Salt Institute for Documentary Studies in Portland, Maine in 2012, and is now enrolled in the film program at Virginia Commonwealth University.

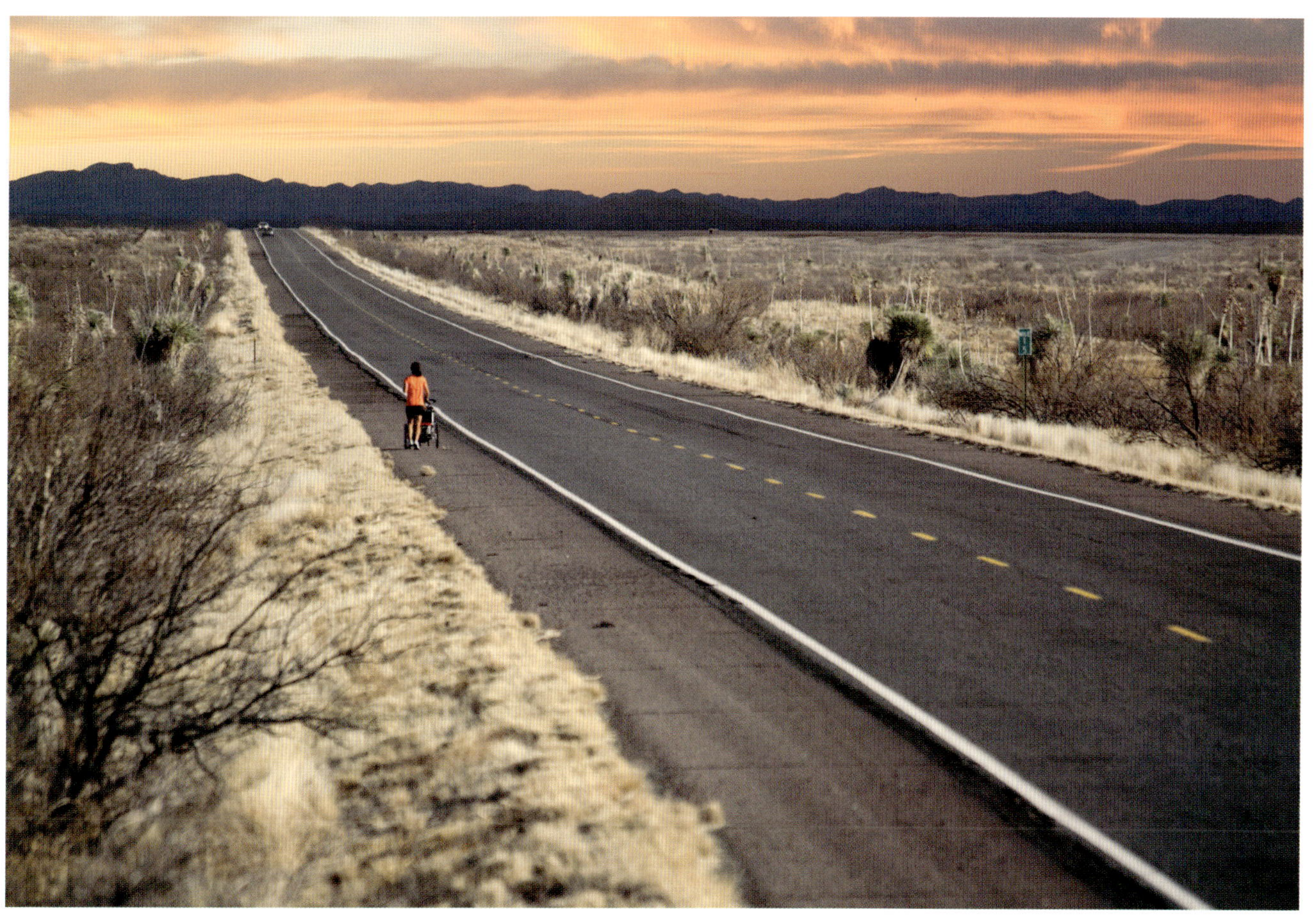

1. G. Ligaiya Romero
2. Maria M. Litwa

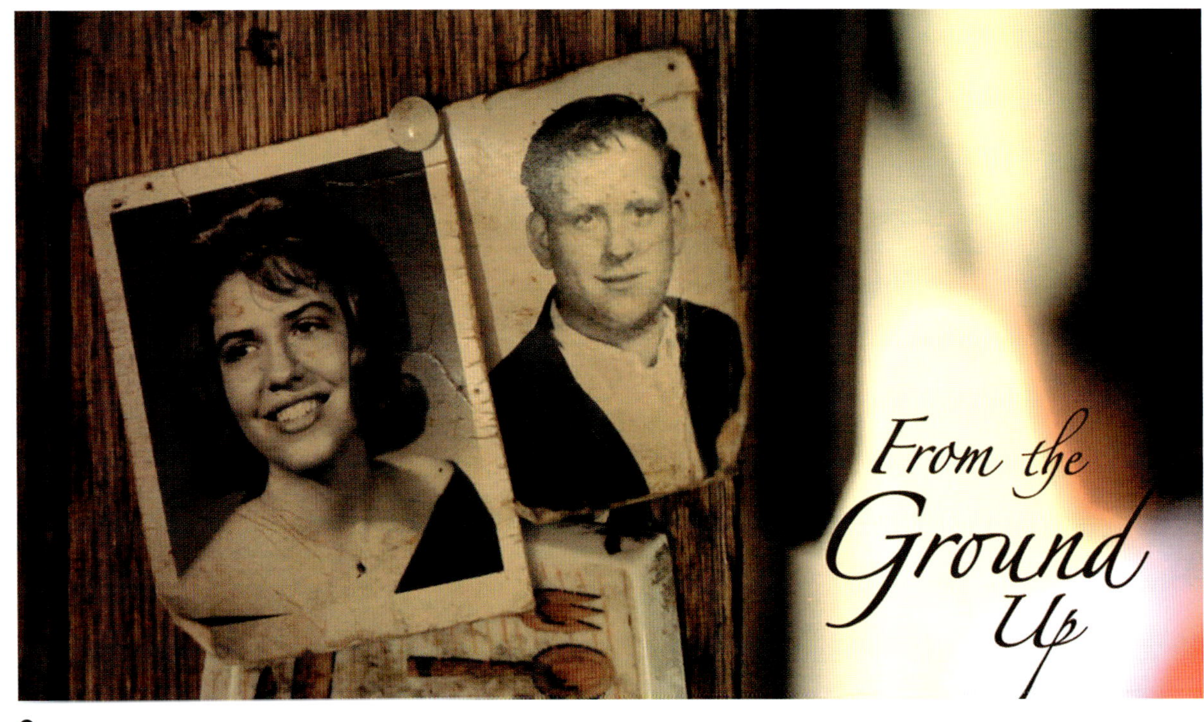

❶

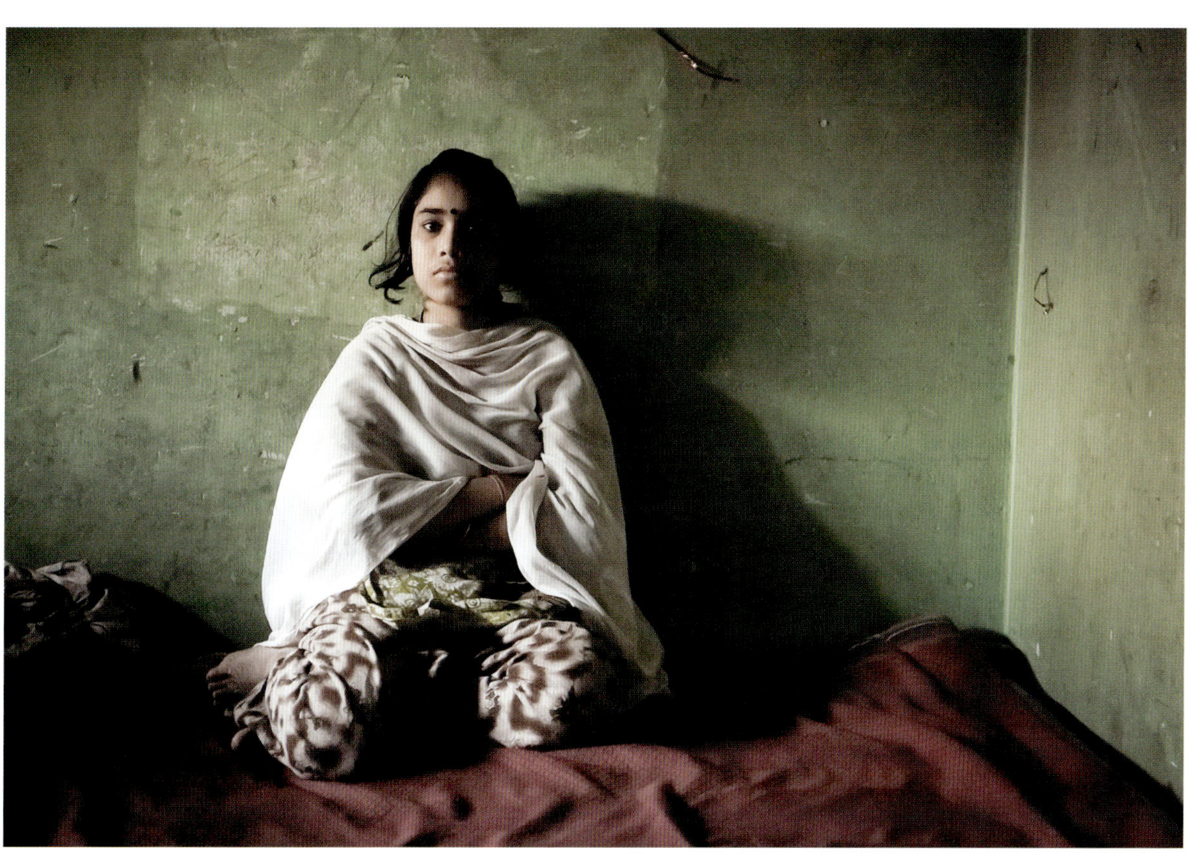

❷

Adam Hinton
Nike-Make It Count

WINNER
ADVERTISING

When **Adam Hinton** was 15, he received the first installment of compensation from the government following a knife attack (his attacker had a thing against punks) and instinctively knew what he was going to spend the money on: cameras. From that moment onwards, photography has been his focus. It has enabled Hinton to comment on his other interest: politics.

Studying photojournalism in the 1980s enabled him to articulate his feelings, beliefs, and values in a visual medium that could communicate to others. Hinton hoped—and still does—that his images could portray something of the way we live today, how each action has a reaction, and that nothing is without cause or response.

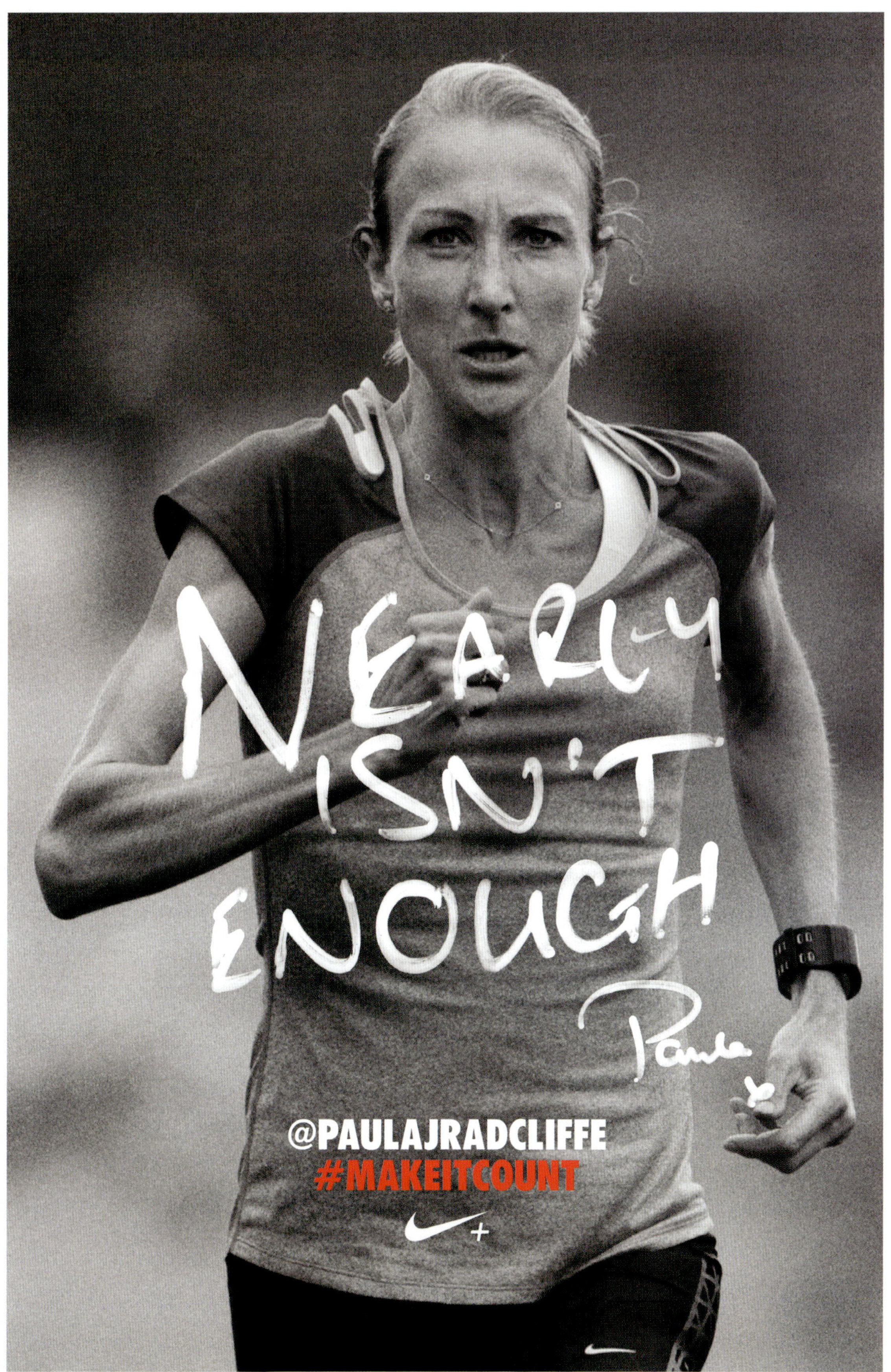
NEARLY ISN'T ENOUGH
Paula
@PAULAJRADCLIFFE
#MAKEITCOUNT

Adam Hinton

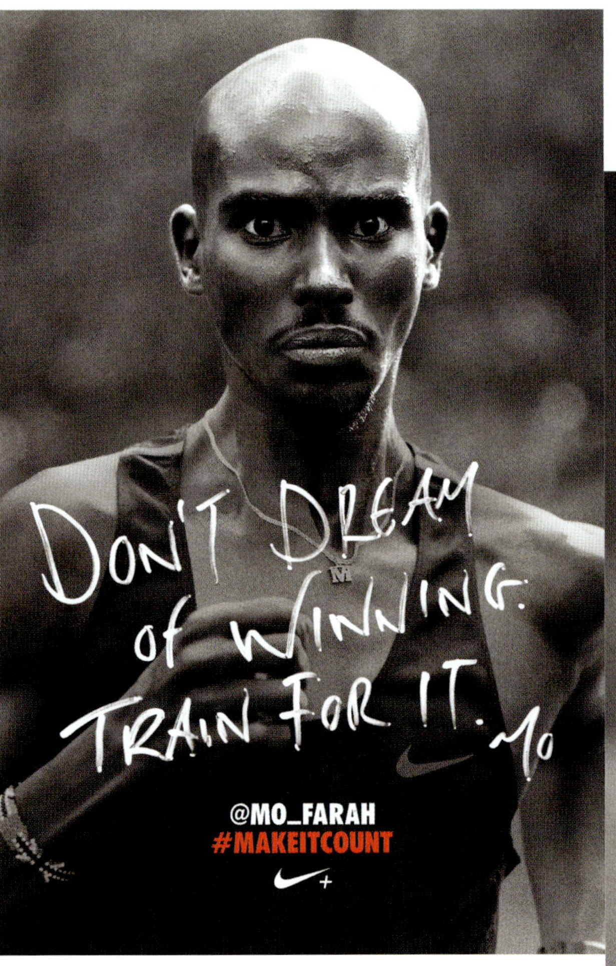
DON'T DREAM
of WINNING.
TRAIN FOR IT. Mo
@MO_FARAH
#MAKEITCOUNT

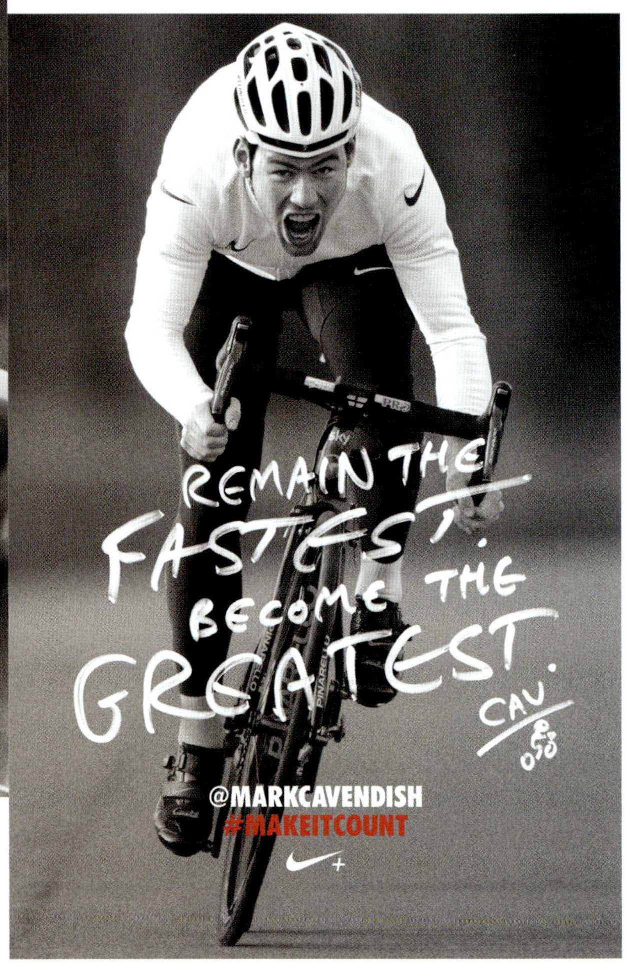
REMAIN THE
FASTEST.
BECOME THE
GREATEST.
CAV
@MARKCAVENDISH
#MAKEITCOUNT

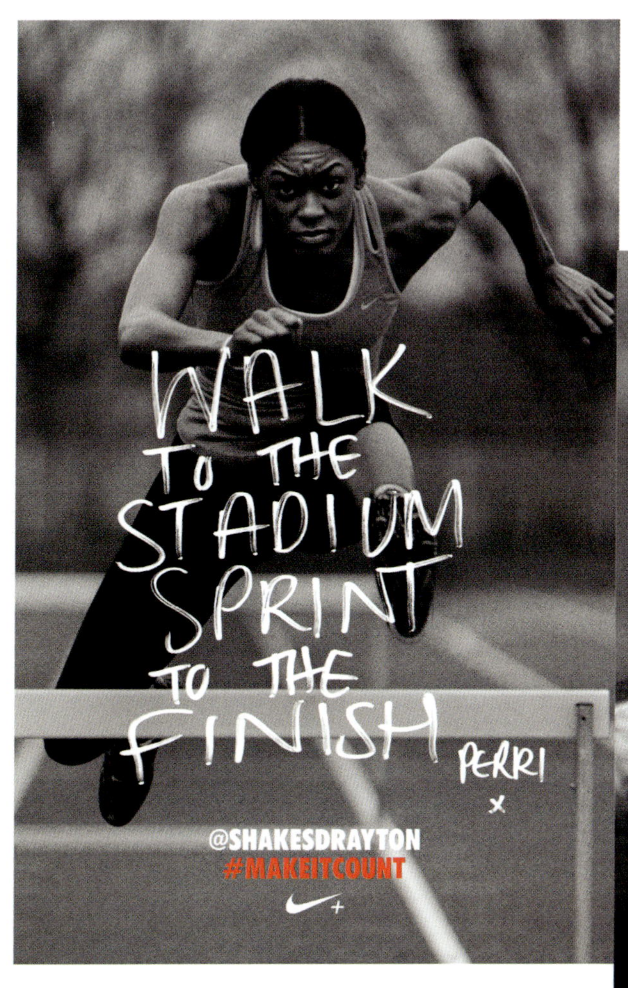
WALK
TO THE
STADIUM
SPRINT
TO THE
FINISH
PERRI
x
@SHAKESDRAYTON
#MAKEITCOUNT

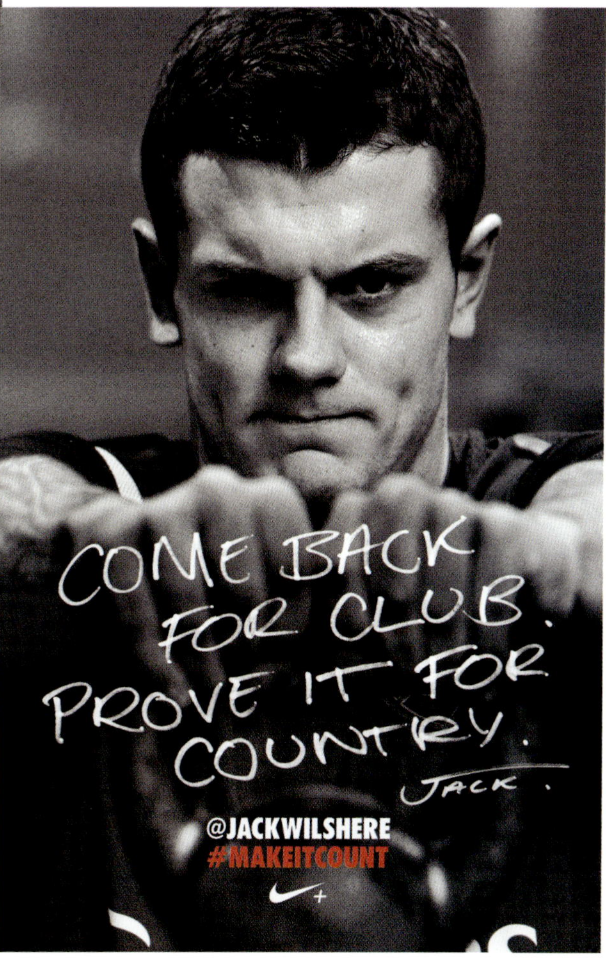
COME BACK
FOR CLUB.
PROVE IT FOR
COUNTRY.
JACK.
@JACKWILSHERE
#MAKEITCOUNT

1. Bára Prášilová
2. Laura Pannack
3. Arthur Mebius

❶

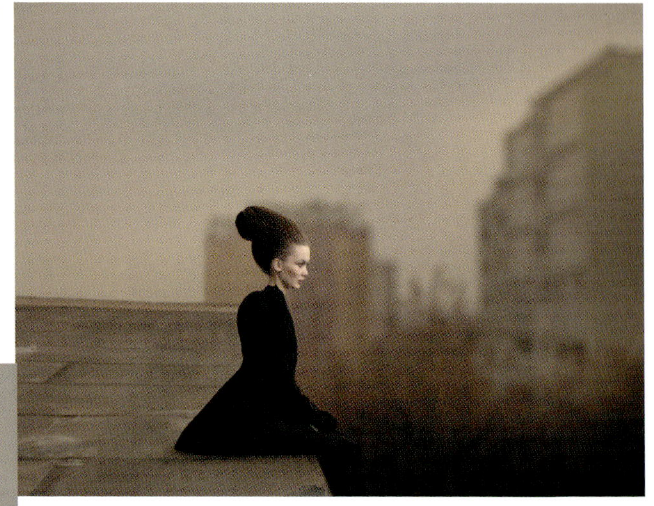

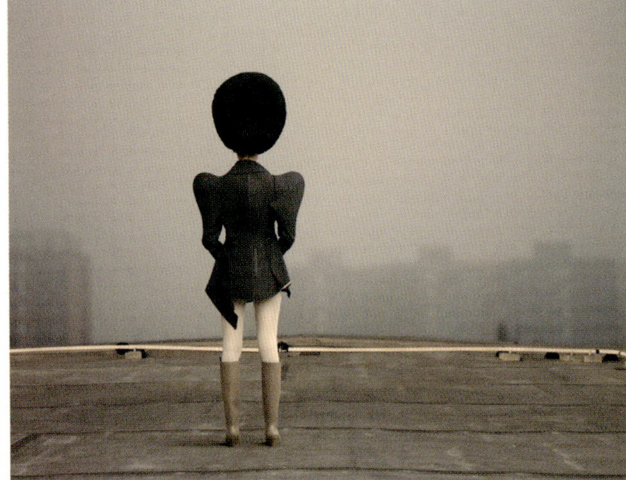

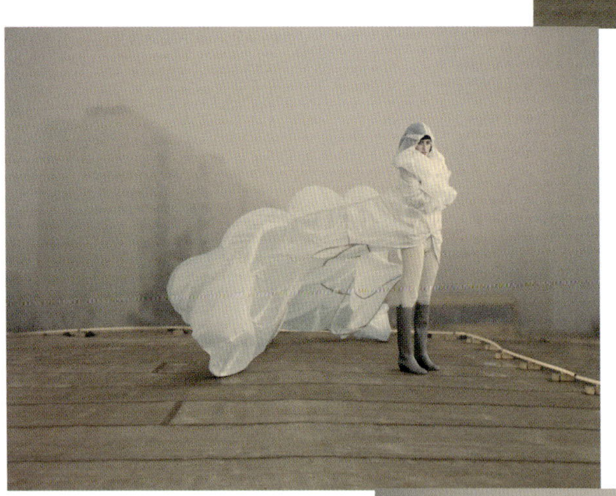

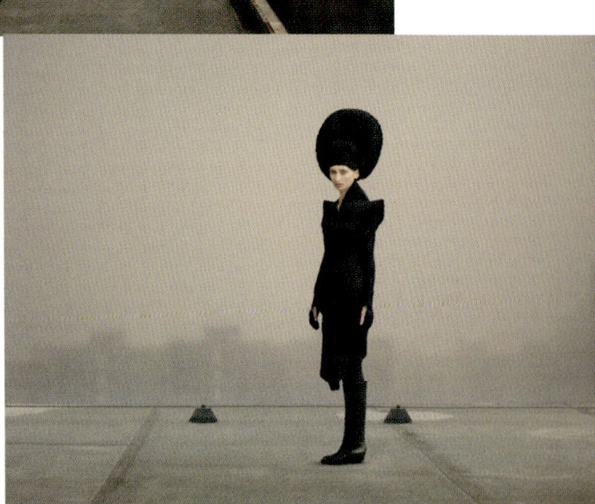

2

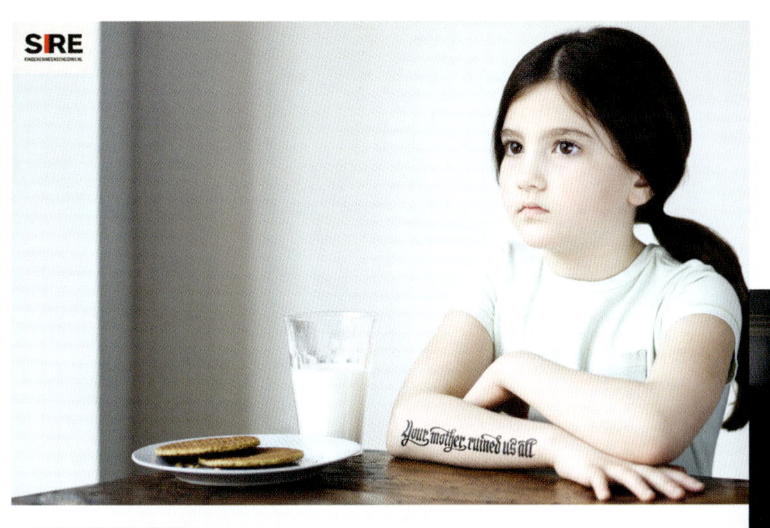
SIRE
Your mother ruined us all
WHAT YOU SAY DURING DIVORCE LASTS FOREVER.

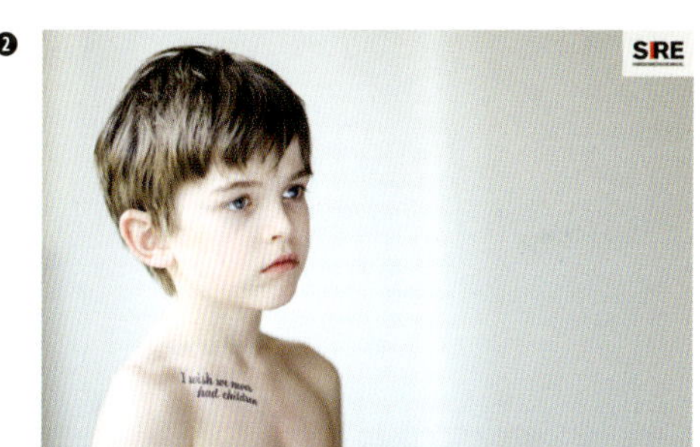
SIRE

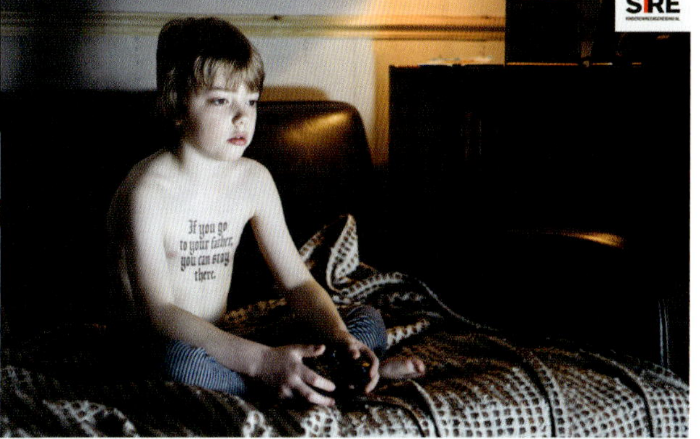
SIRE
If you go
to your father,
you can stay
there.
WHAT YOU SAY DURING DIVORCE LASTS FOREVER.

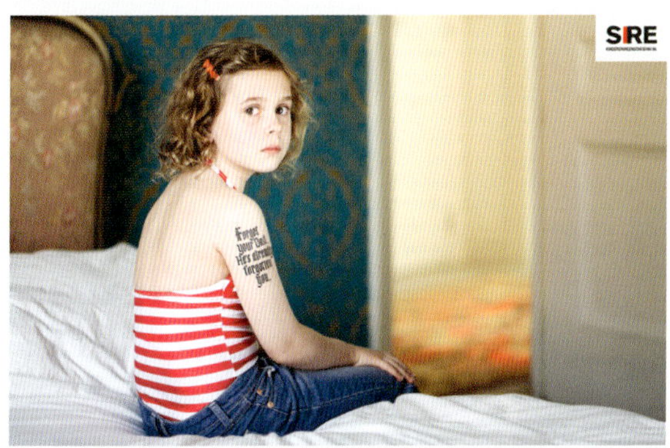
SIRE
Forget
your Dad.
WHAT YOU SAY DURING DIVORCE LASTS FOREVER.

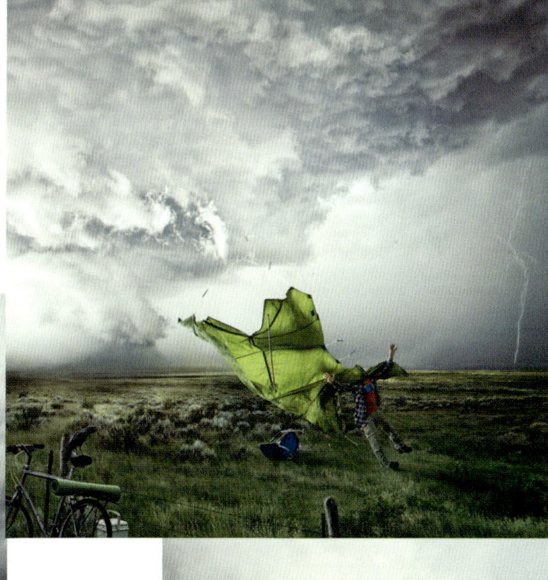

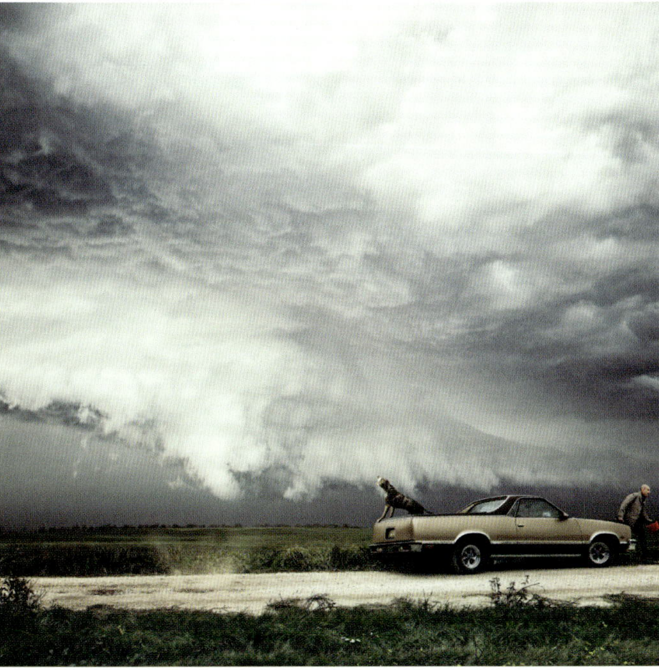

3

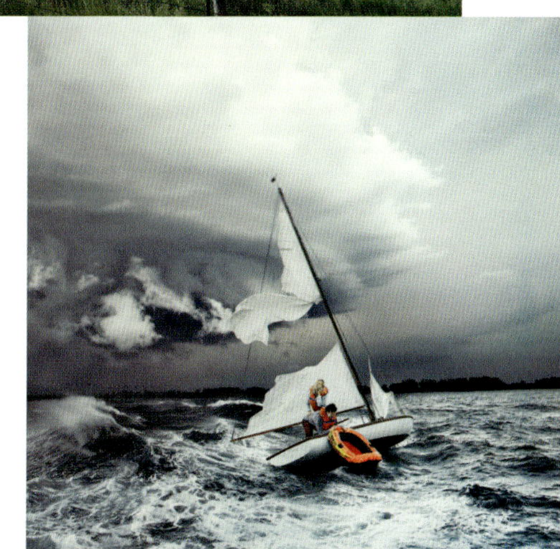

Annabel Clark
Carmen and Lupita

WINNER
DOCUMENTARY

Annabel Clark was born in Topanga, California in 1981. She received her BFA in photography from Parsons School of Design in 2003. During her final term at Parsons, she photographed her mother, the late actress Lynn Redgrave, during her treatment and initial recovery from breast cancer. In 2004, the project was published in the *New York Times Magazine* and then as the book *Journal: A Mother and Daughter's Recovery from Breast Cancer*, by Umbrage Editions. Her work has been exhibited at the MPLS Center for Photography, Michael Mazzeo Gallery, and the Southeast Museum of Photography, as well as at hospitals and medical schools across the country. Her editorial work has appeared in *The New York Times*, *The Guardian*, *Marie Claire*, *Redbook*, and *Money Magazine*. She also teaches photography at the Creative Center, a nonprofit organization that provides free art workshops to people living with cancer and other chronic illnesses.

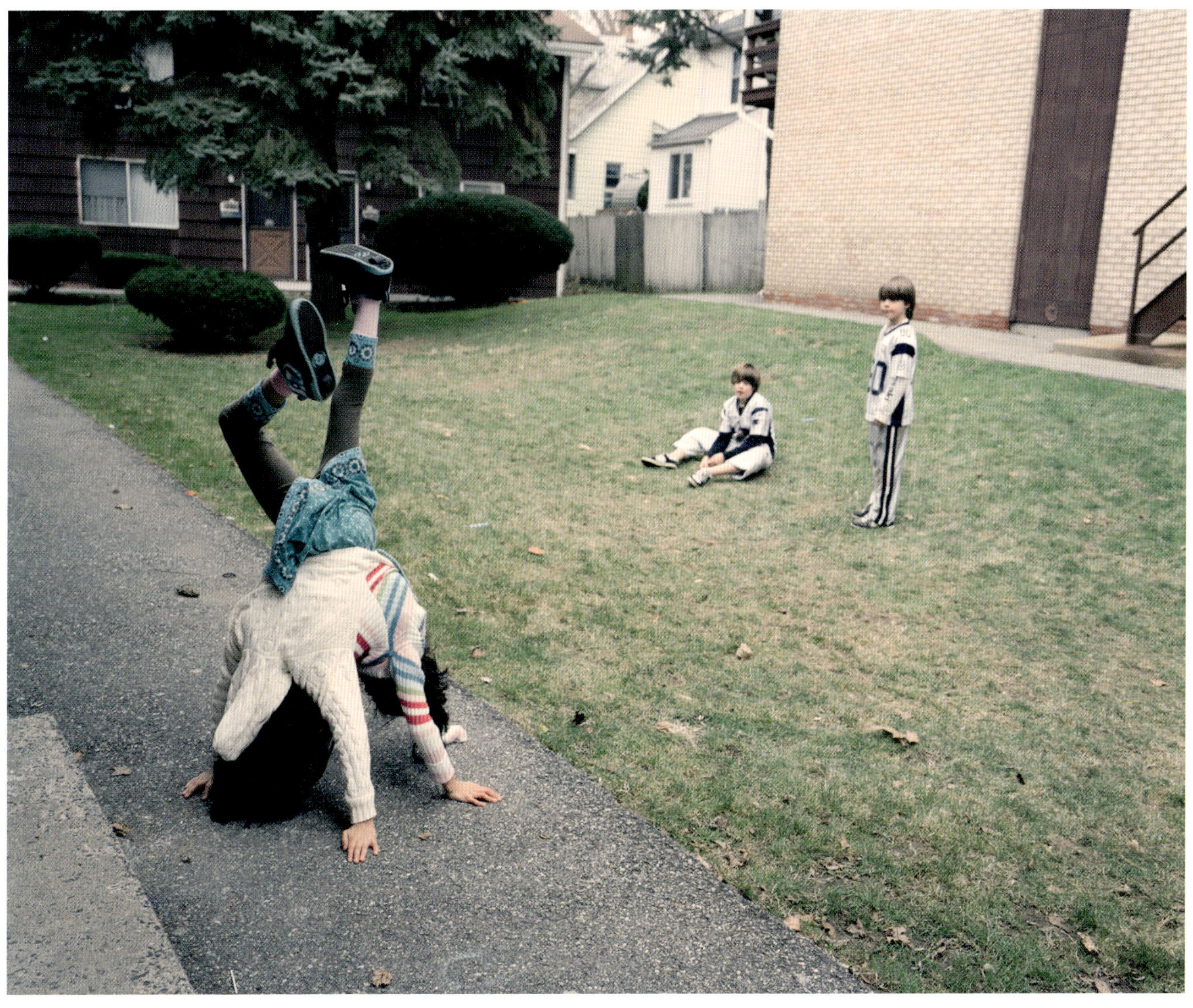

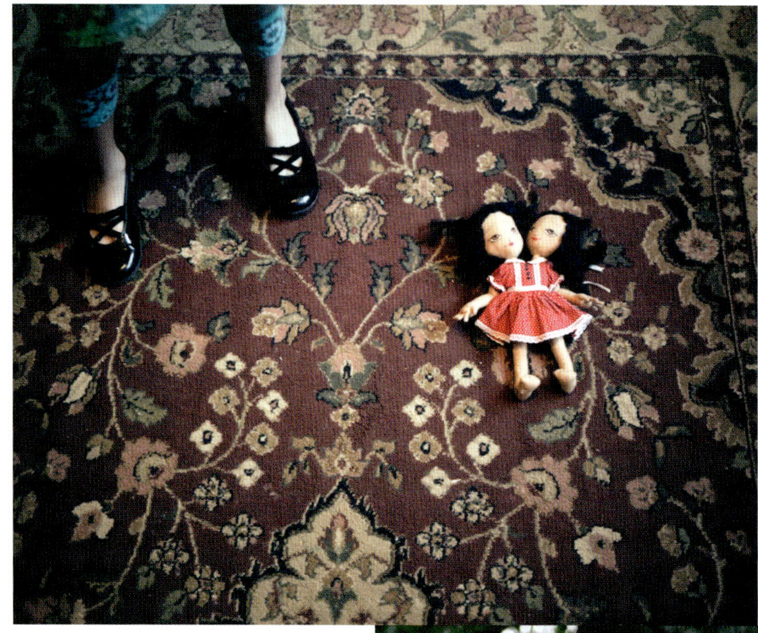

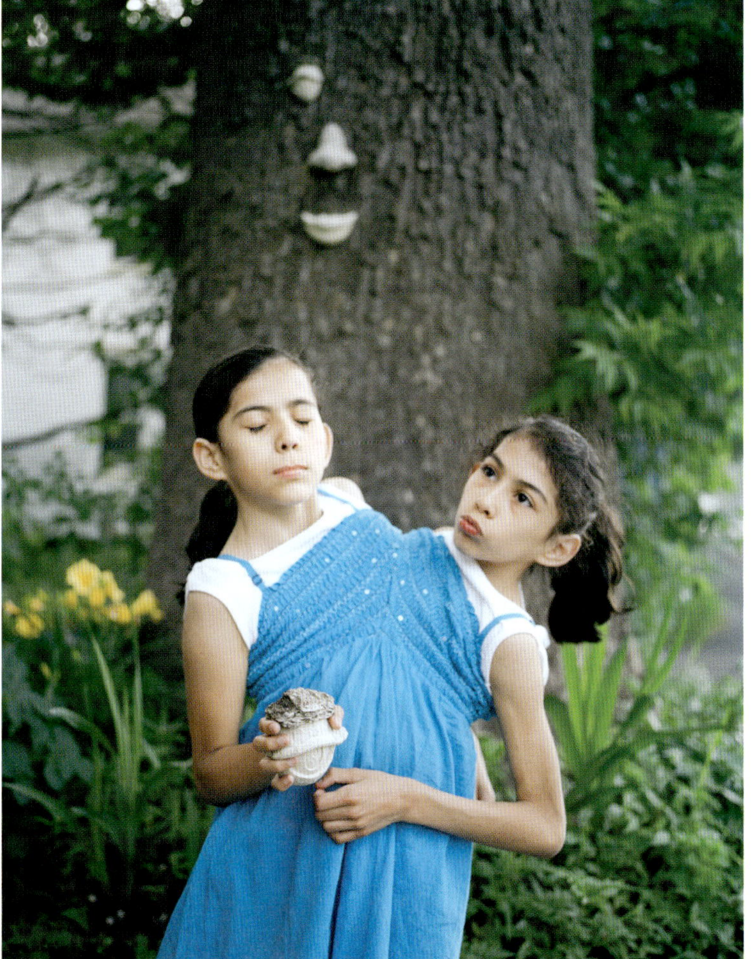

Carmen and Lupita

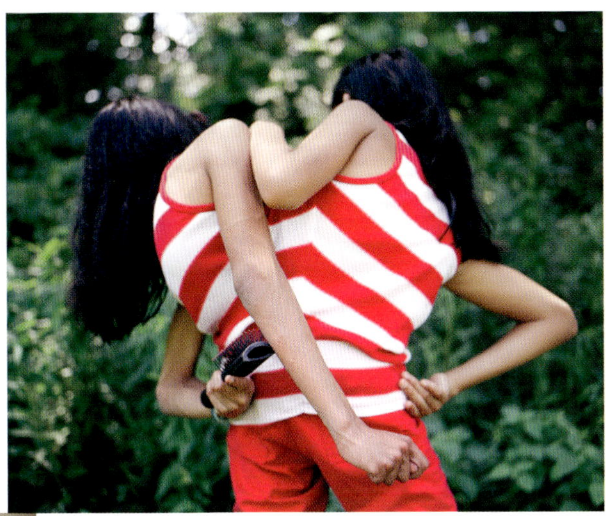

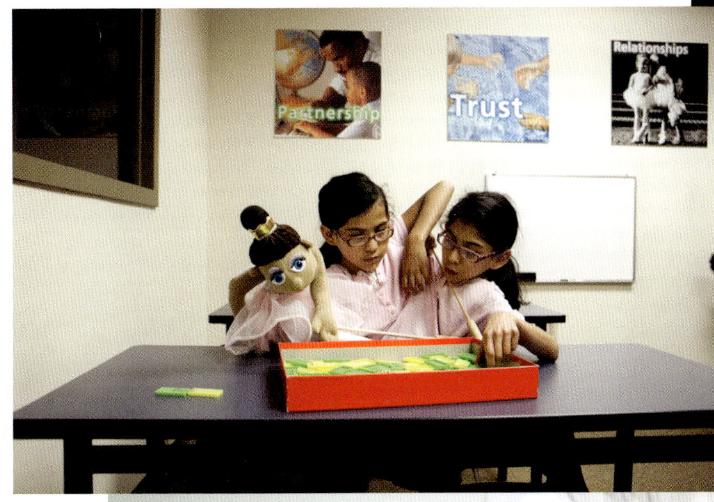

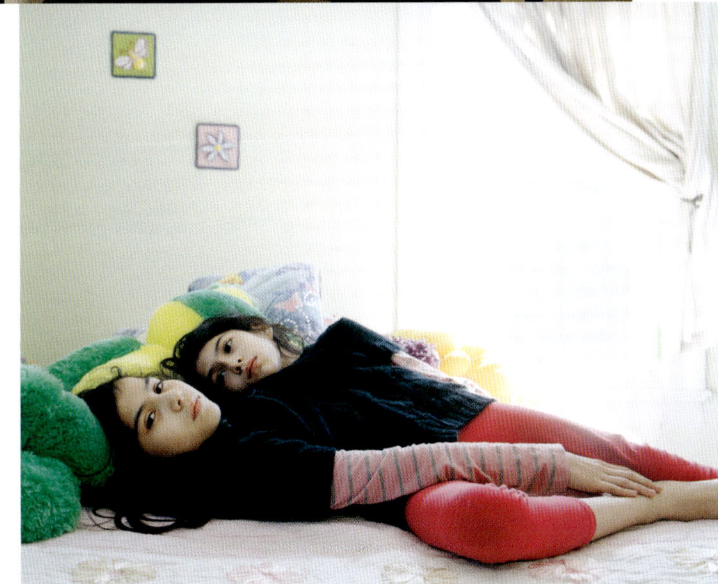

1. Arian Camilleri & Rodney White
2. Brian Driscoll
3. Linda Bournane Engelberth
4. Kerry Mansfield

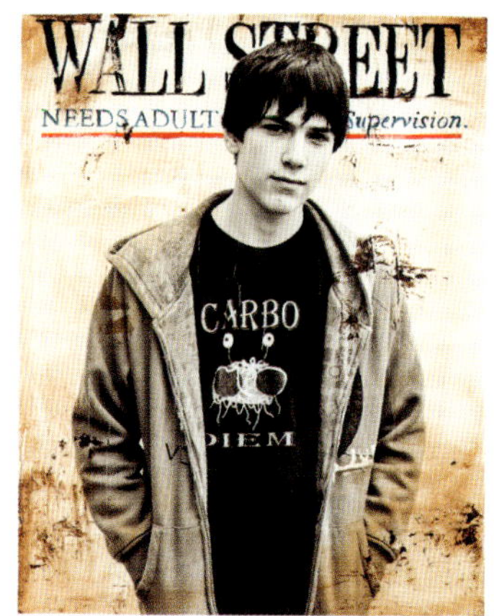

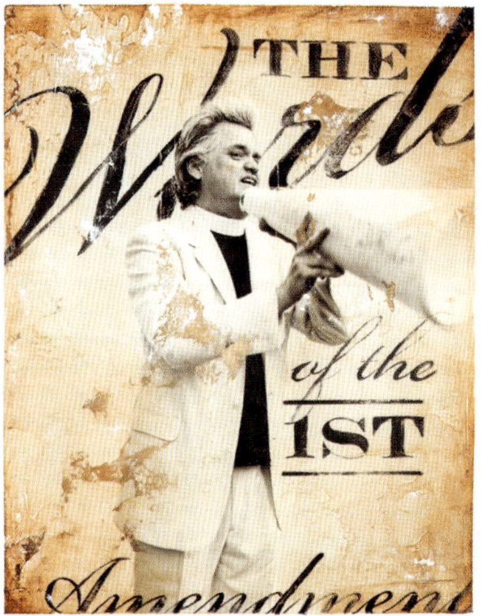

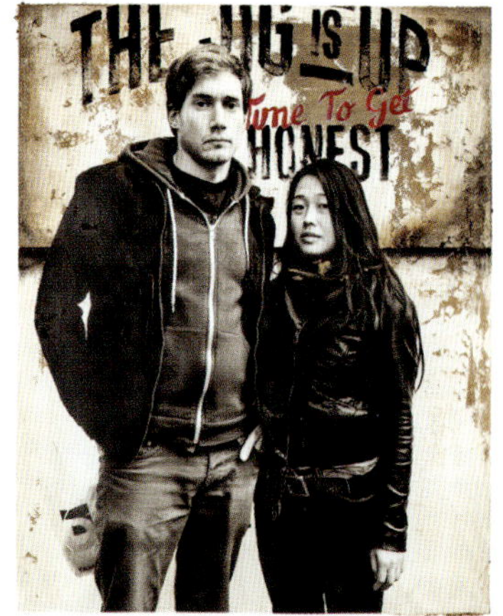

1

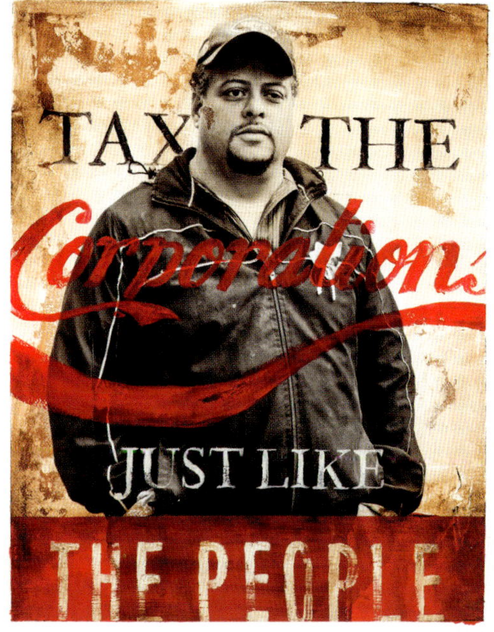

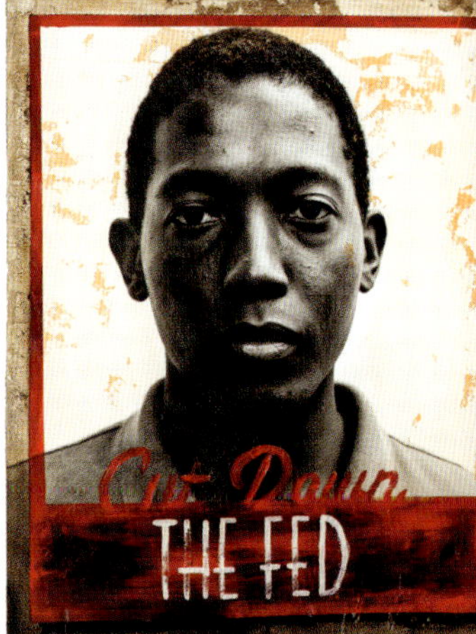

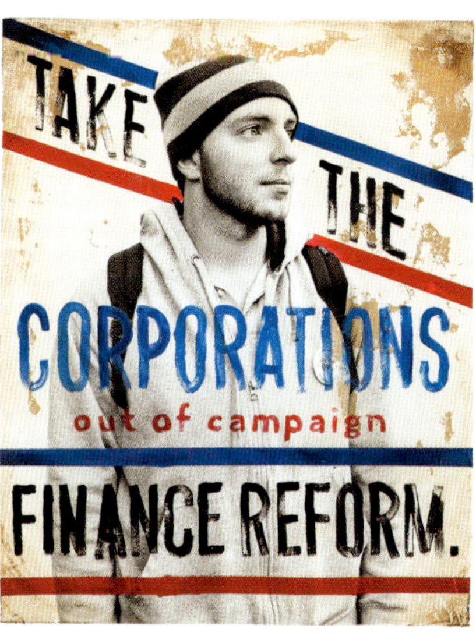

❷

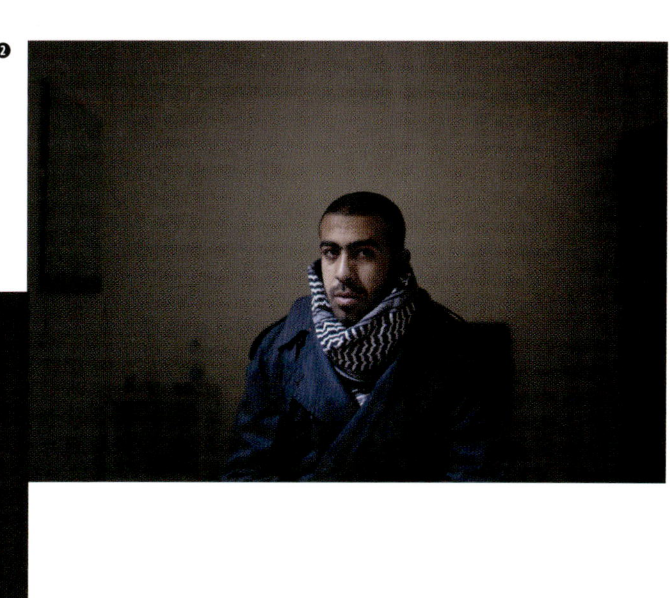

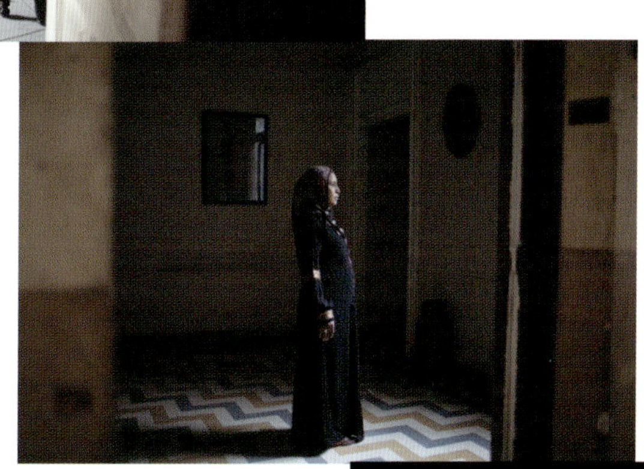

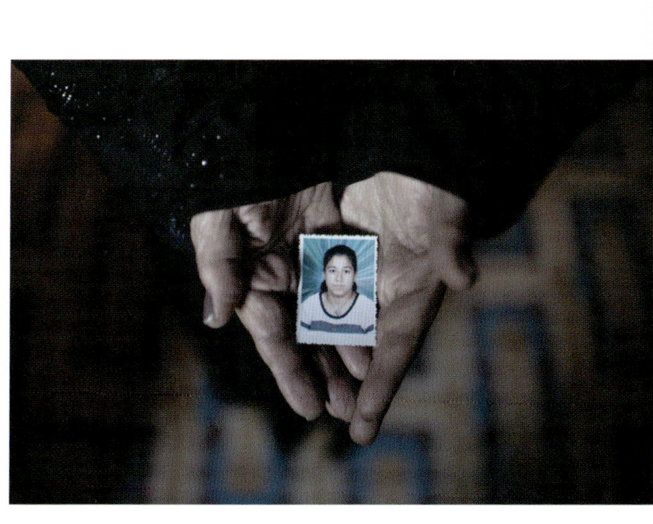

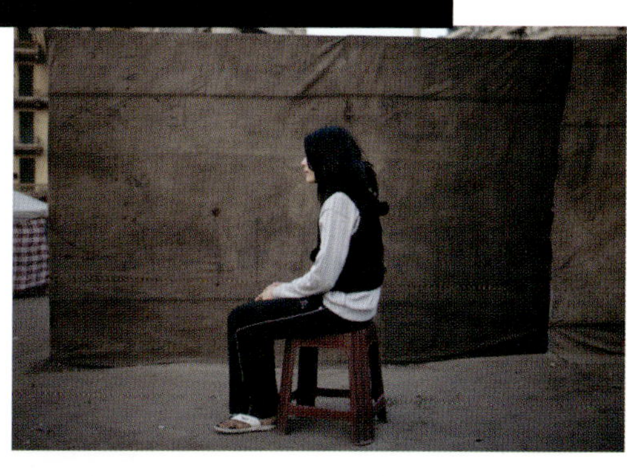

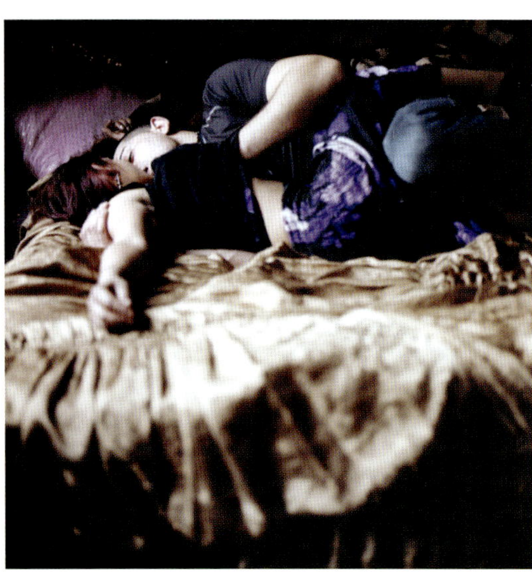

3

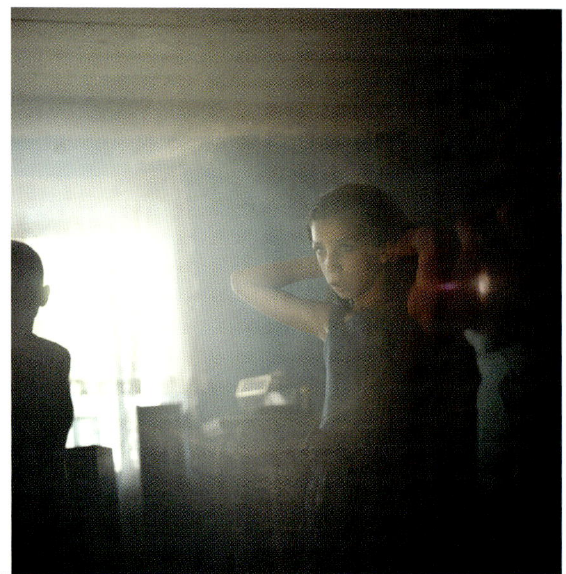

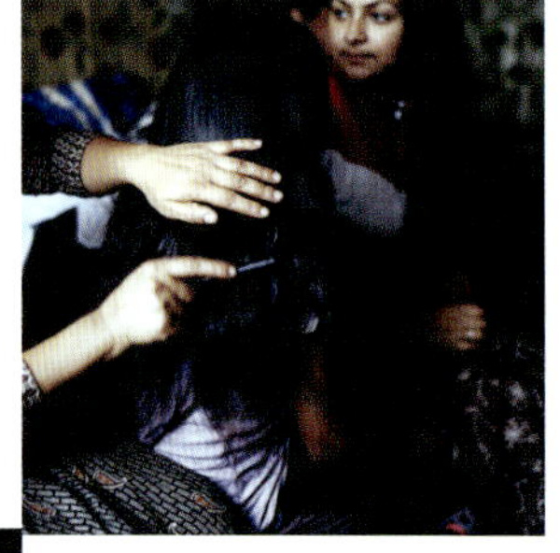

FINALISTS
DOCUMENTARY

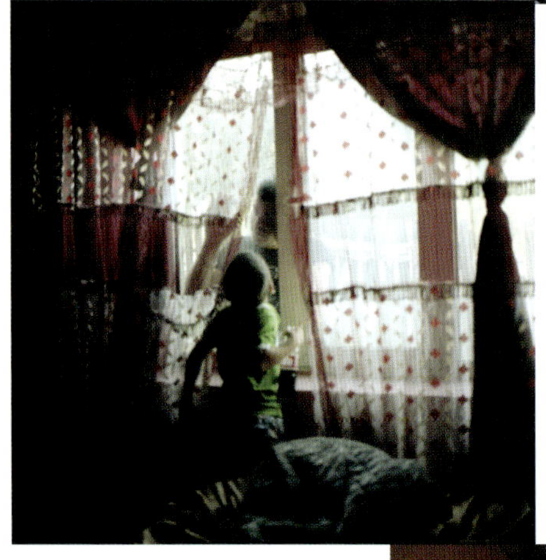

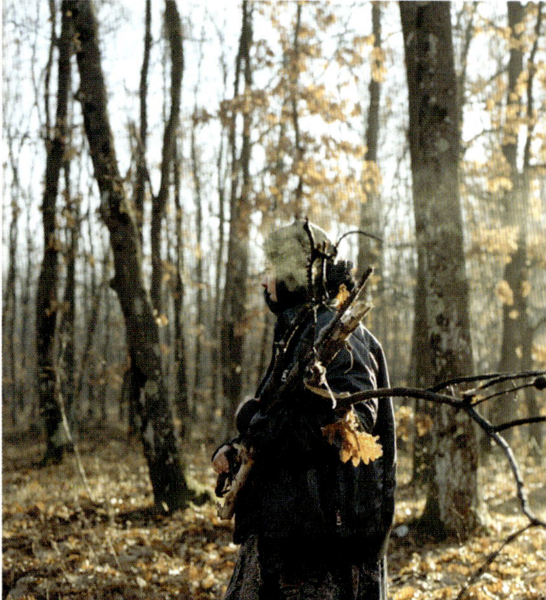

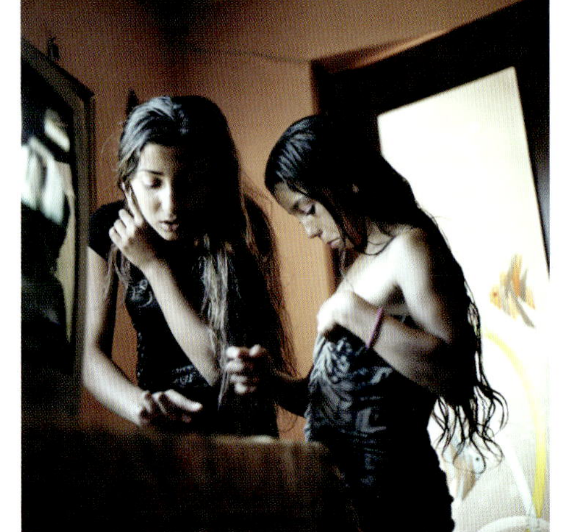

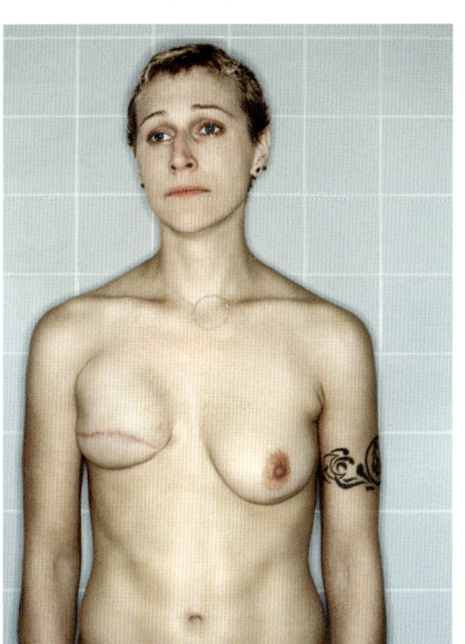

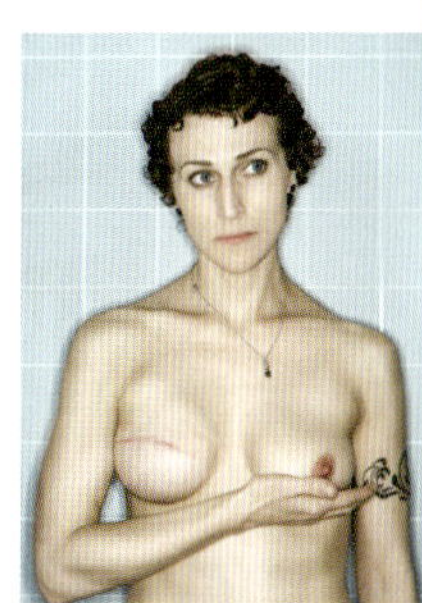

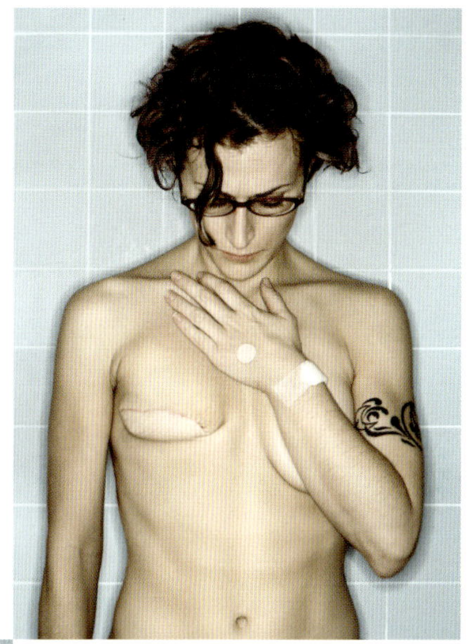

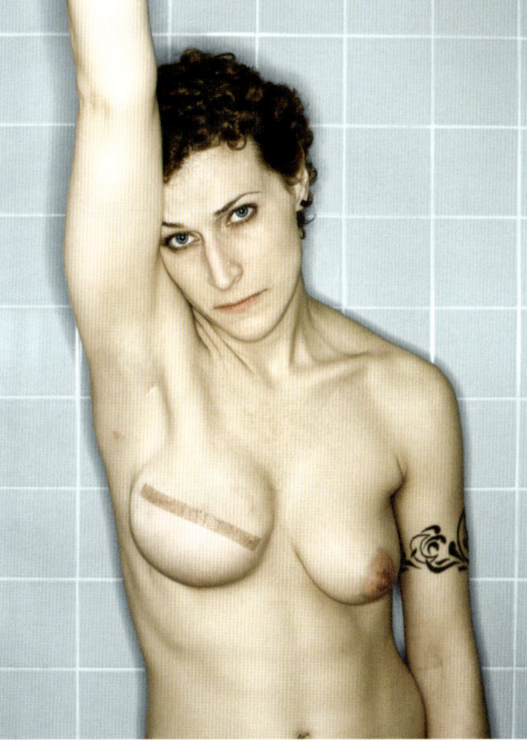

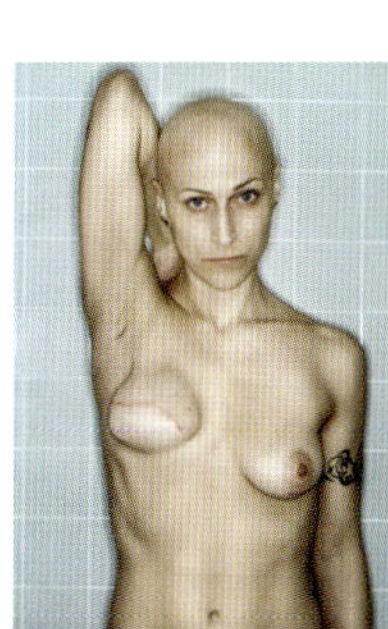

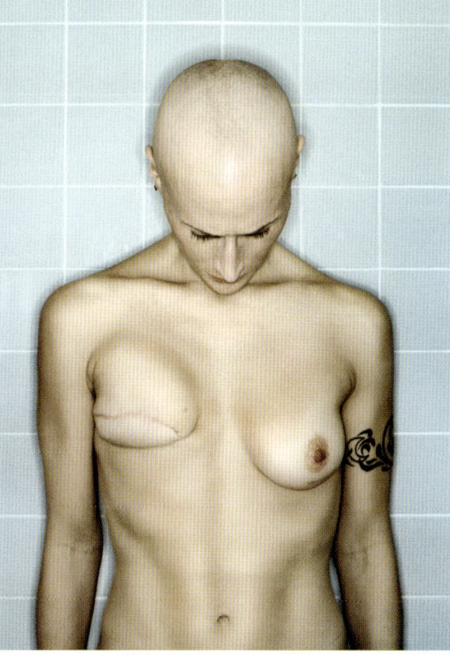

4

Christopher Dawson
Coverage

WINNER
FINE ART

Christopher Dawson was born in 1972 in New York City. His work is represented in the permanent collections of the Smithsonian American Art Museum, the Nelson-Atkins Museum of Art, and la Maison Européenne de la Photographie, among others. Pictures from his series *Coverage* were selected for the 2011 Critical Mass Top 50, and included in the recent exhibition *Crime Unseen* at the Museum of Contemporary Photography in Chicago. He lives in New York with his family.

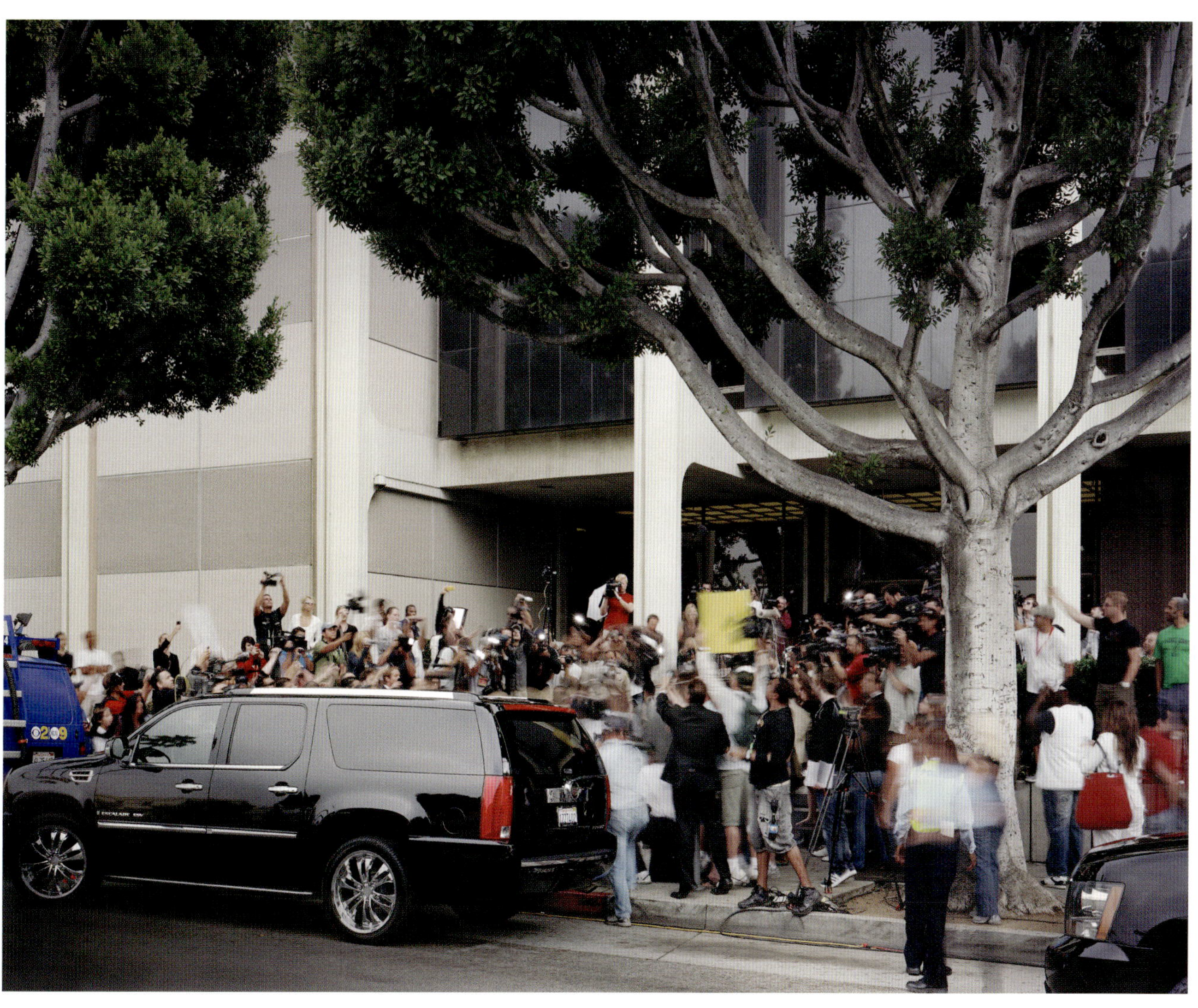

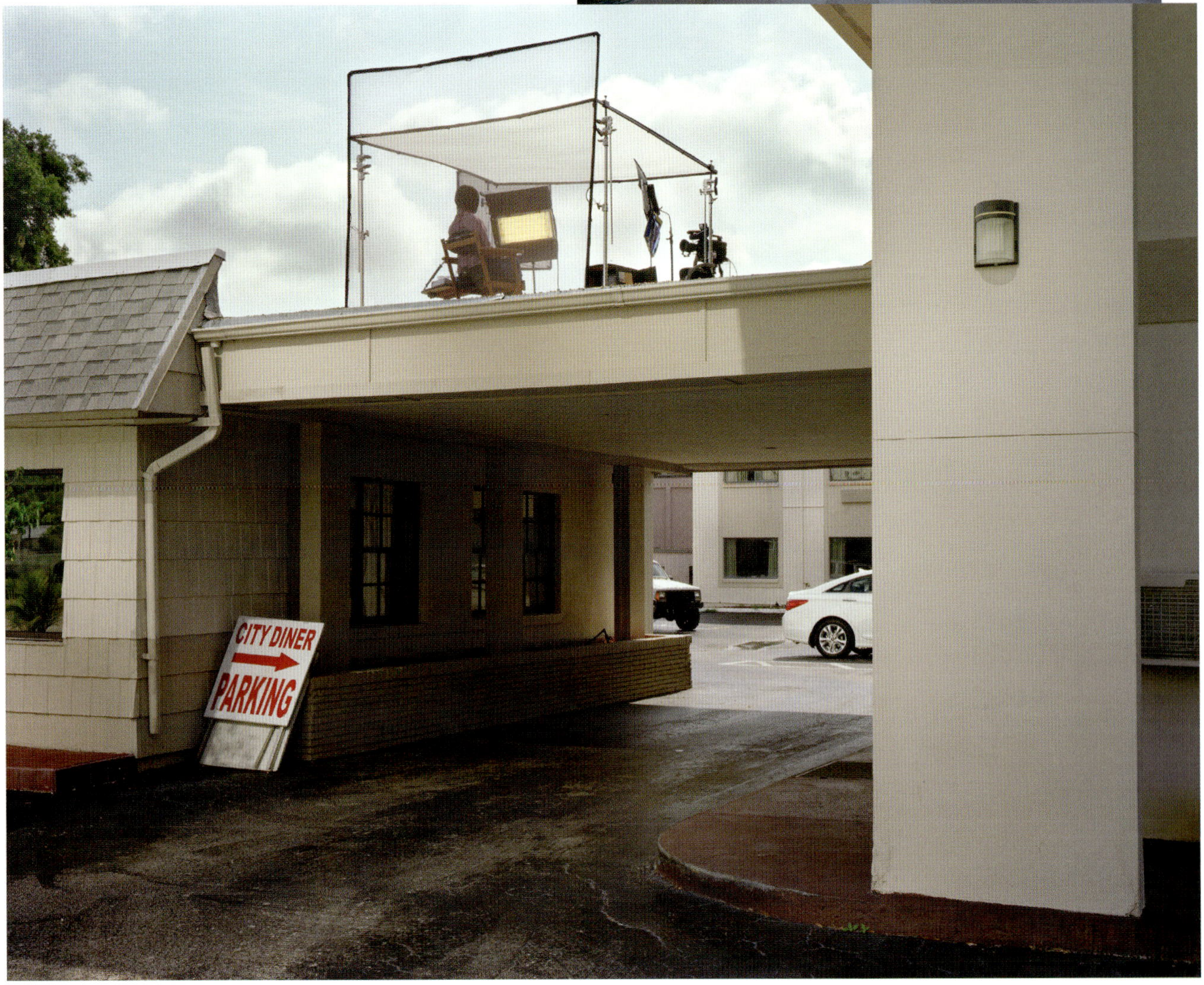

Christopher Dawson

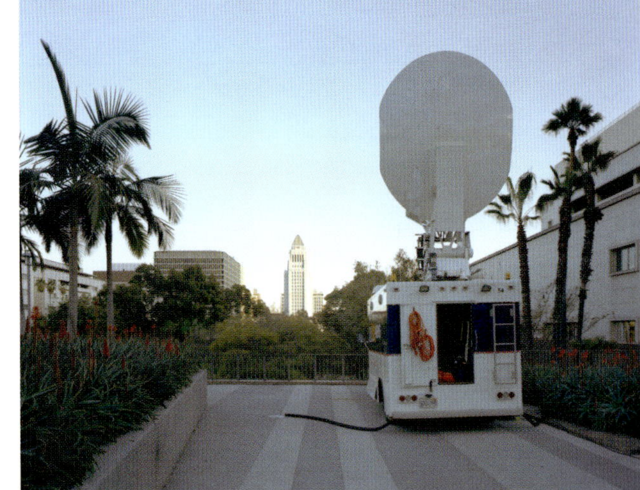

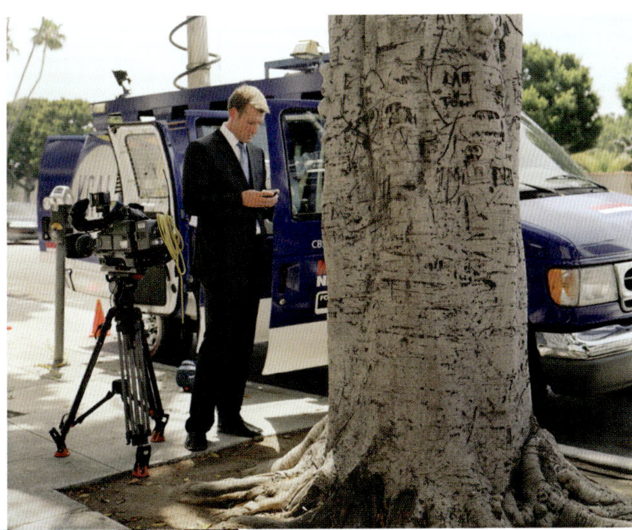

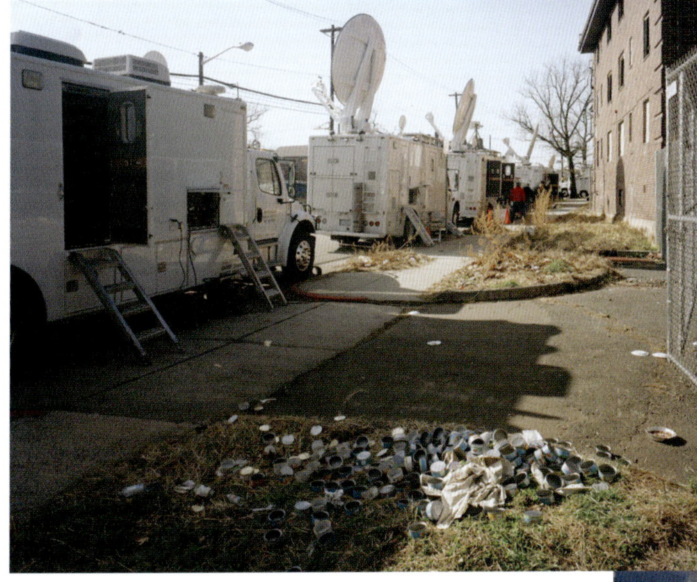

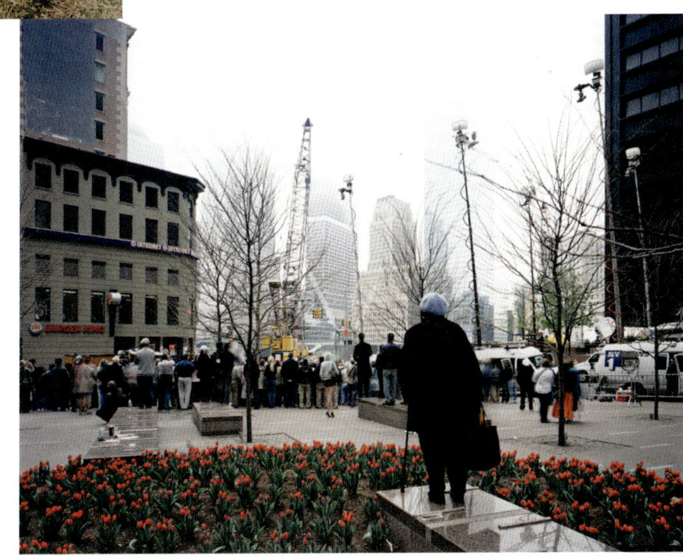

1. Andres Gonzalez
2. Emily Schiffer
3. Katrin Koenning
4. Shane Lavalette

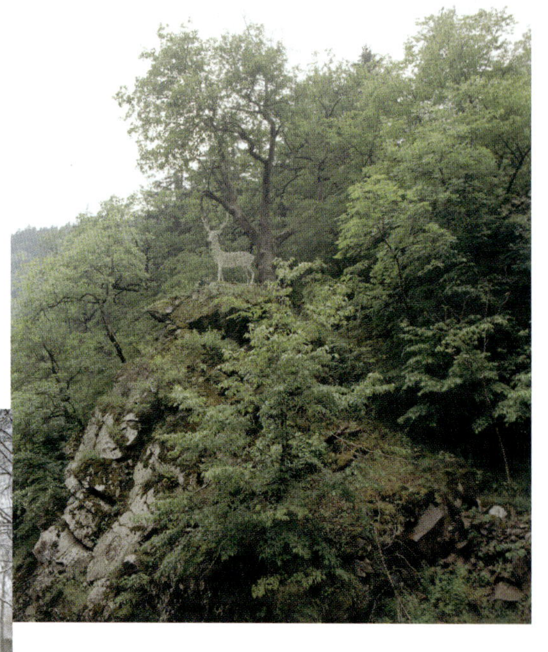

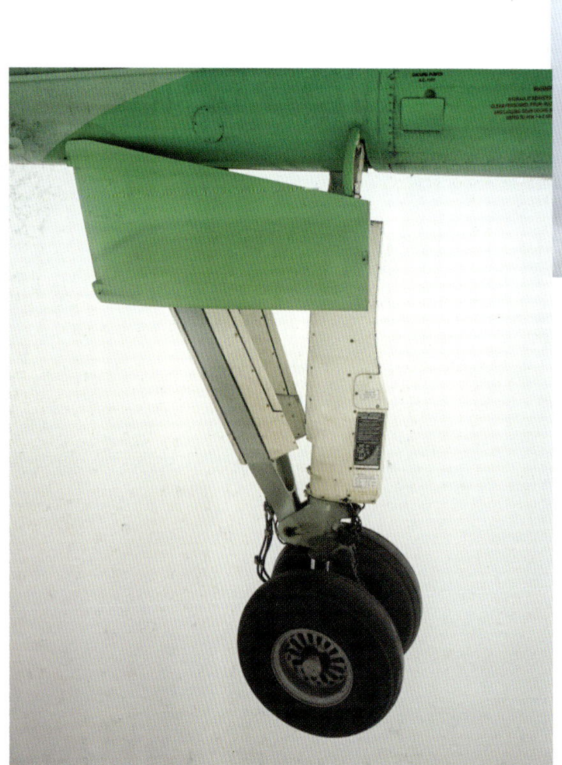

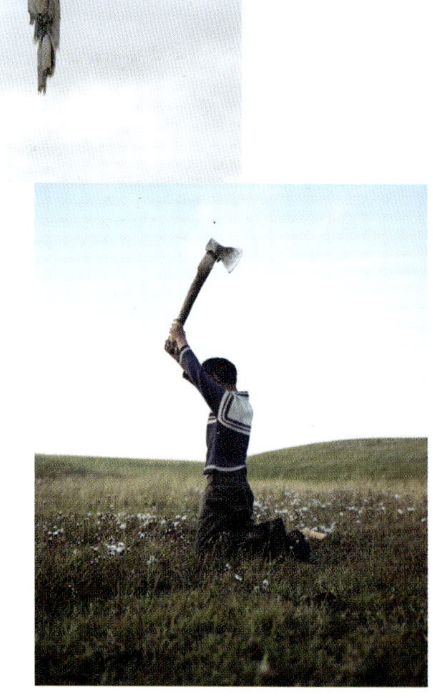

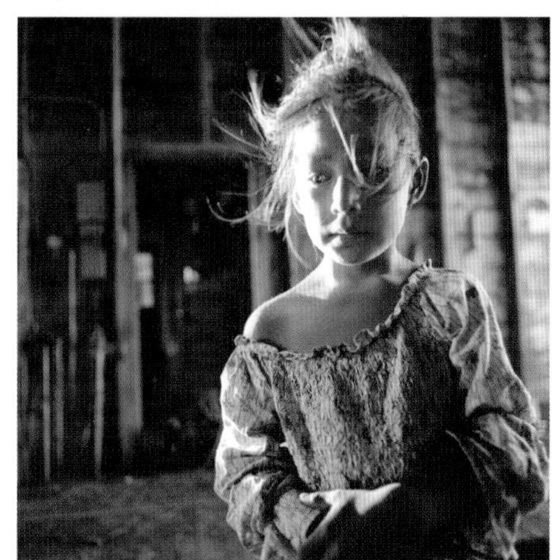

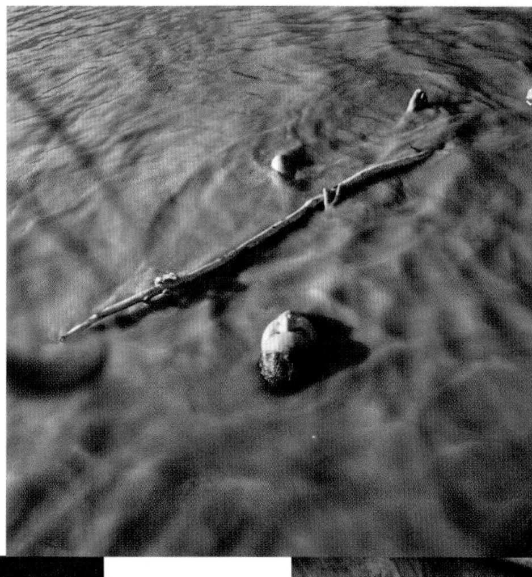

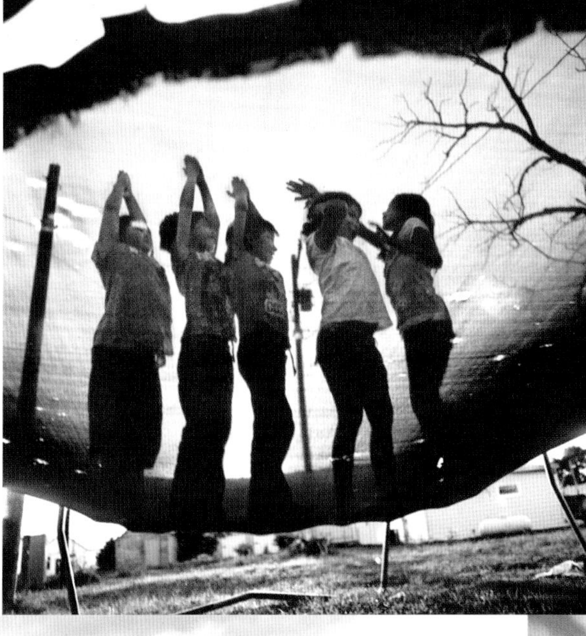

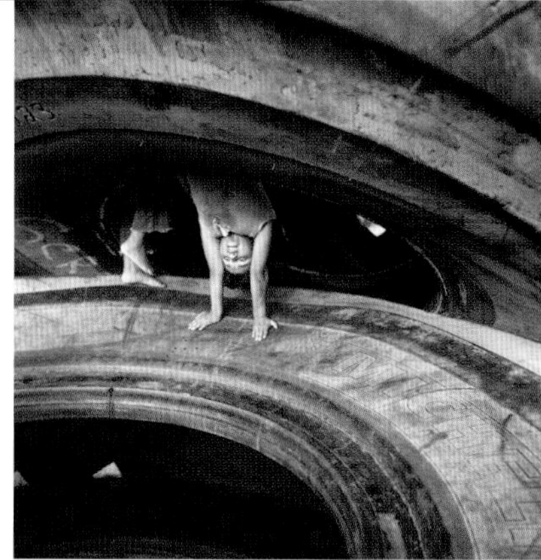

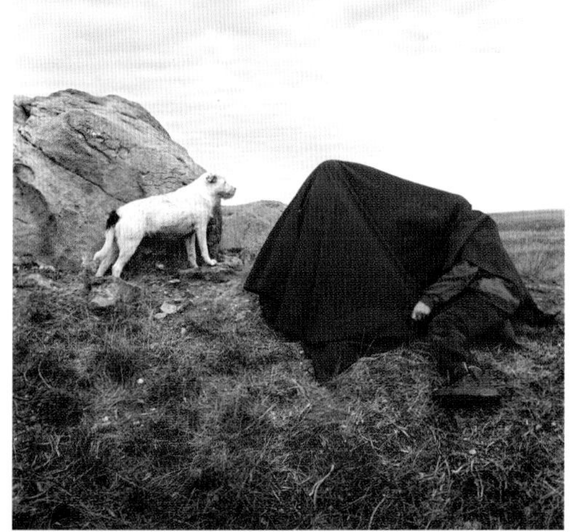

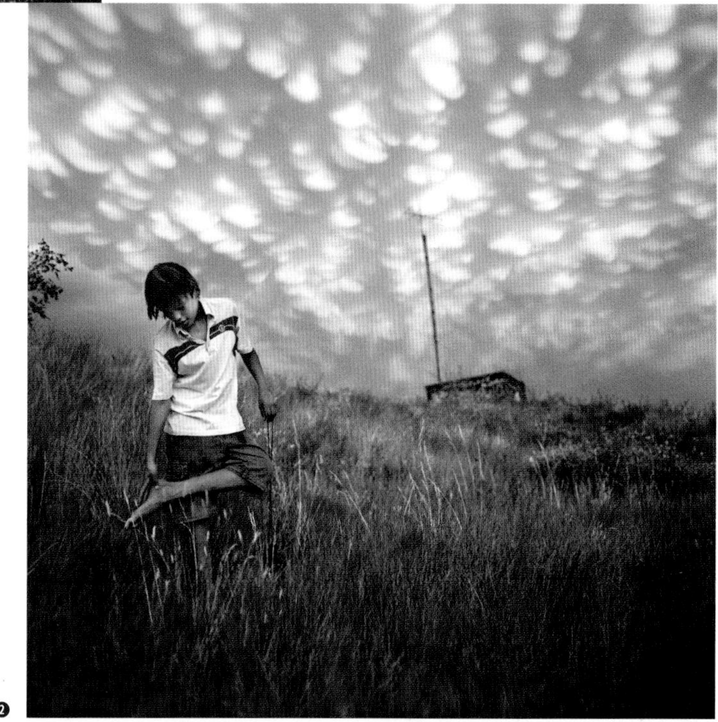

2

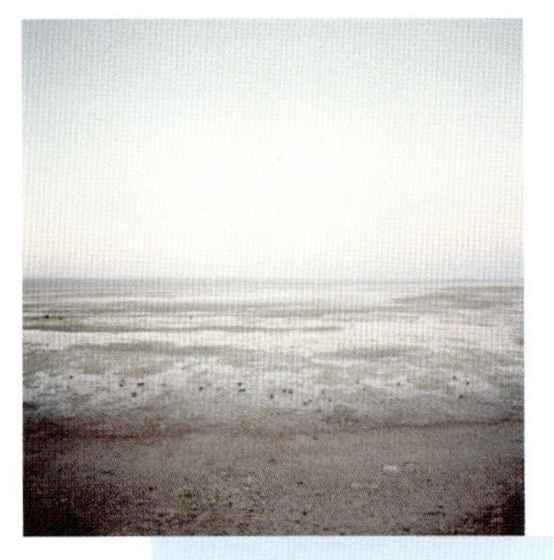

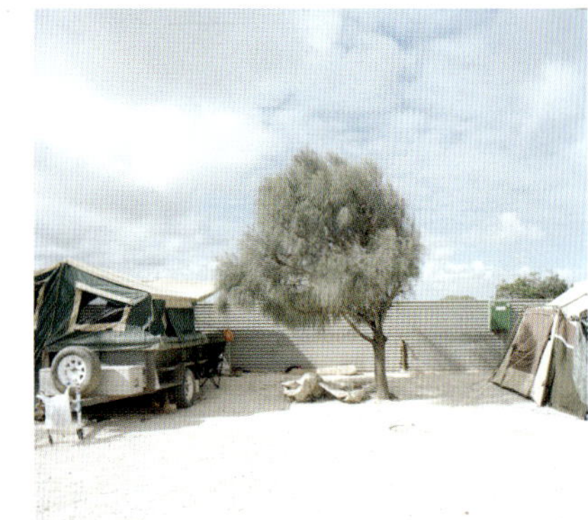

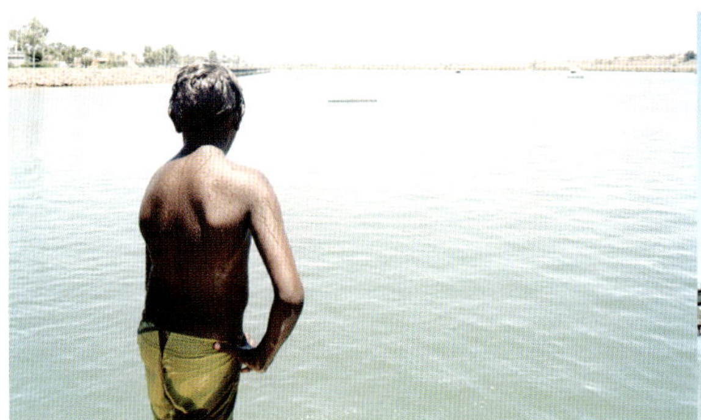

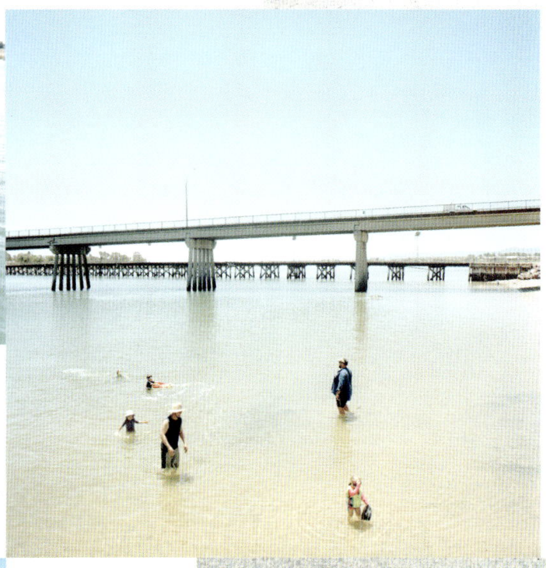

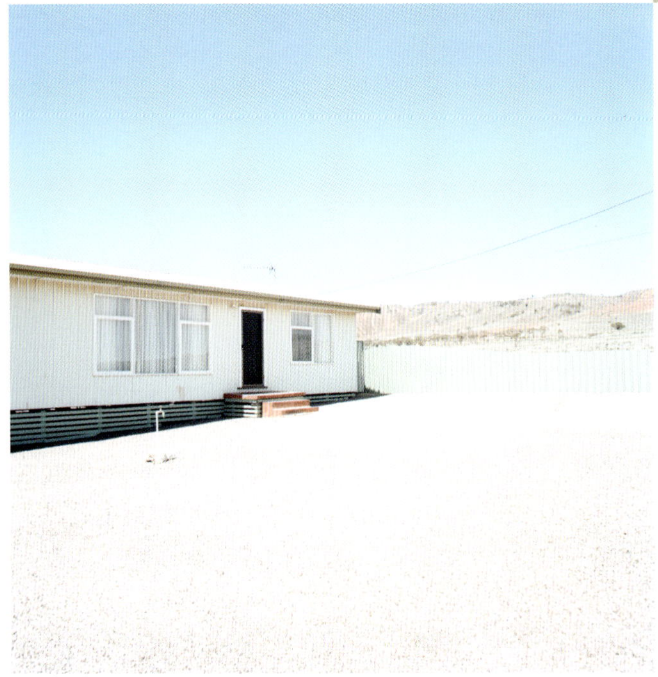

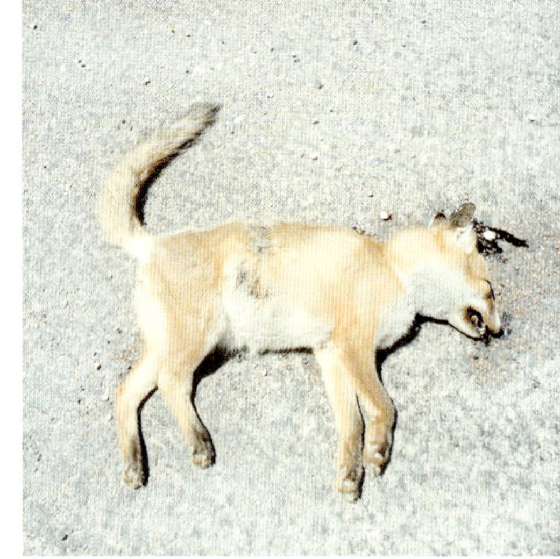

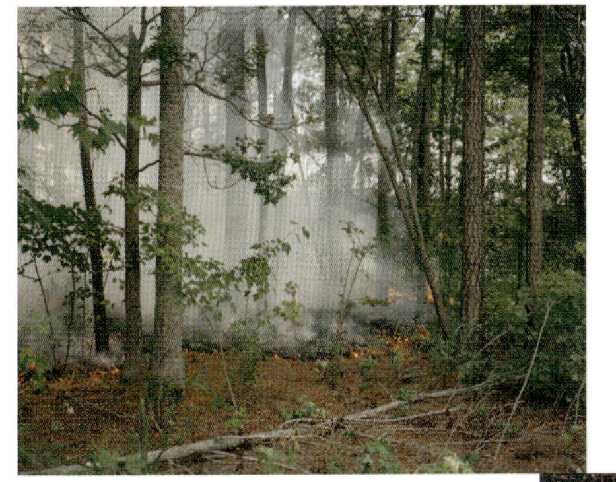

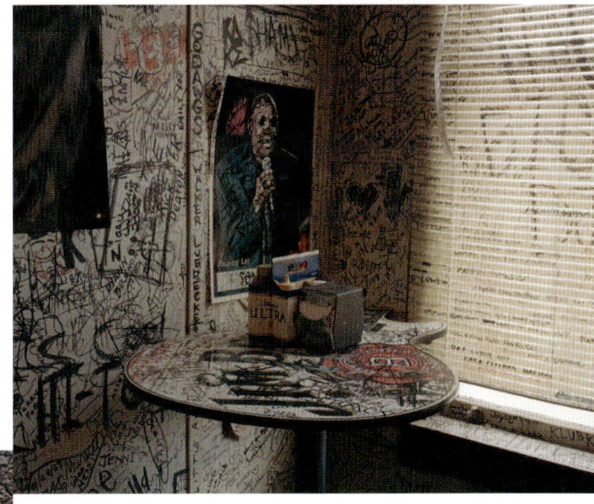

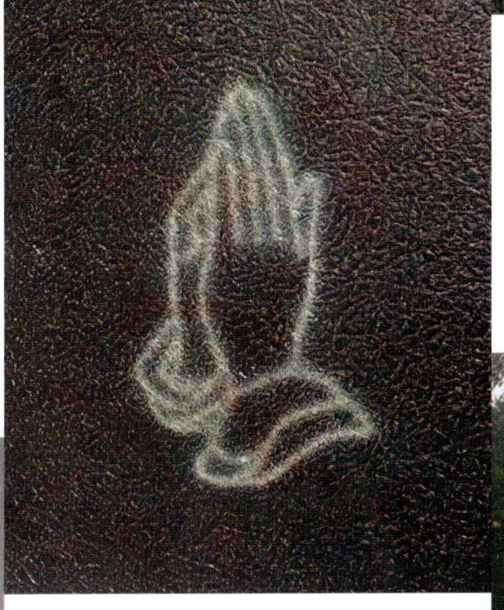

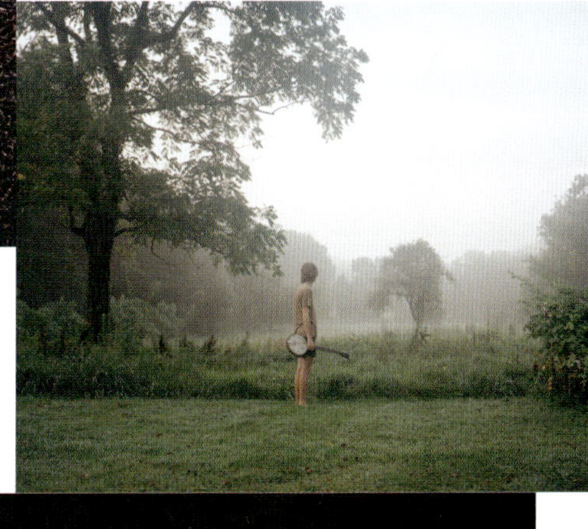

❹

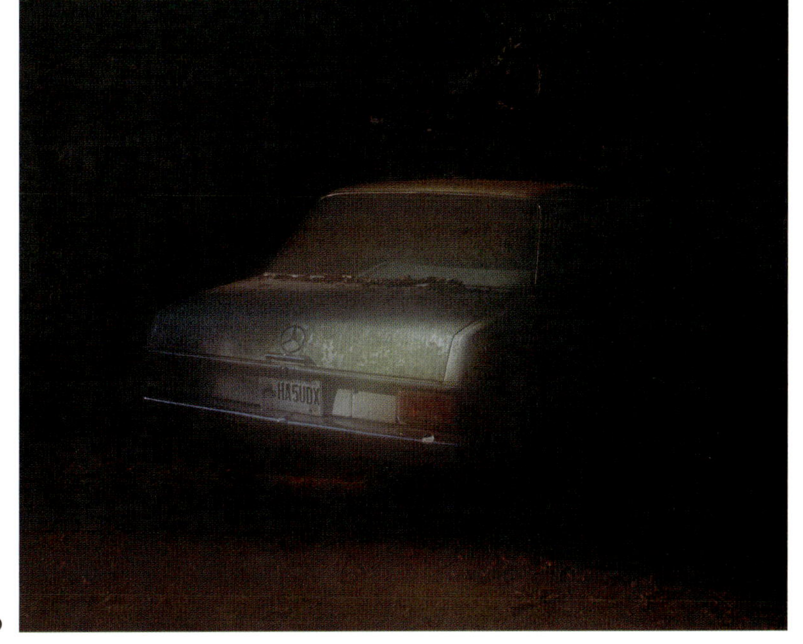

Benjamin Lowy
Iraq | Perspectives

WINNER
PHOTOBOOK

Benjamin Lowy received a BFA from Washington University in St. Louis in 2002 and began his career covering the Iraq War in 2003. In 2004 Lowy attended the World Press Joop Swart Masterclass, that same year he was named in the Photo District News 30. Lowy has received awards from World Press Photo, POYi, *PDN*, Communication Arts, *American Photo*, the Society of Publication Designers, and has been a finalist for the Oskar Barnack Award, among many other distinctions. Lowy's work from Iraq, Darfur, and Afghanistan has been exhibited at the Tate Modern, SF MoMA, Houston Center for Photography, Invalides, and Arles.

In 2011 Lowy's *Iraq | Perspectives* was selected by William Eggleston for the Center for Documentary Studies/Honickman First Book Prize in Photography. In 2012, Lowy was awarded the Magnum Foundation Emergency Fund to continue his work in Libya. In the same year, he received the International Center of Photography Infinity Award for Photojournalism.

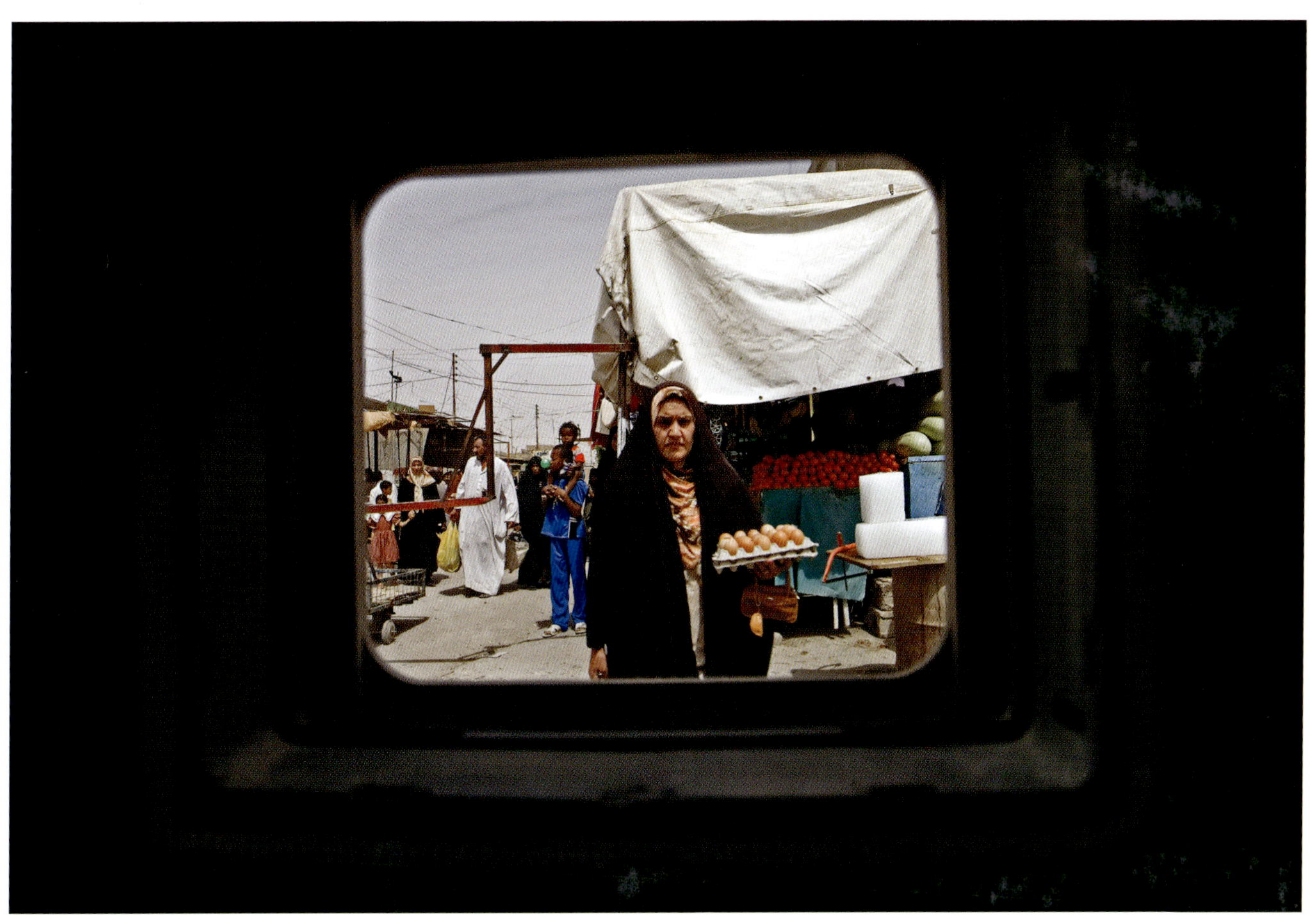

Benjamin Lowy

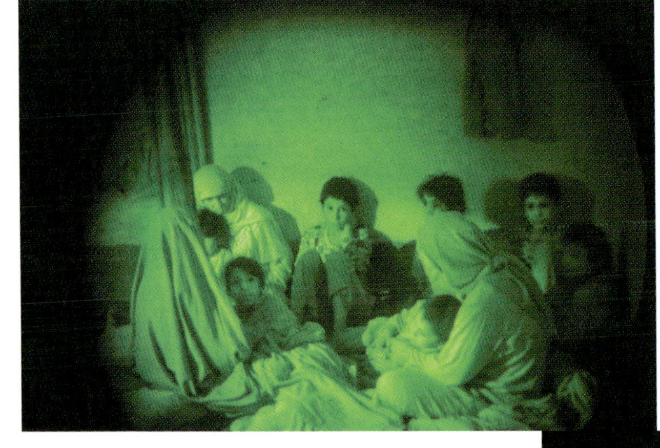

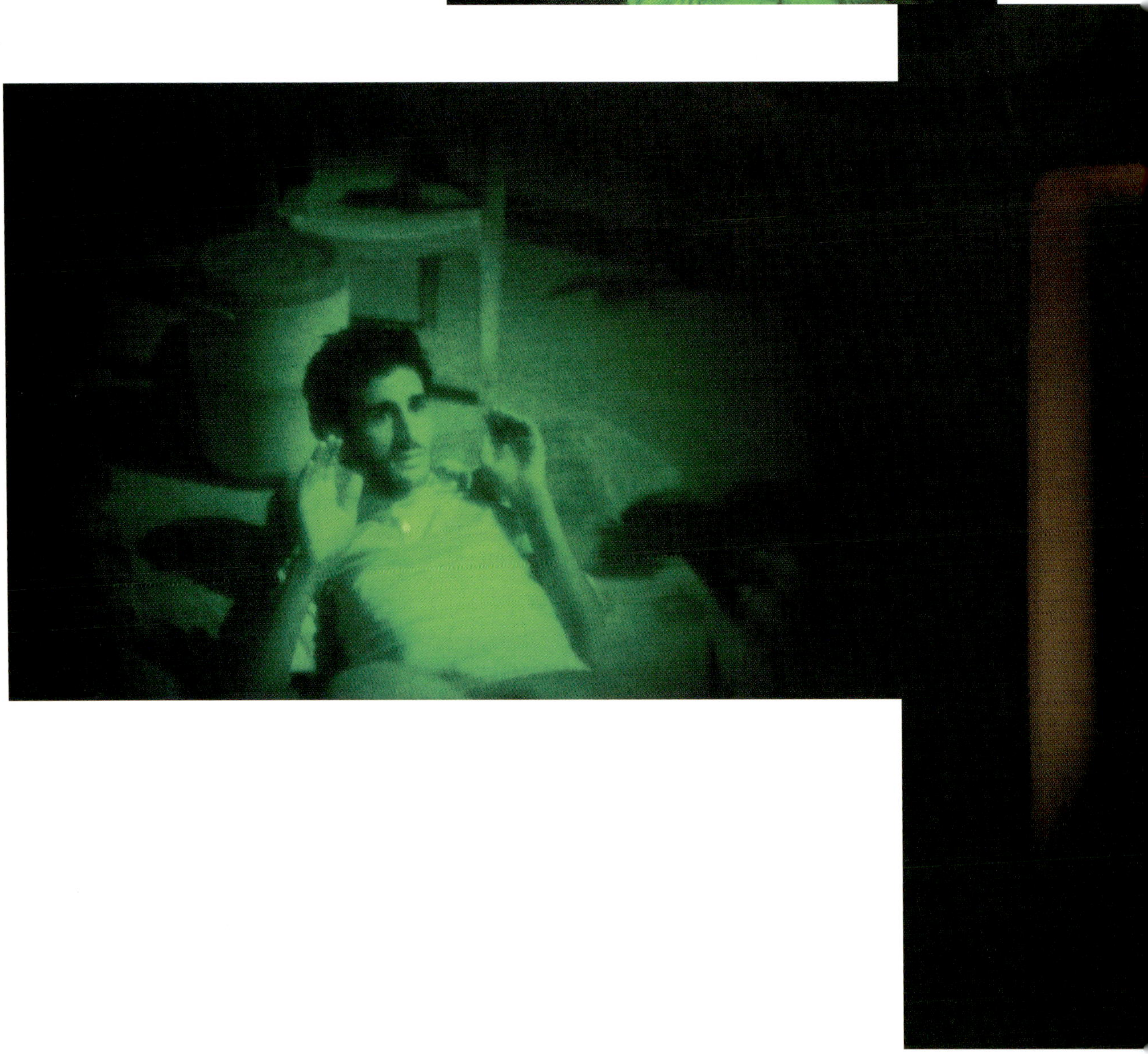

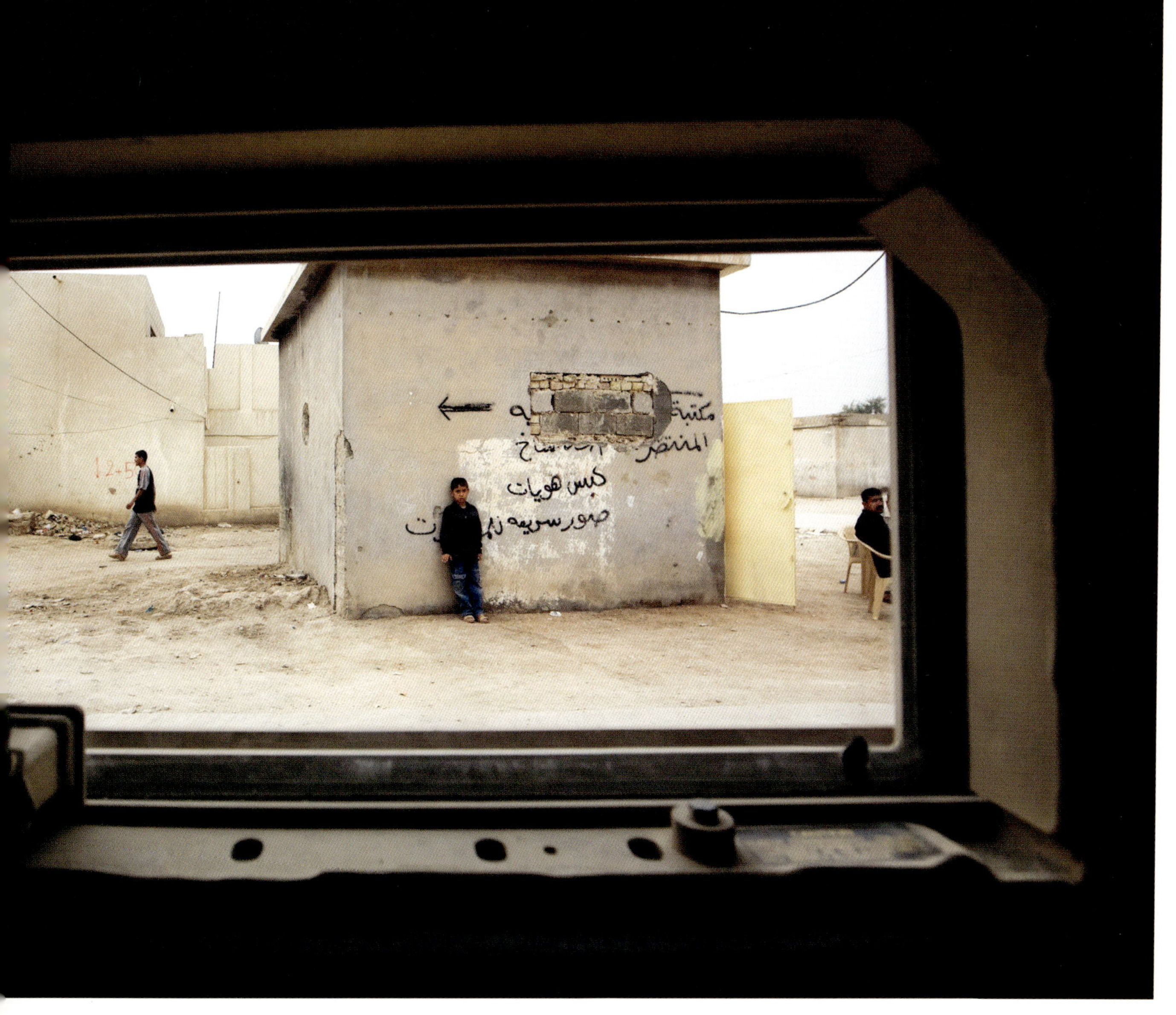
مكتبة
المنتصر
كبس هويات

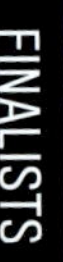

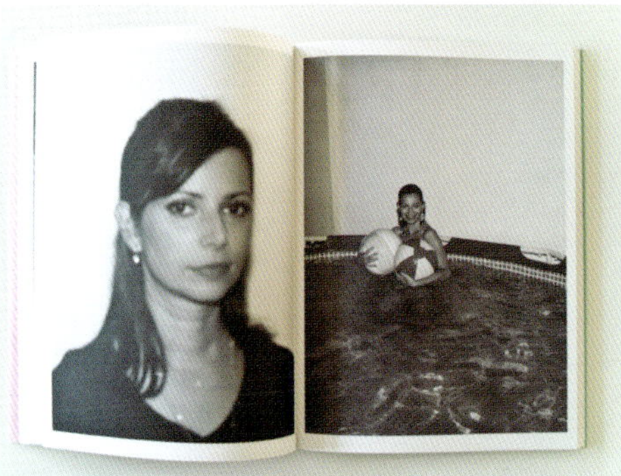

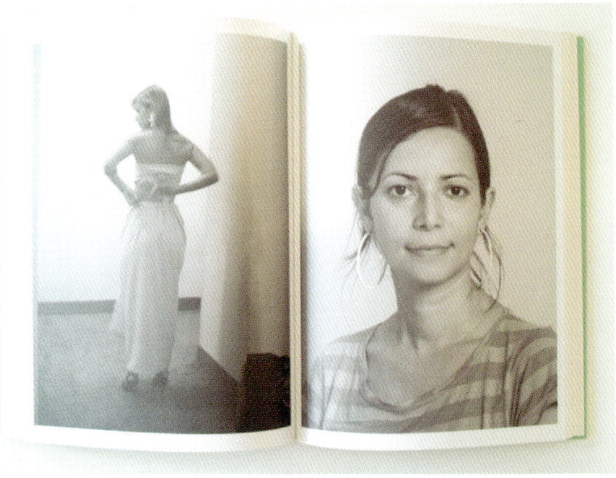

❶

THIS IS NOT MY WIFE

Erik van der Weijde

Rollo Press

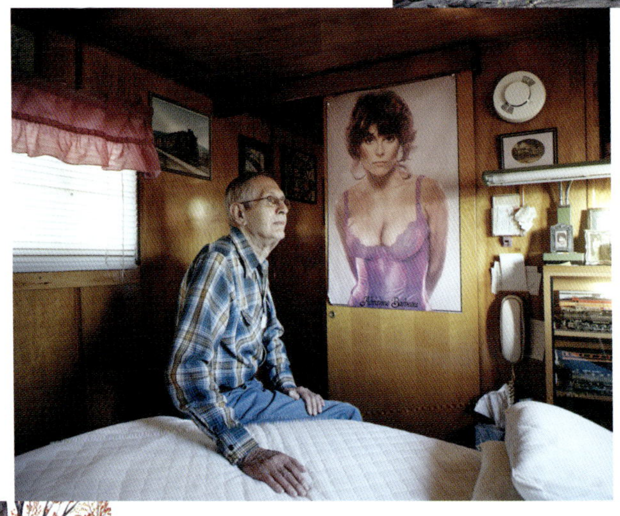

❷

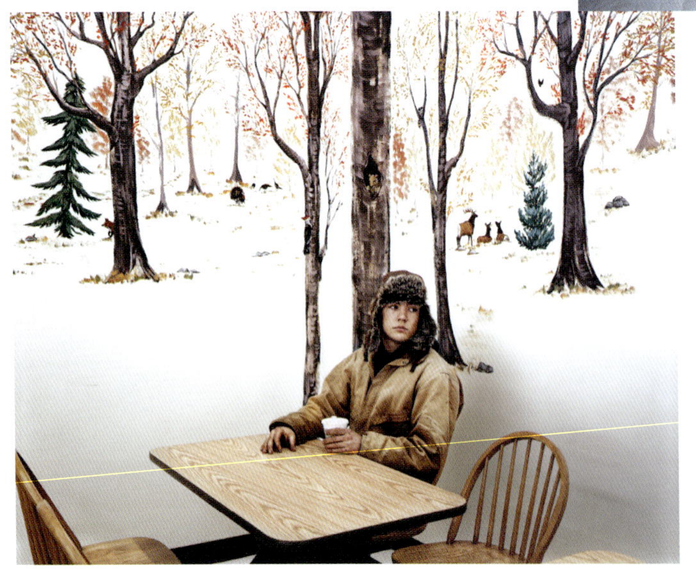

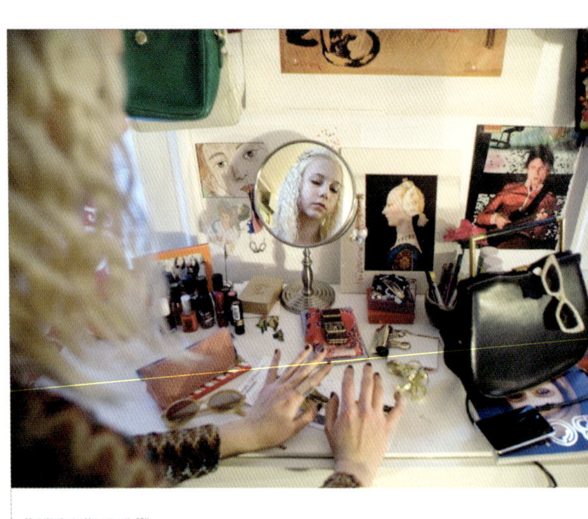

Mimi, Winchester, Massachusetts 2011

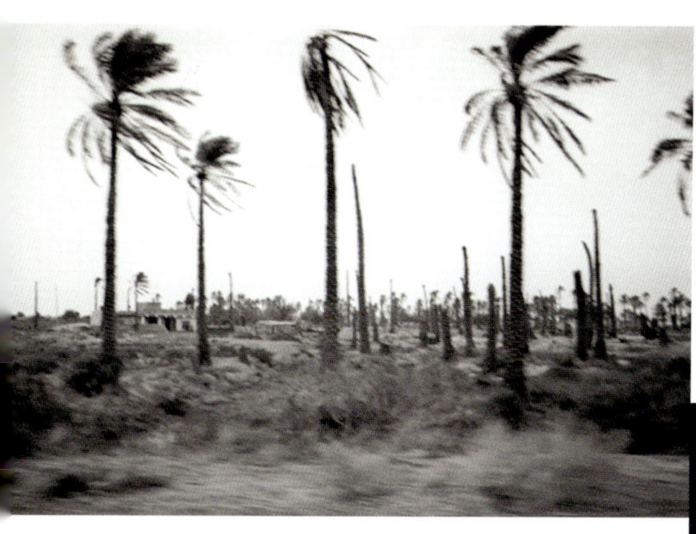

3

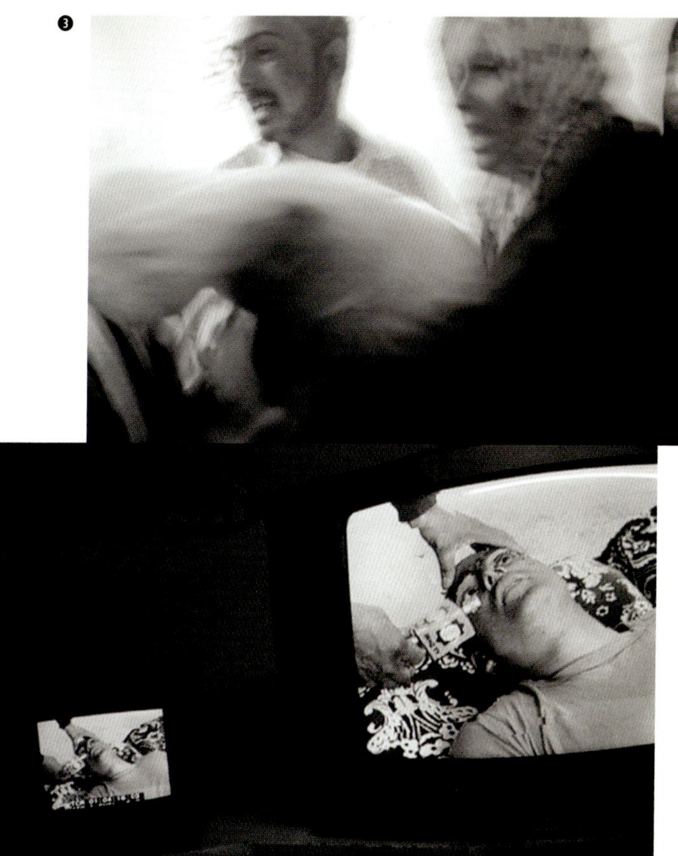

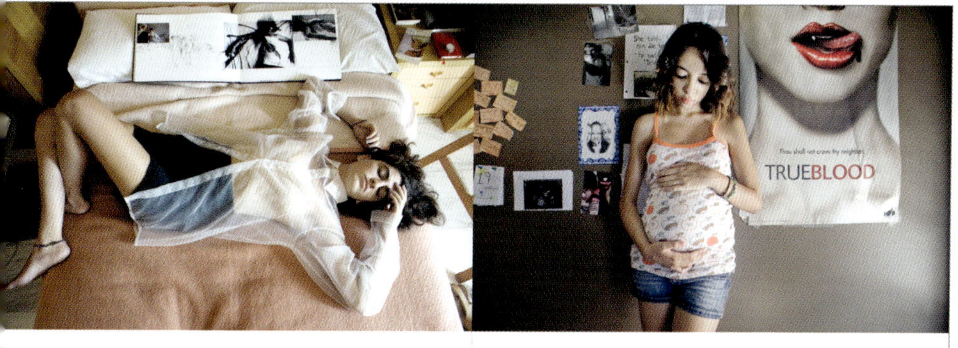

4

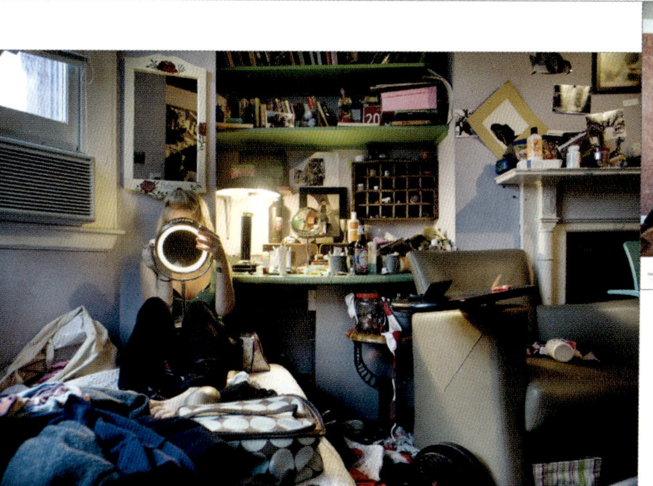

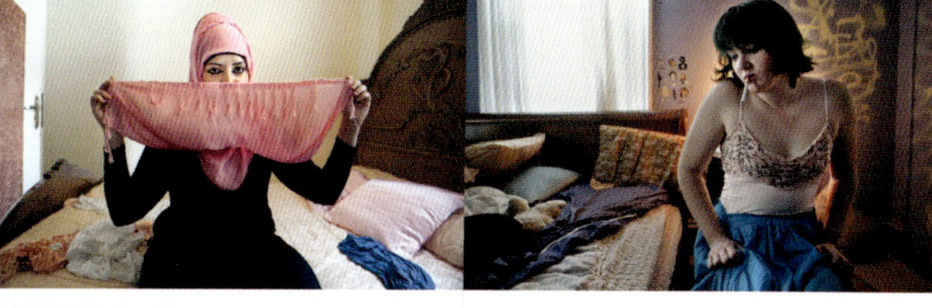

1. Erik van der Weijde
2. Thomas Gardiner
3. Ilkka Uimonen
4. Rania Matar

Kai Löffelbein
Kids of Sodom: E-waste in Ghana

WINNER
STUDENT DOCUMENTARY

Kai Löffelbein is a freelance photographer from Germany. He studied political science in Berlin and later photojournalism and documentary photography in Hanover and has worked in various countries in South America, Asia, Africa, and Eastern Europe.

Through documentary photography, Löffelbein shows the effects of socio-political and economic processes on common people. His work has been exhibited internationally in numerous shows and festivals and won several prizes including Unicef Photo of the Year, 2011; The New York Photo Awards, 2012; DAYS JAPAN International Photojournalism Awards, 3rd prize; FotoVisura Spotlight Grant 2012; *PDN* Photo Annual, Student 2012; Px3-Prix de la Photographie, Paris, Honorable Mention; PhotoPhilanthropy Activist Awards, Student, 2013, Canon Portfolio Award; and is one of Critical Mass, Top 50, 2012. He is represented by Laif photo agency.

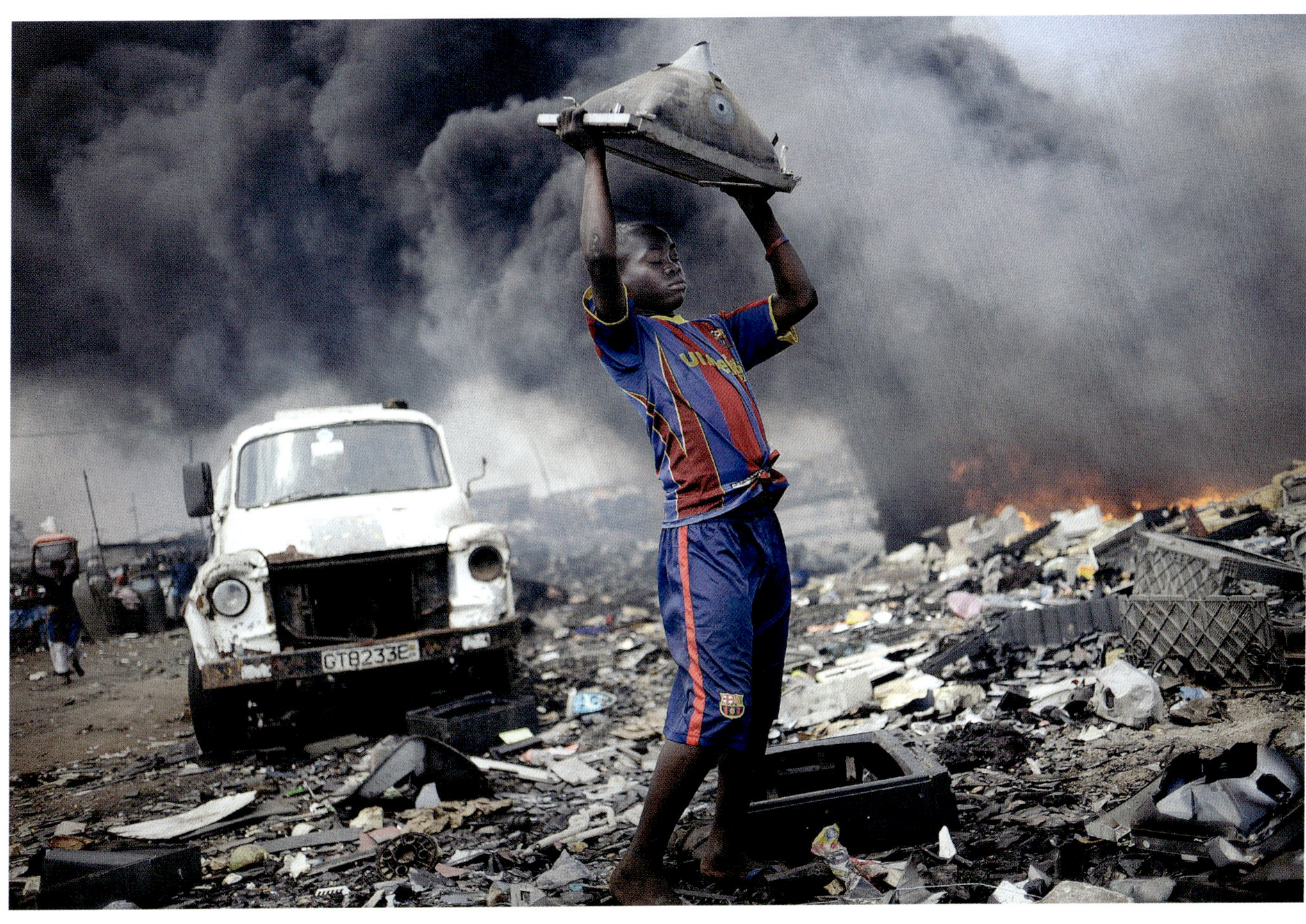
GT8233E

Kai Löffelbein

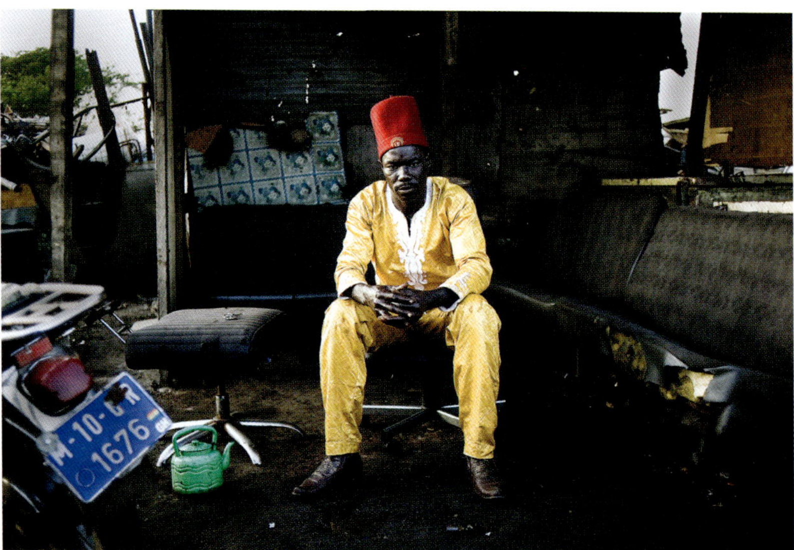

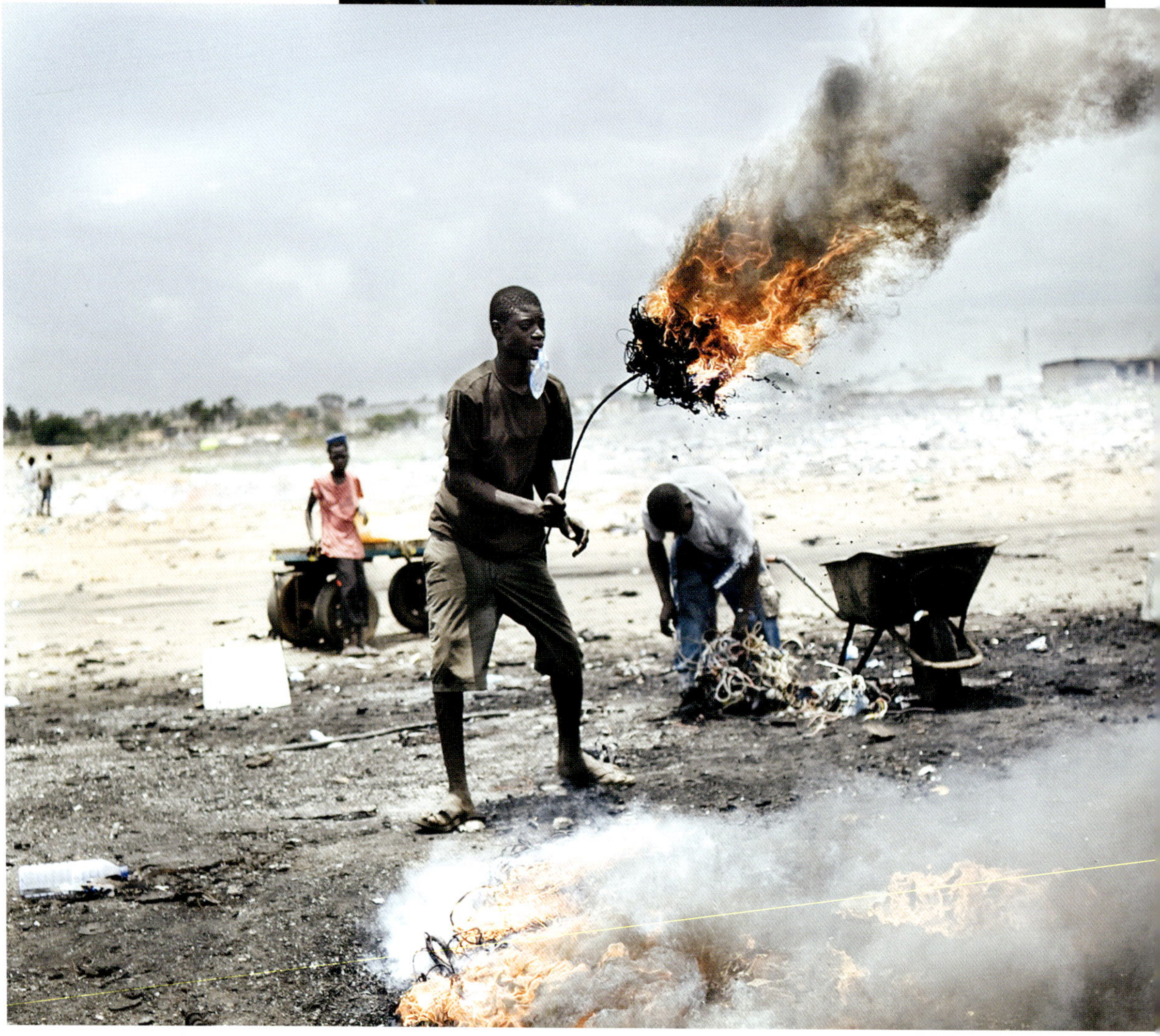

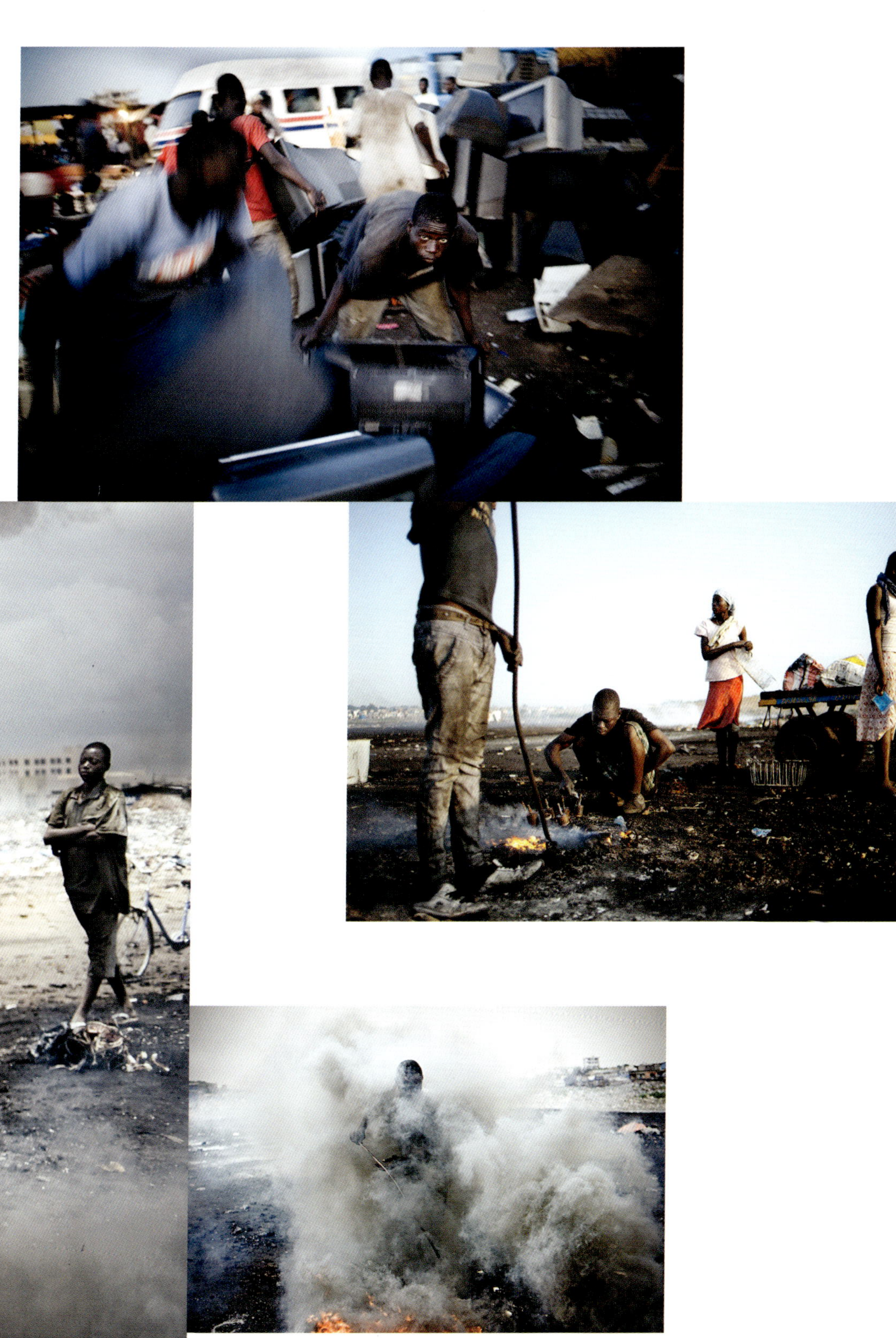

❶

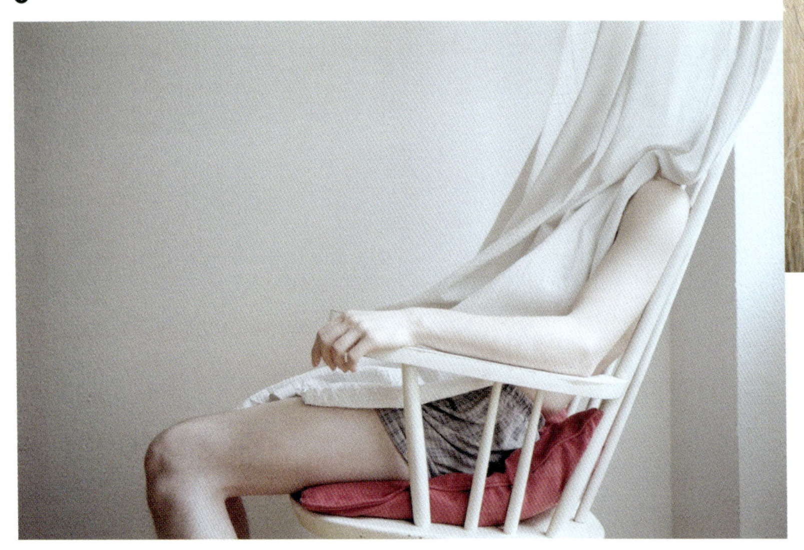

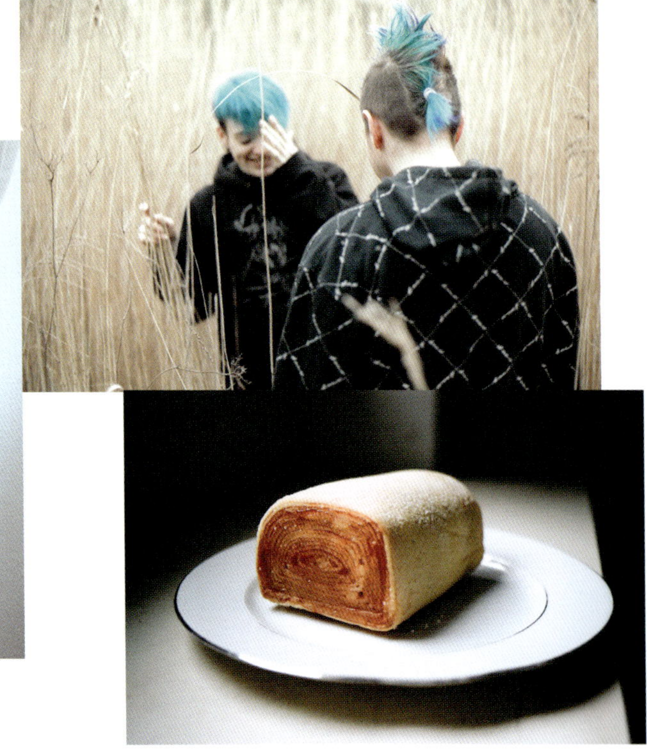

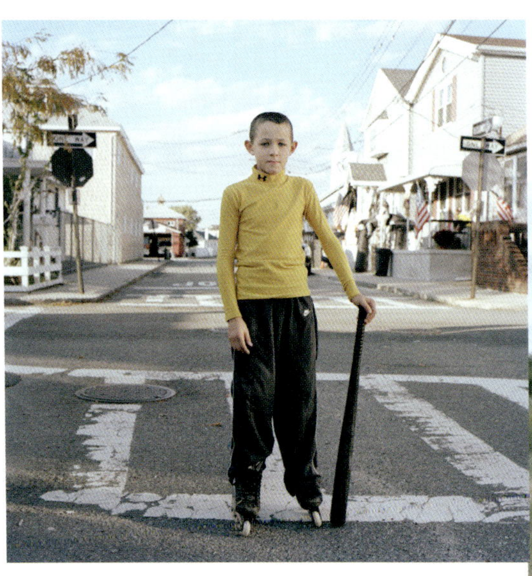

❷

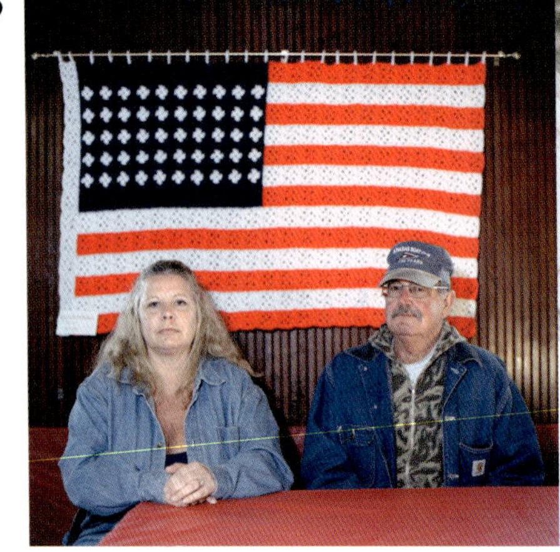

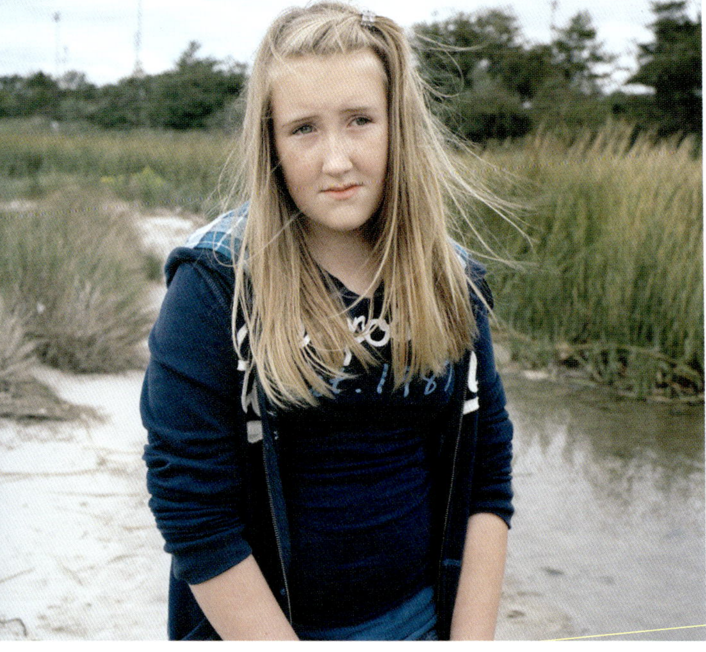

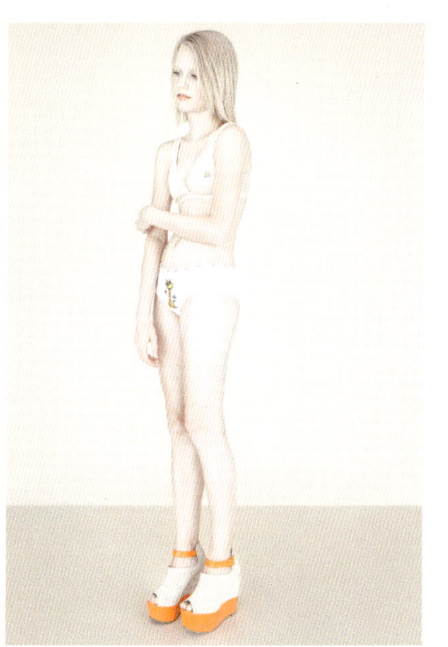

❹

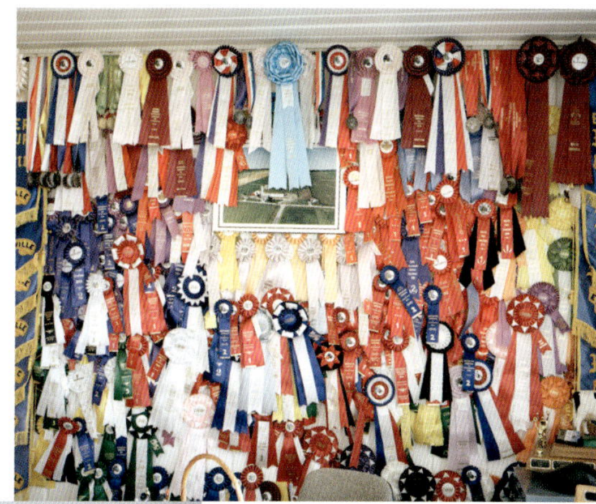

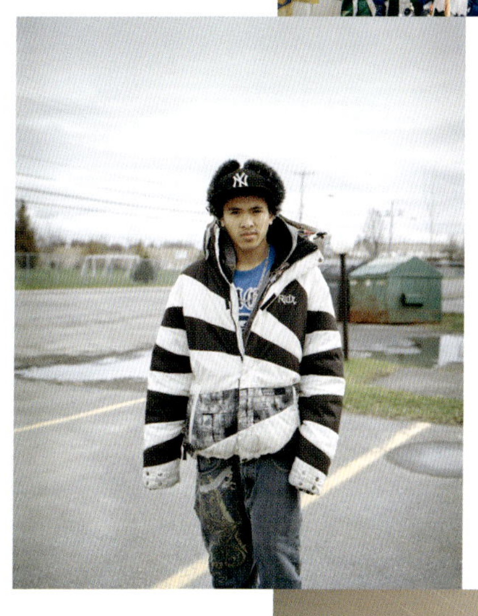

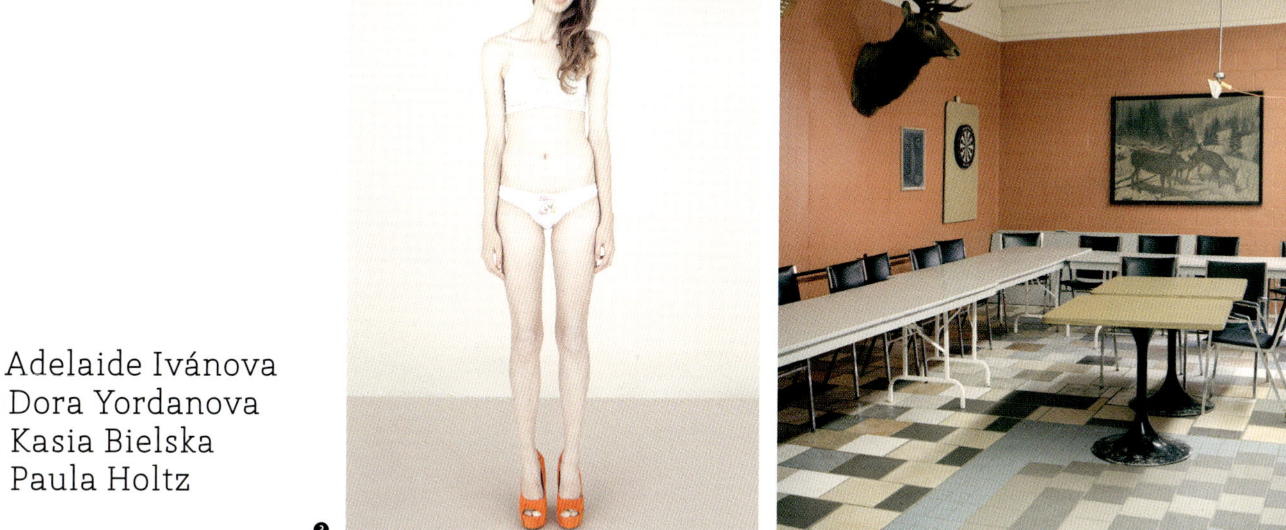

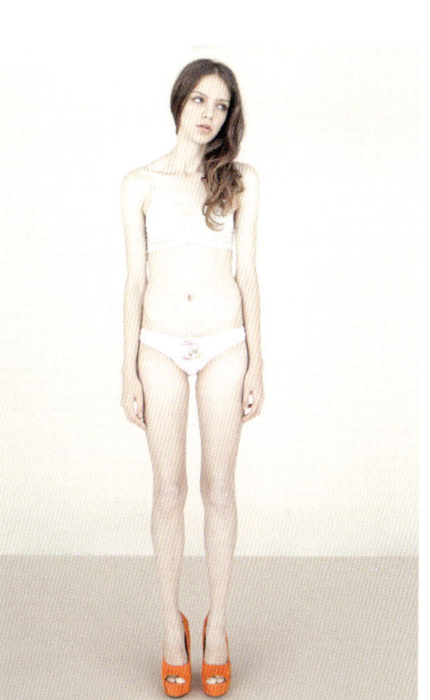

❸

1. Adelaide Ivánova
2. Dora Yordanova
3. Kasia Bielska
4. Paula Holtz

I-Hsuen Chen
Nowhere in Taiwan

WINNER
STUDENT FINE ART

I-Hsuen Chen is a New York-based photographer, born and raised in Taiwan. He received an MFA in photography from Pratt Institute in 2012. His work has been selected for the 2012 New York Photo Festival Invitational and his series *Nowhere in Taiwan* is in the permanent collection at The Museum of Fine Arts, Houston. Chen was chosen as one of Magenta Foundation's Flash Forward Emerging Photographers 2012. He was also an honorable mention Hot Shot in Jen Beckman's Hey Hot Shot! competition. Chen's work has been published in magazines and online, including *Photograph Magazine*, *Conveyor Magazine*, *PHOTONews*, *The New Yorker's Photo Booth*, *American Photo*, and the CCNY blog. His work has also been shown at hpgrp Gallery New York; Foley Gallery; Ed. Varie Gallery; 25CPW Gallery; and ISE Cultural Foundation in New York. Before coming to the U.S. he was a professional opera and choir singer in Taiwan.

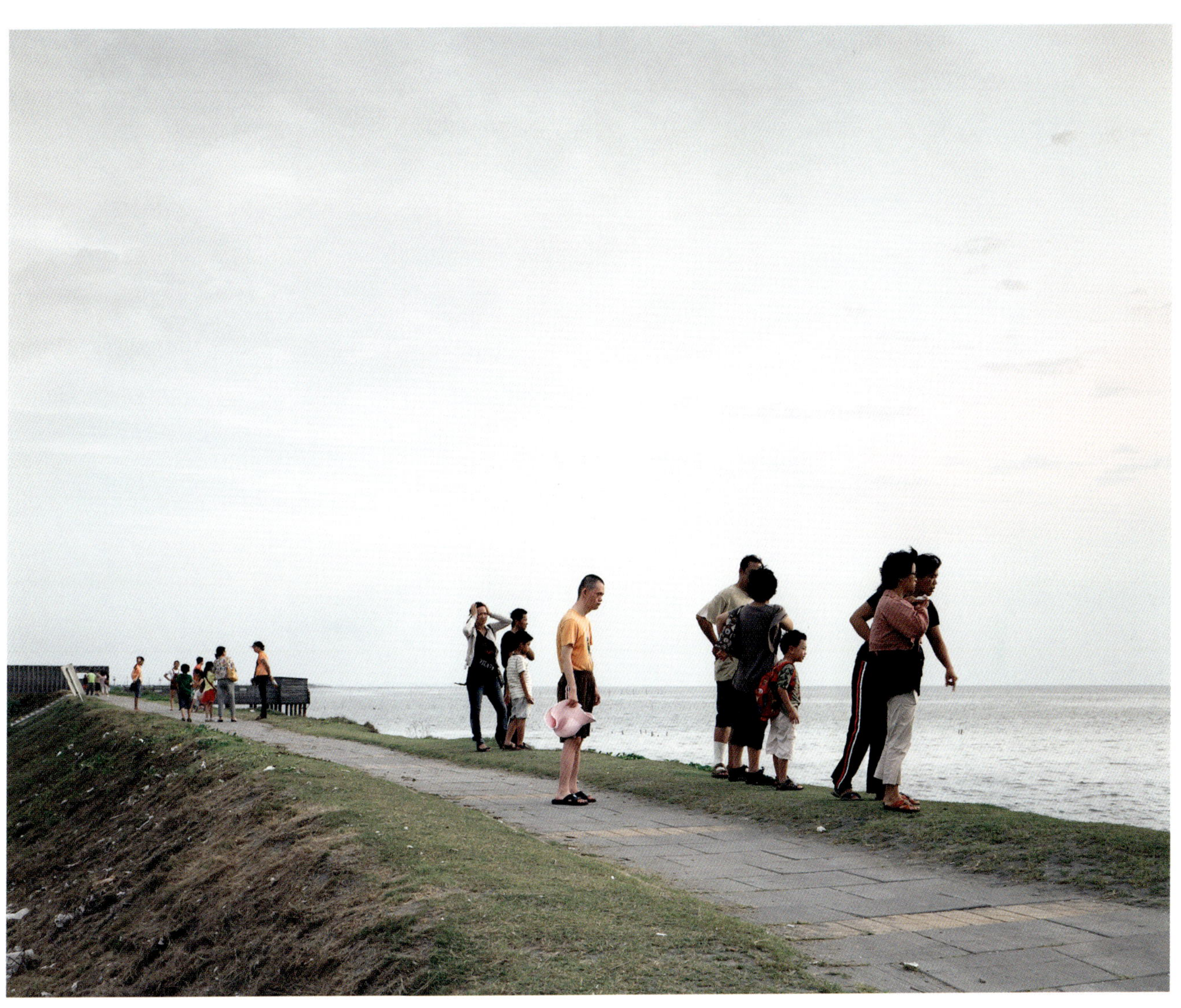

I-Hsuen Chen

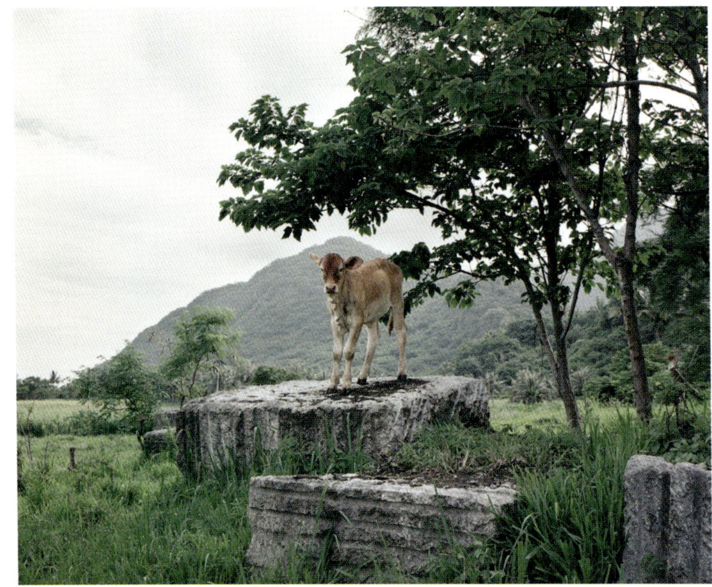

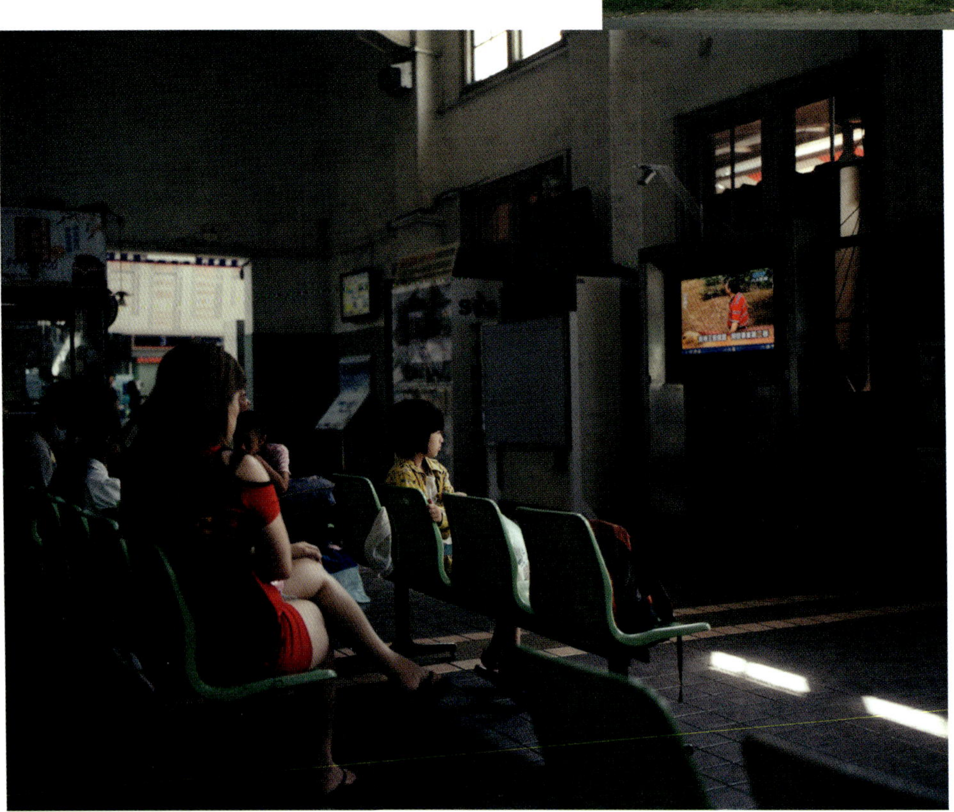

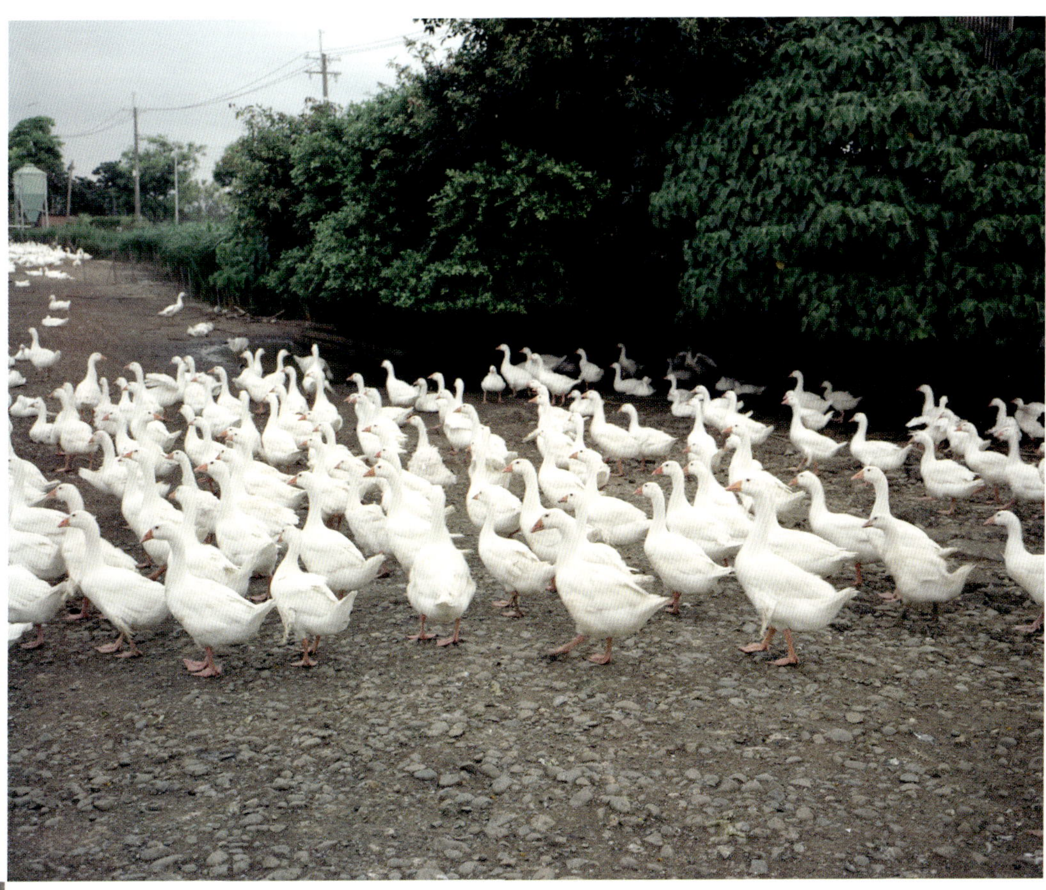

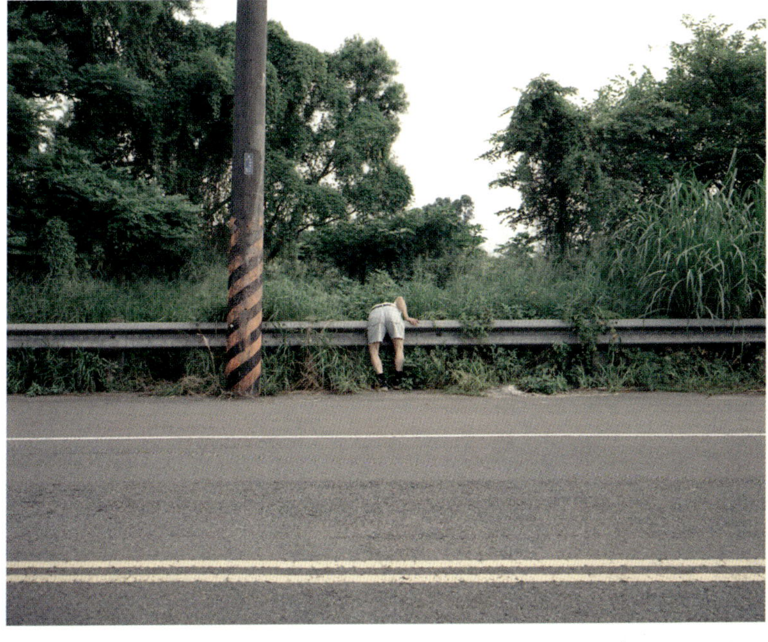

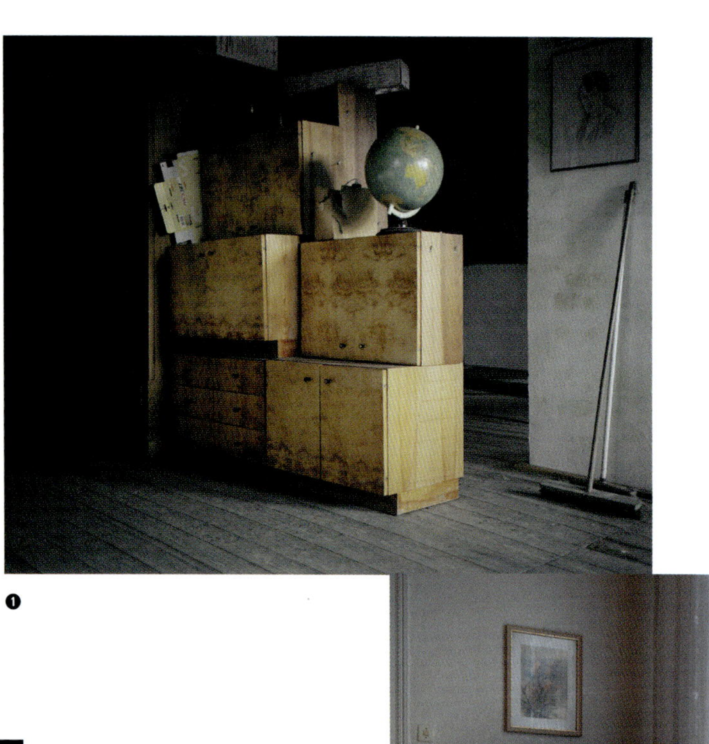

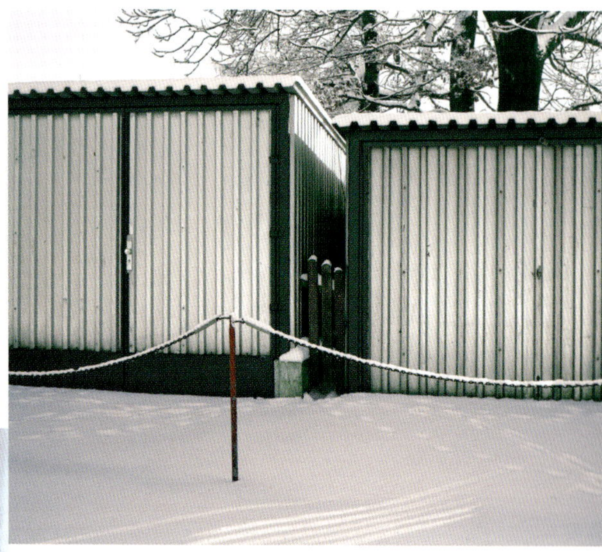

❶

❷

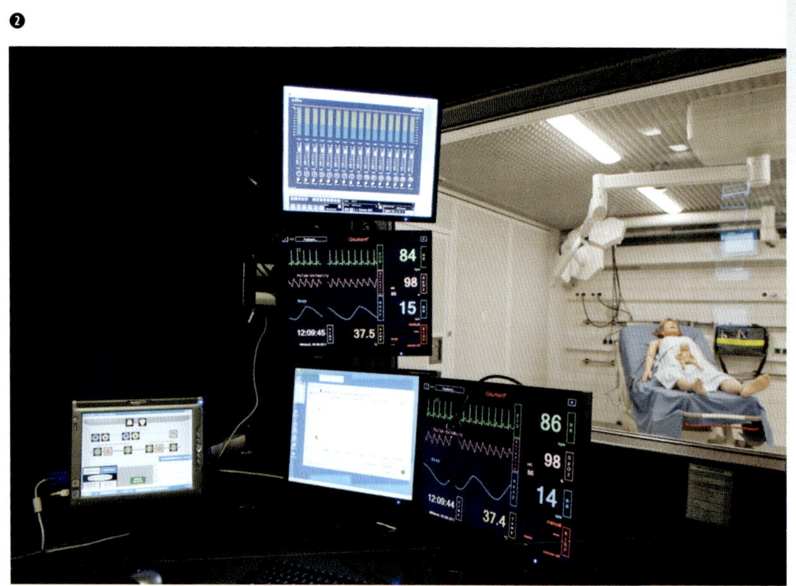

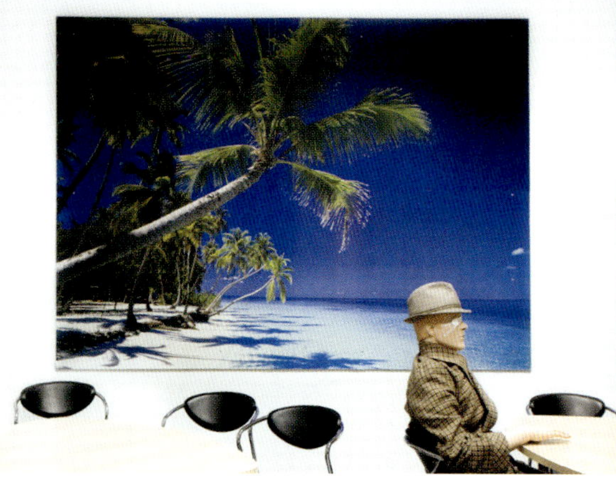

1. Christoph David Drange
2. Linda Dreisen
3. Louise Åkebrand

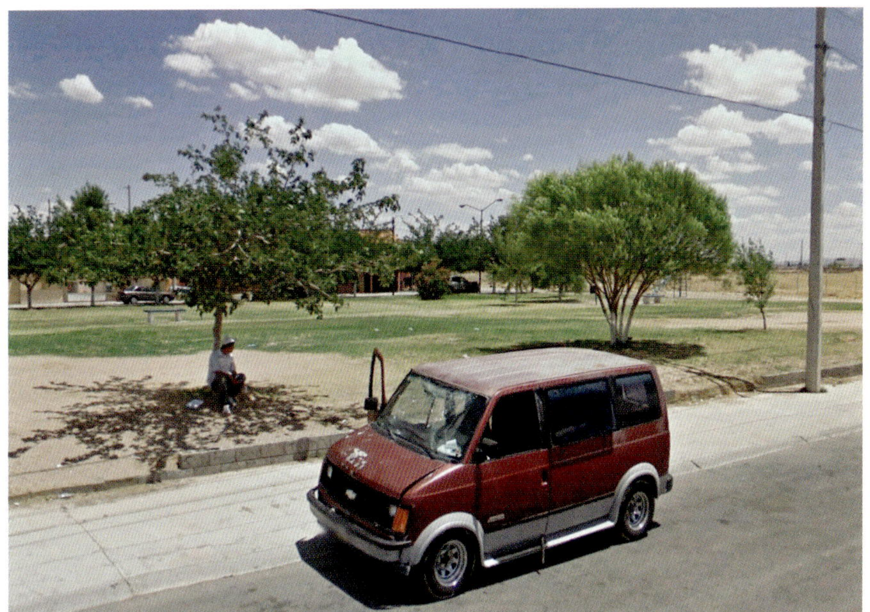

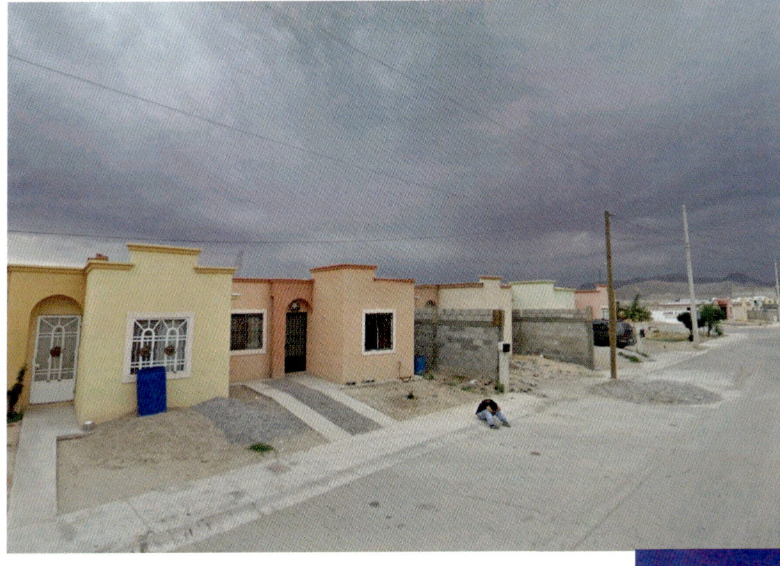

3

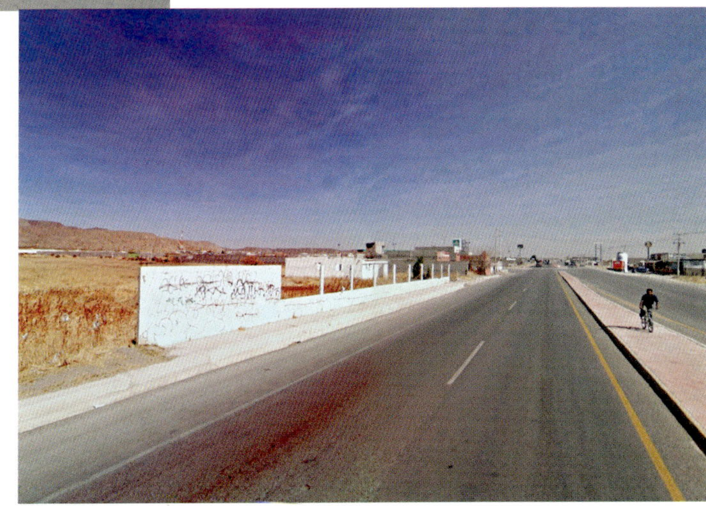

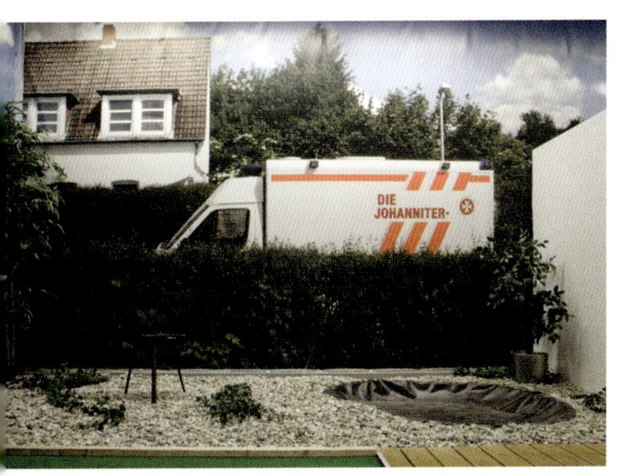

Steph Martyniuk
These are Them: Part I

WINNER
STUDENT PERSONAL PORTFOLIO

Steph Martyniuk is a commercial photographer based in Toronto, Canada. She uses portraiture and documentary photography to convey the divide between realism and imagination. She began her career in New York working with Ryan McGinley, who also served as a mentor. Martyniuk currently lives and works in Toronto.

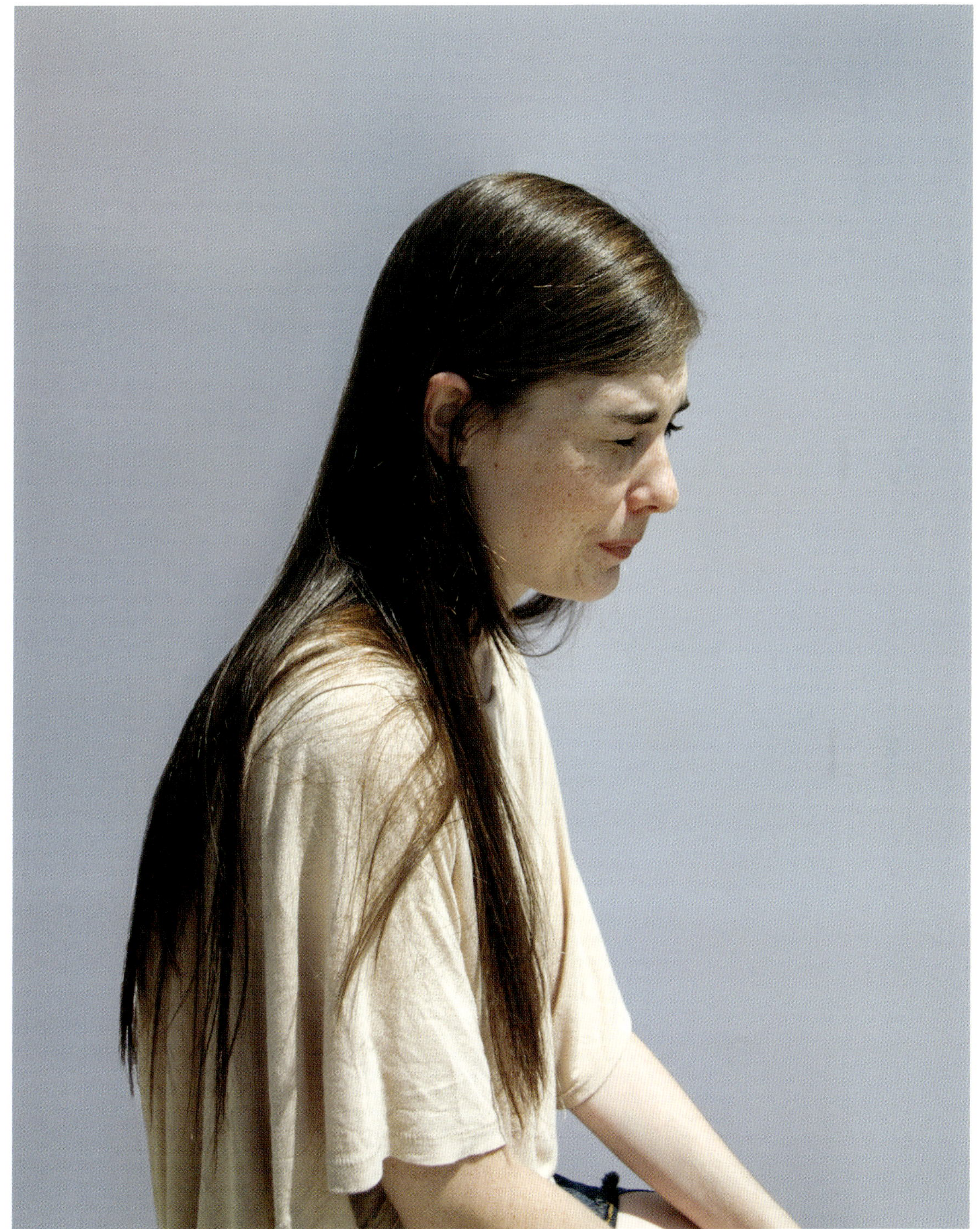

Steph Martyniuk

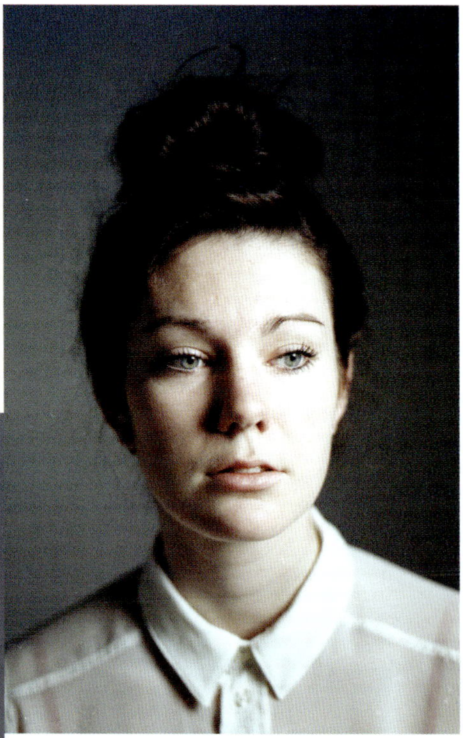

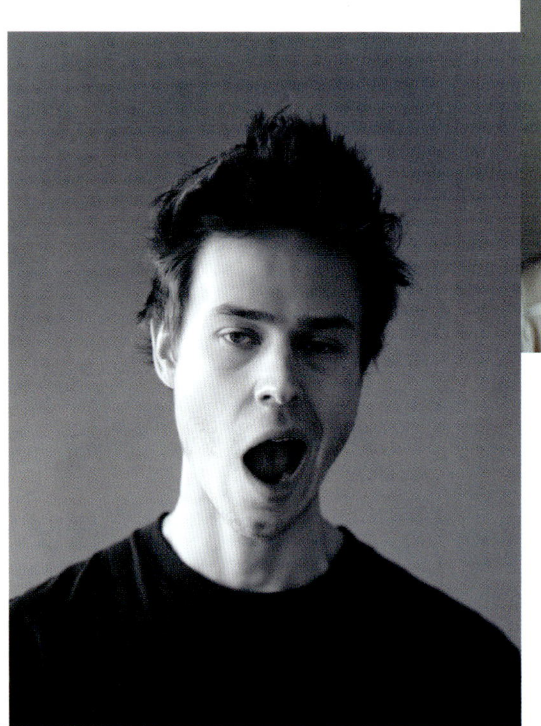

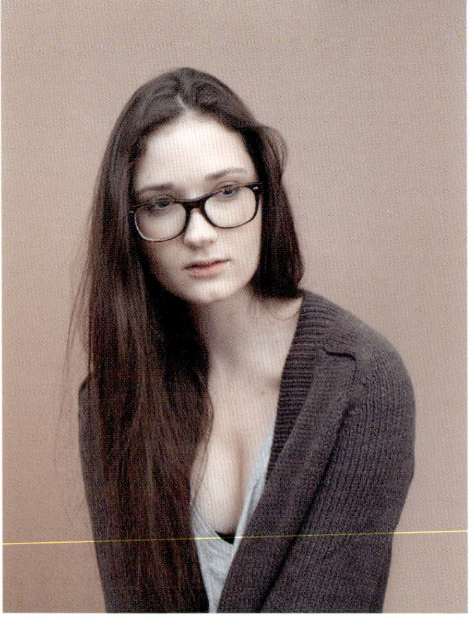

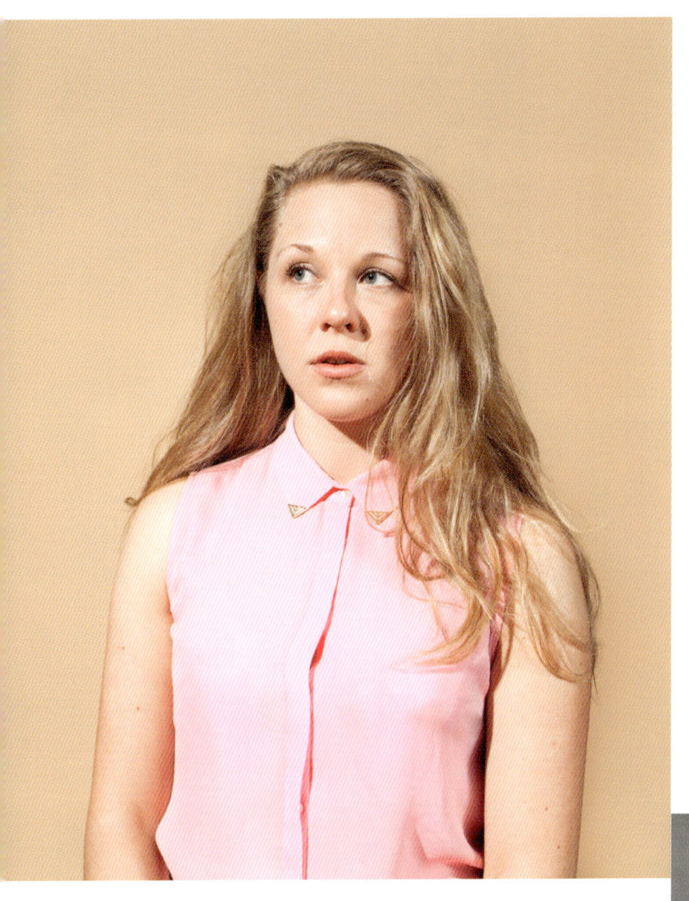

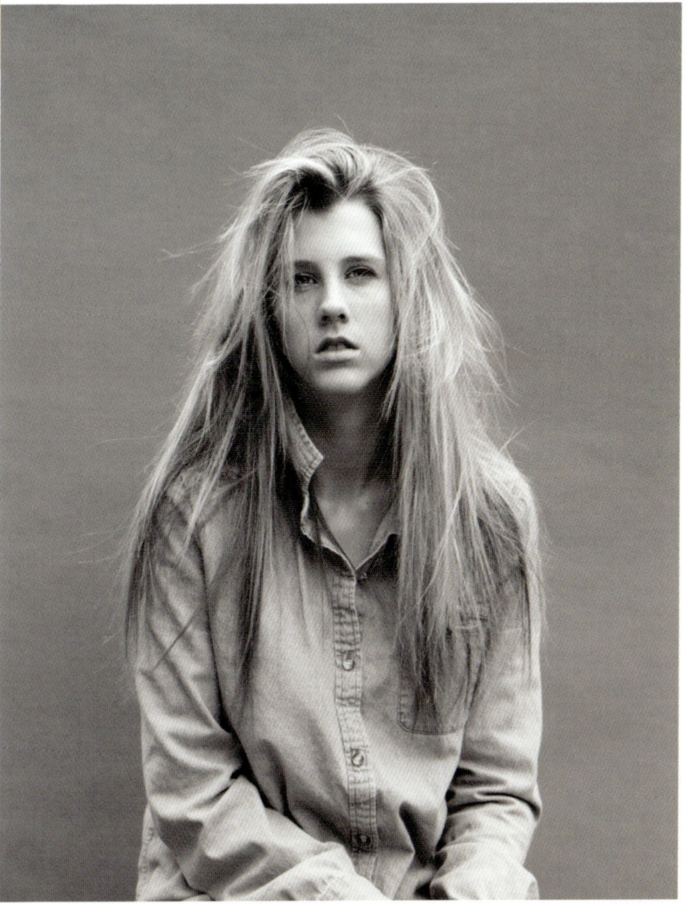

1. Anne Golaz
2. Ina Jang
3. Michelle Walls
4. Wynn Myers

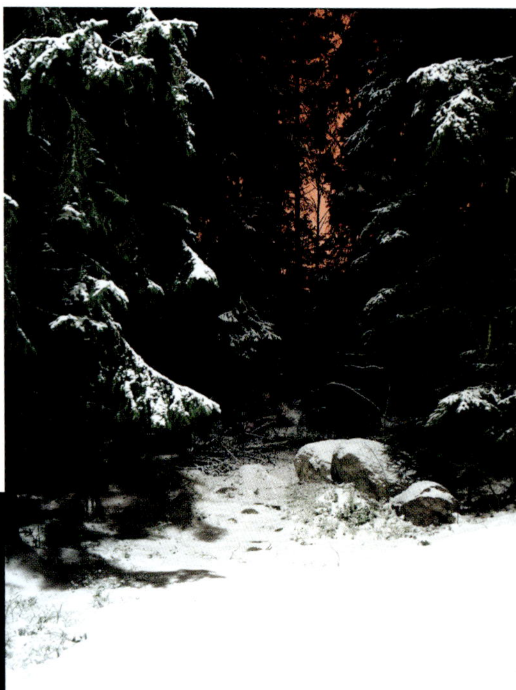

1

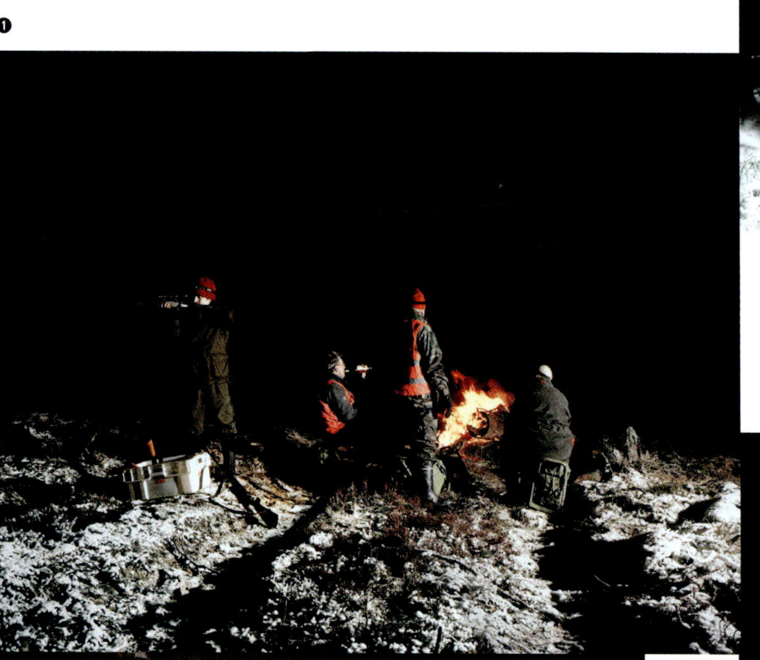

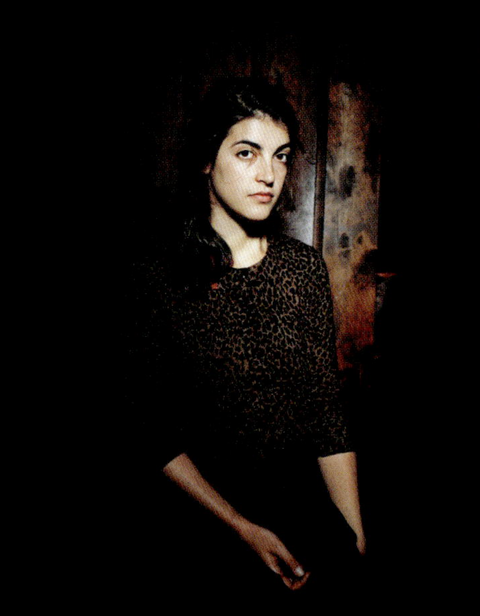

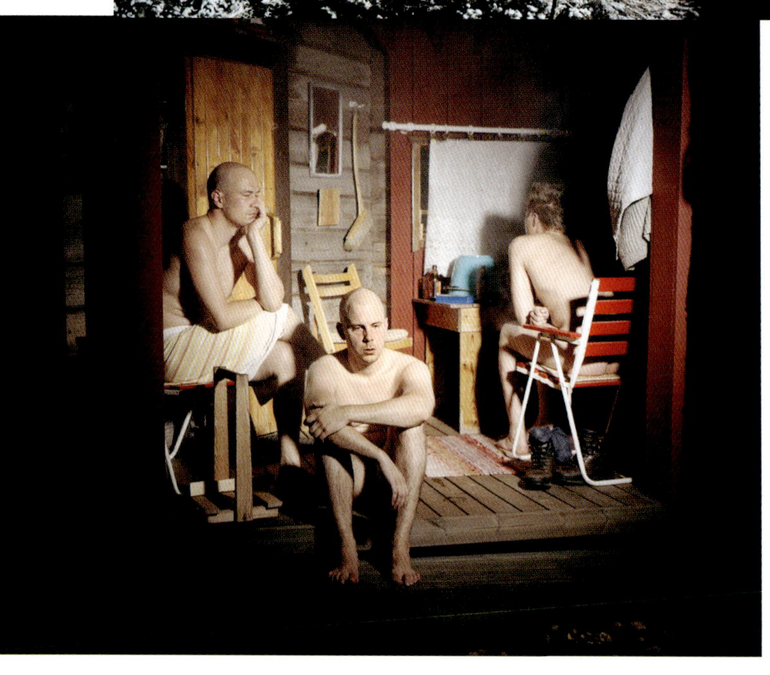

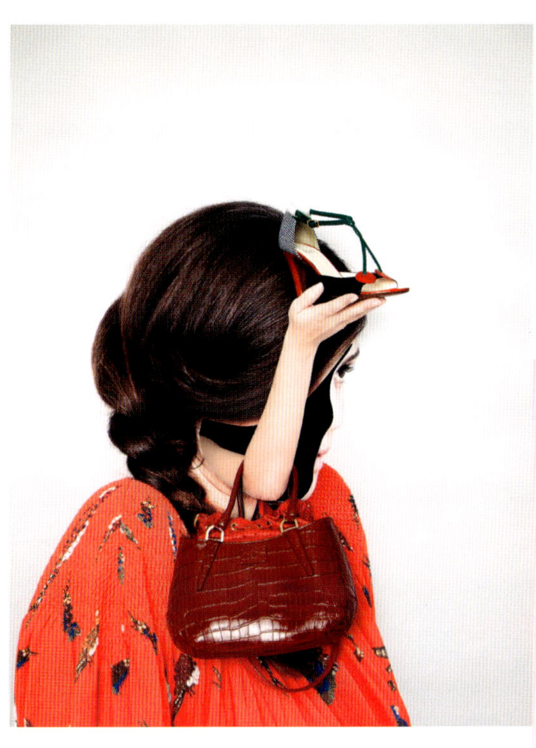

❷

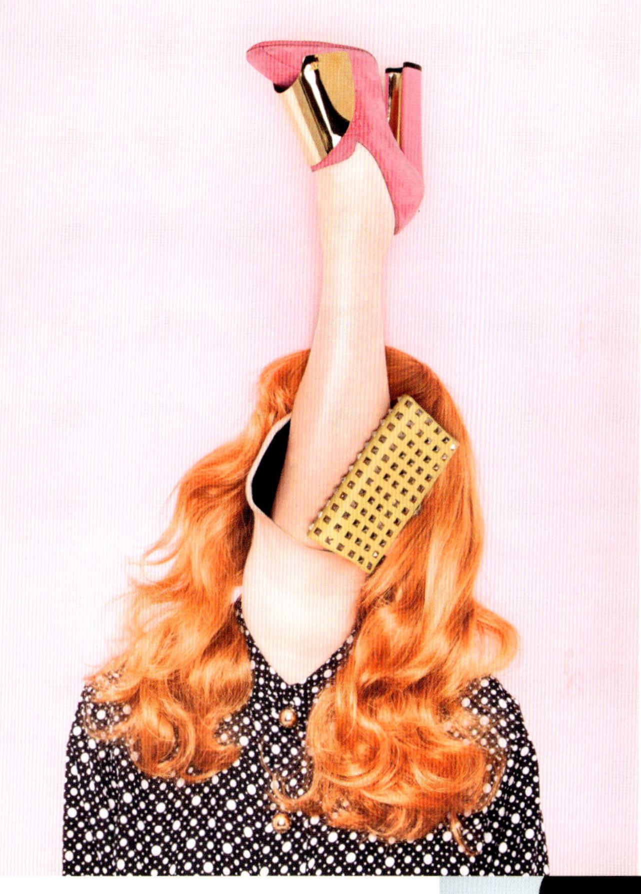

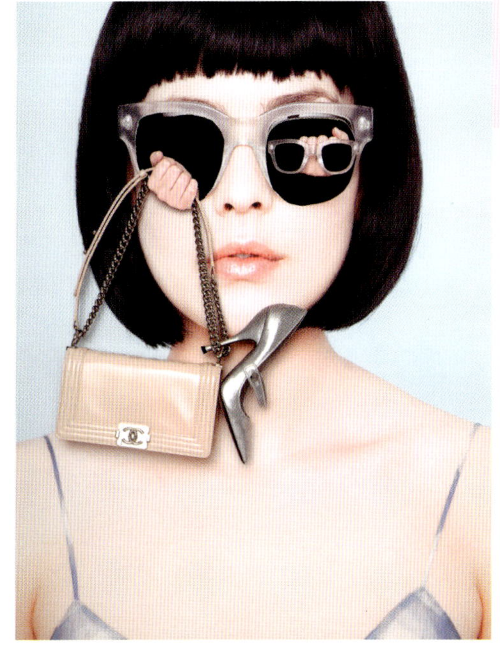

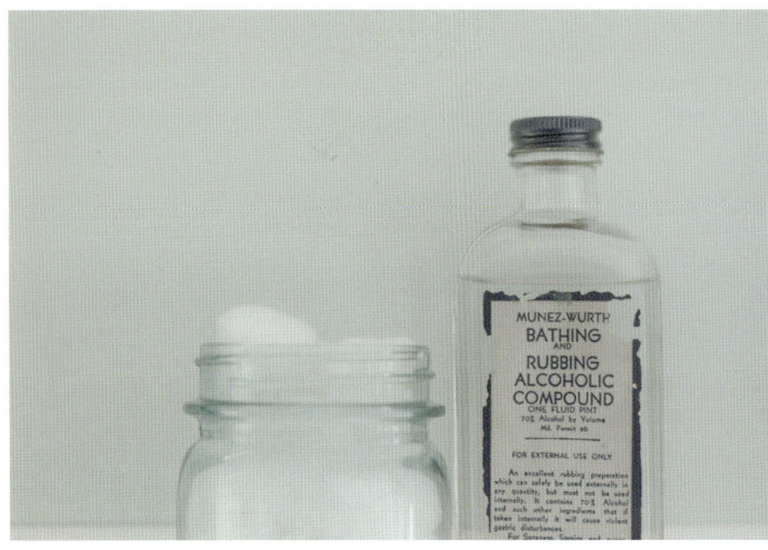
MUNEZ-WURTH
BATHING
AND
RUBBING
ALCOHOLIC
COMPOUND
ONE FLUID PINT
70% Alcohol by Volume
Md. Permit 96
FOR EXTERNAL USE ONLY
An excellent rubbing preparation which can safely be used externally in any quantity, but must not be used internally. It contains 70% Alcohol and such other ingredients that if taken internally it will cause violent gastric disturbances.

3

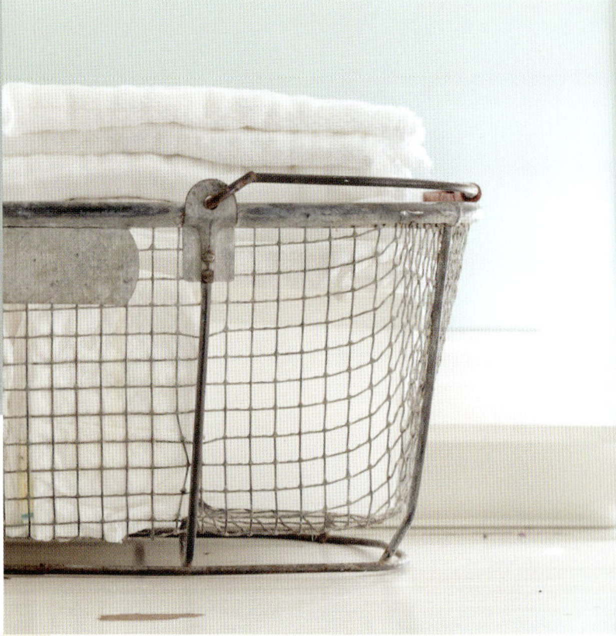

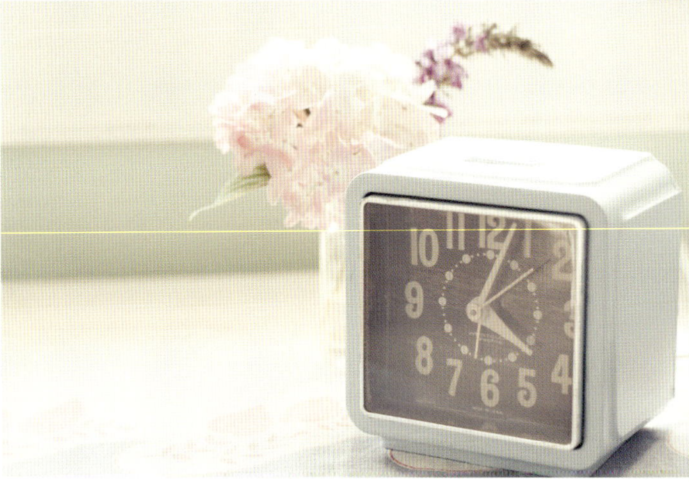

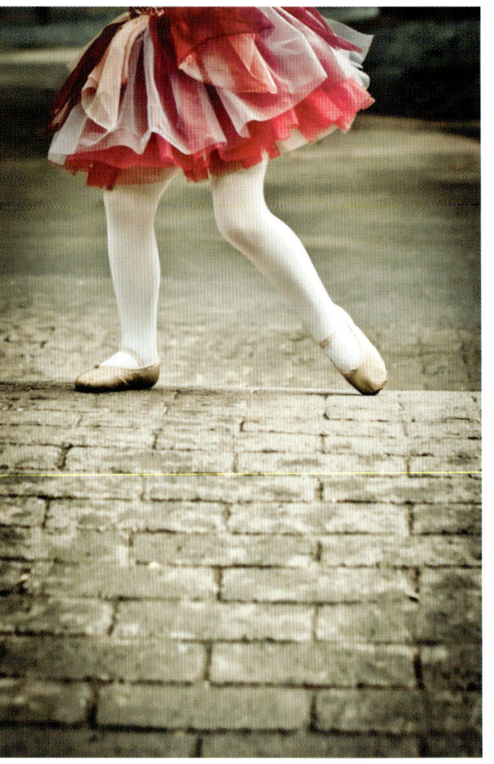

4

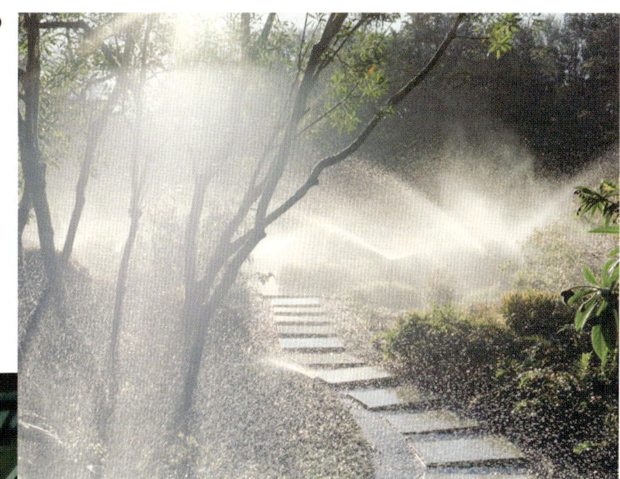

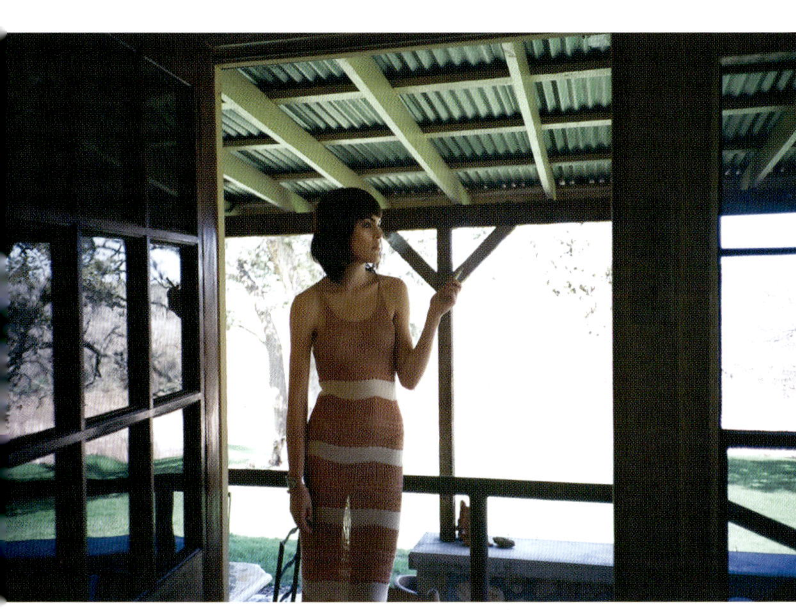

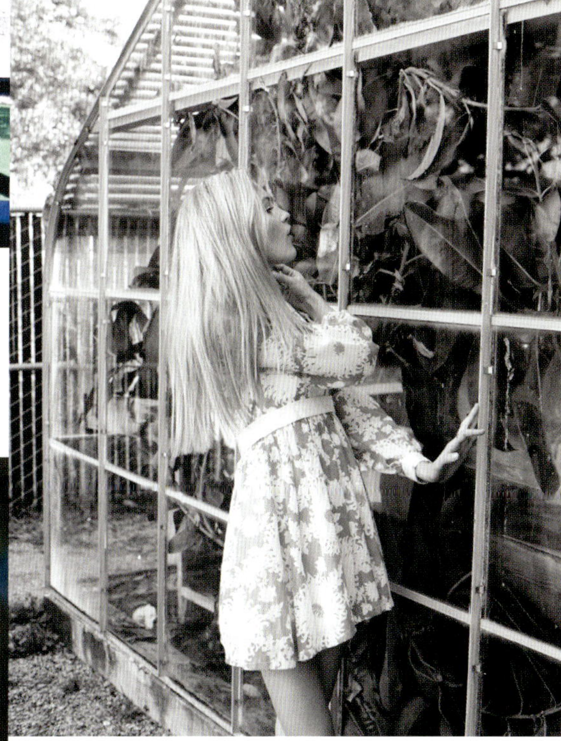

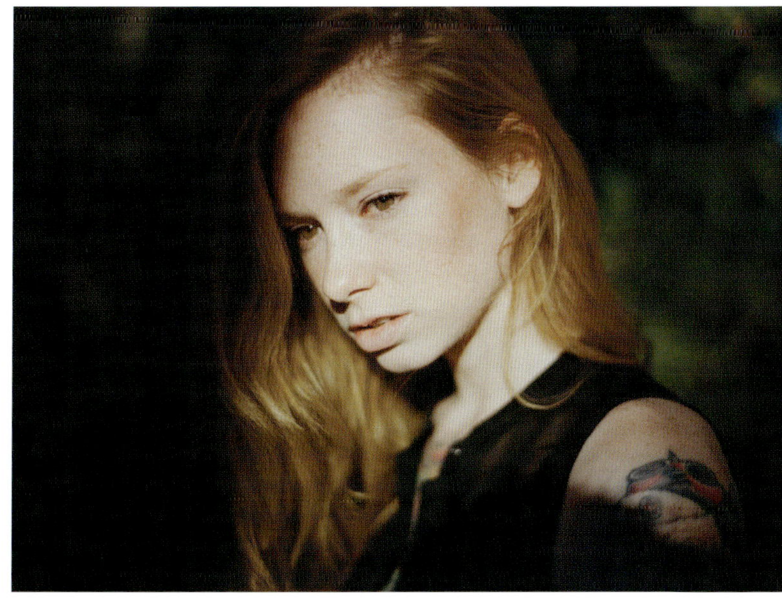

WINNER
STUDENT PHOTOBOOK

Maria Sturm
Be Good

Maria Sturm was born in 1985 in Ploiesti, Romania and moved to Germany in 1991. She received her diploma in photography and media at the University of Applied Sciences Bielefeld in 2012 with her work *Be Good*, which was also awarded third place at the Erstwerk book competition 2012 from the Institut für Buchgestaltung.

Maria was chosen for a residency and workshop with Magnum photographer Antoine D'Agata at Atelier de Visu in Marseille, France in 2012.

Her work has been exhibited internationally and she was shortlisted for Prix Leica 2011, European Schools Photography Awards, was a finalist for the Stern scholarship "Junge Fotografie," and the 54th edition of Bourse du Talent. She is currently based in Bielefeld and Berlin, Germany.

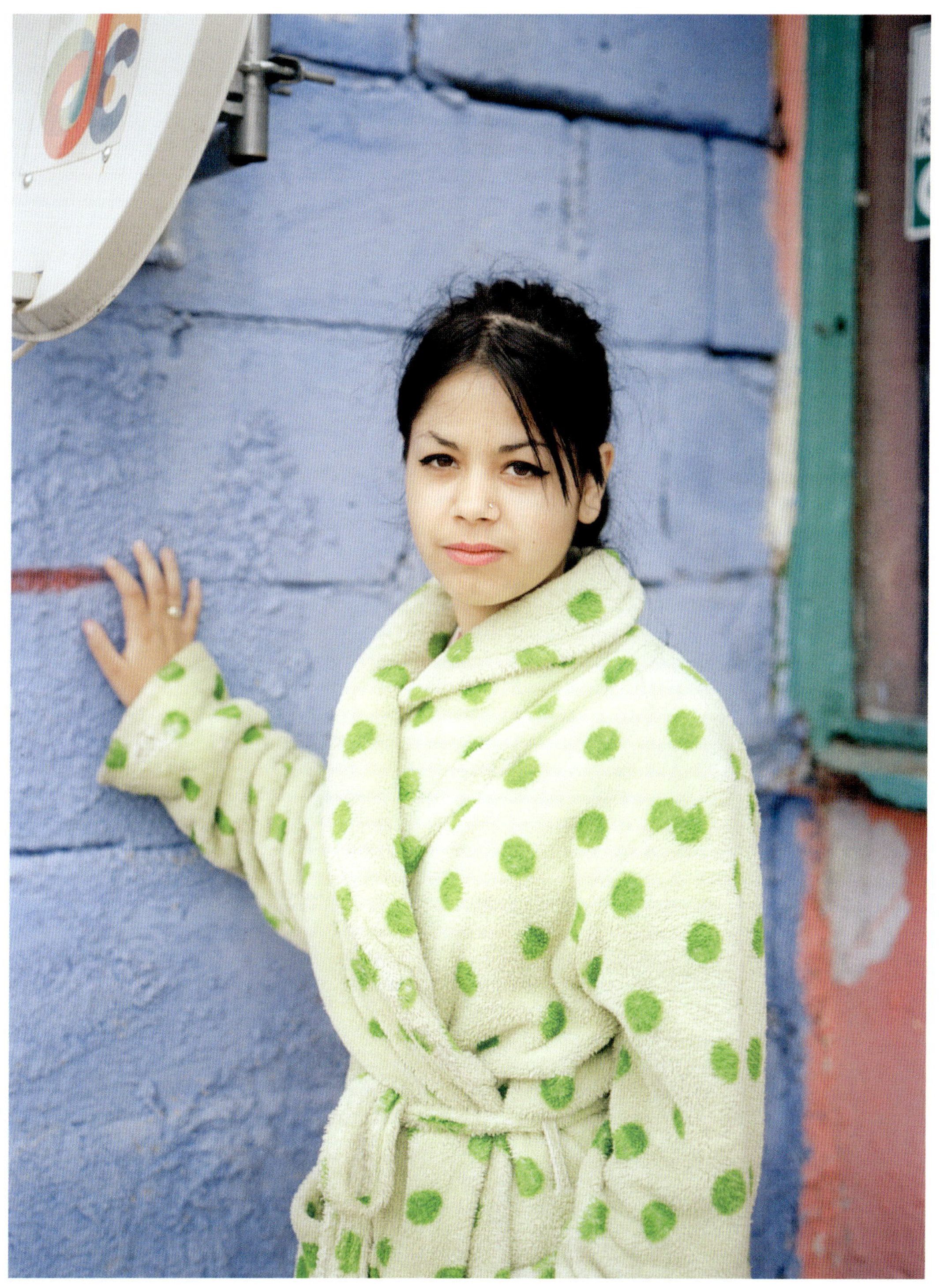

Maria Sturm

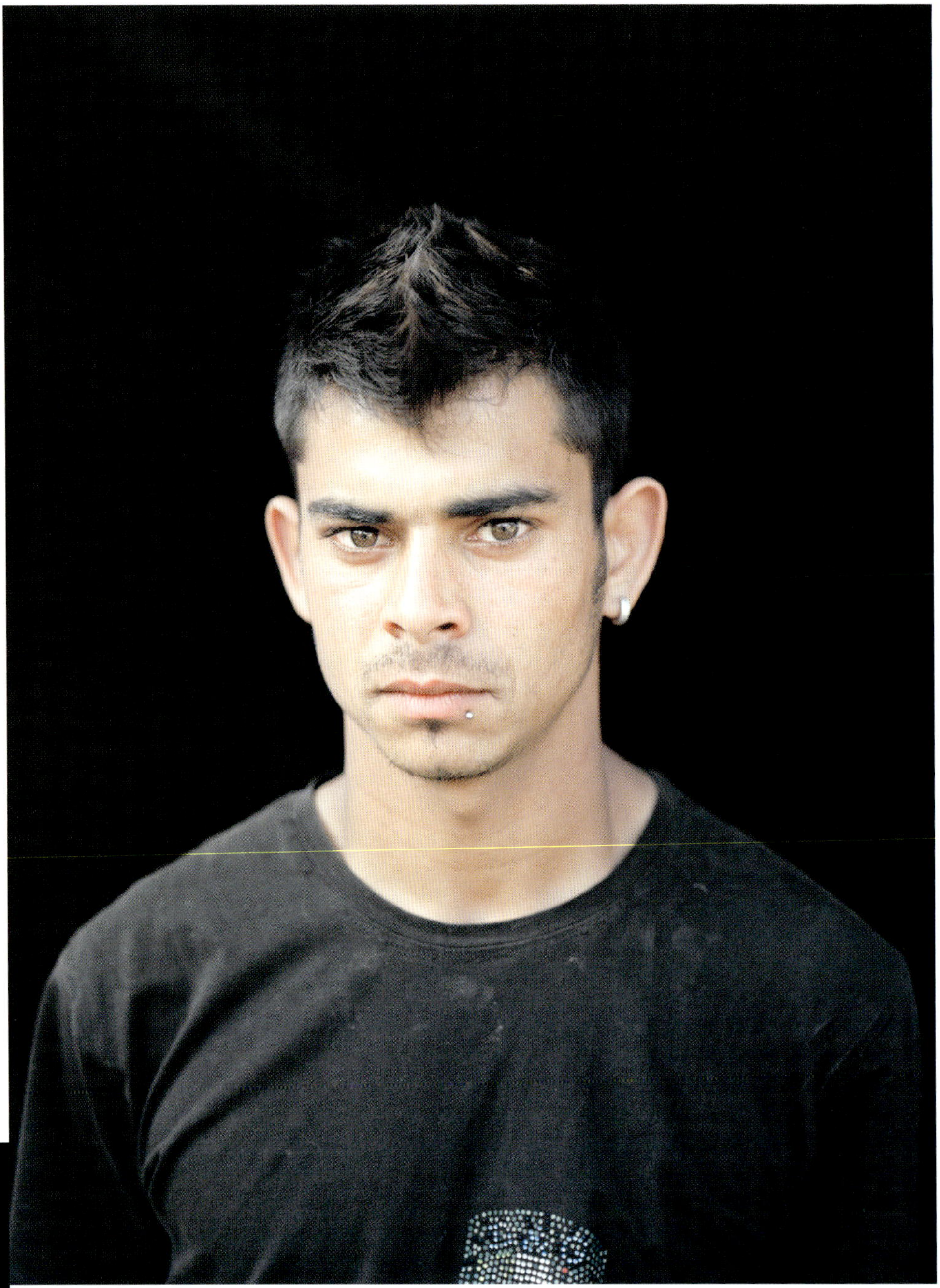

WINNER
STUDENT PHOTOBOOK

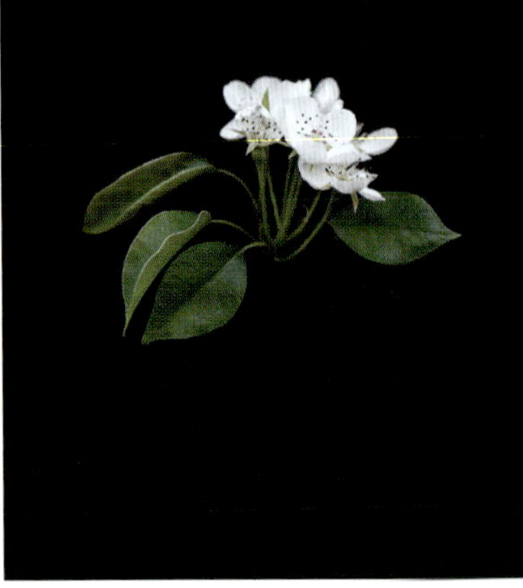

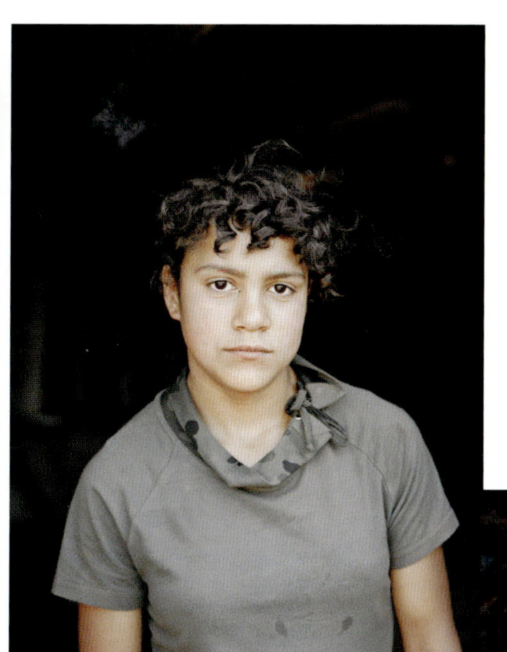

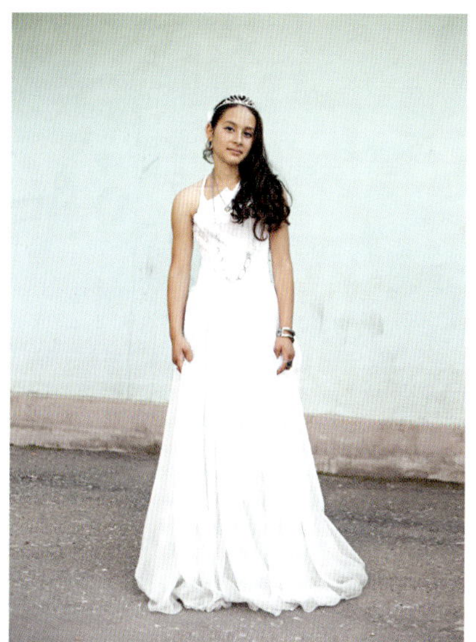

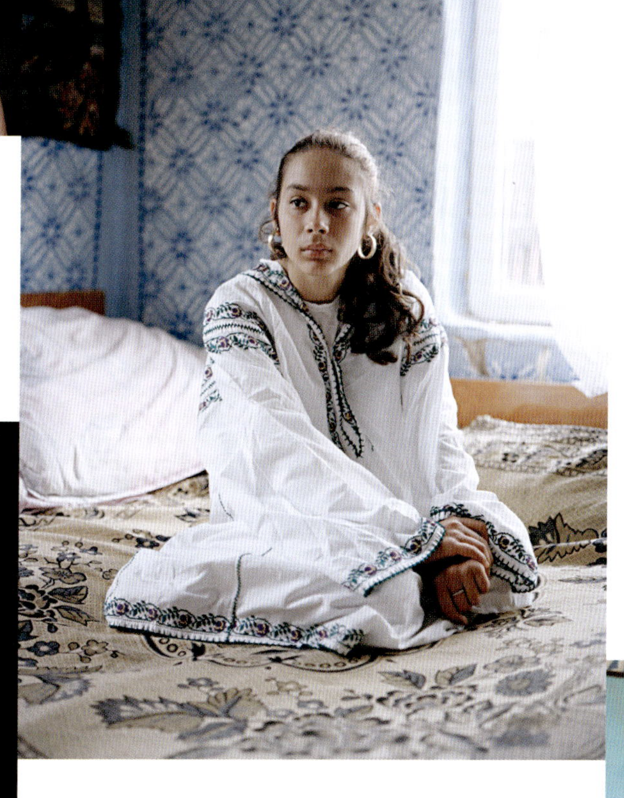

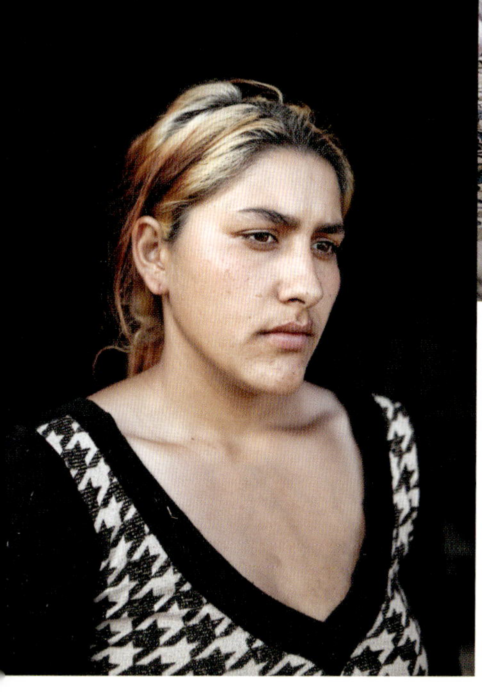

1. Eugen Litwinow
2. Italo Morales & Martina Velenik
3. Yannik Willing

❷

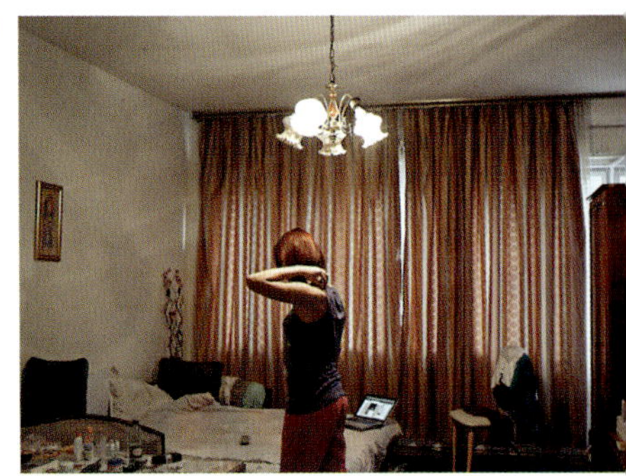

❶

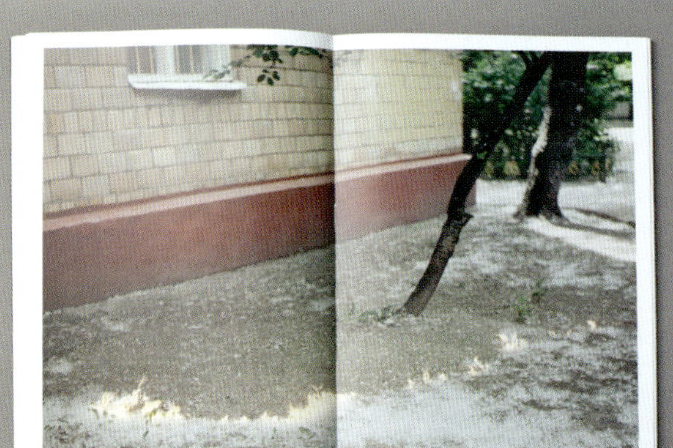

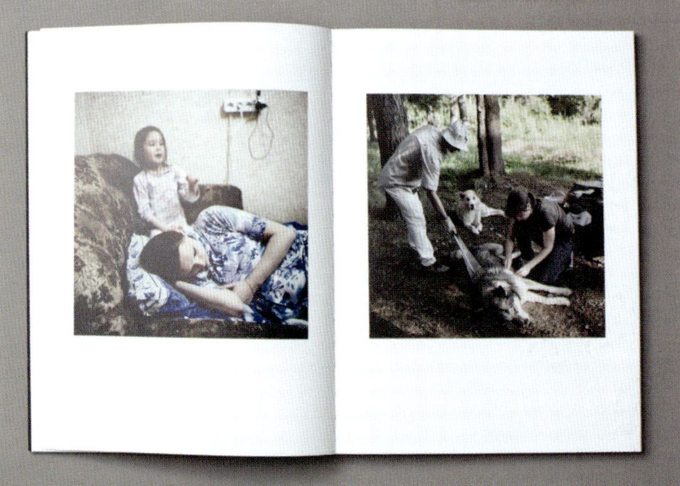

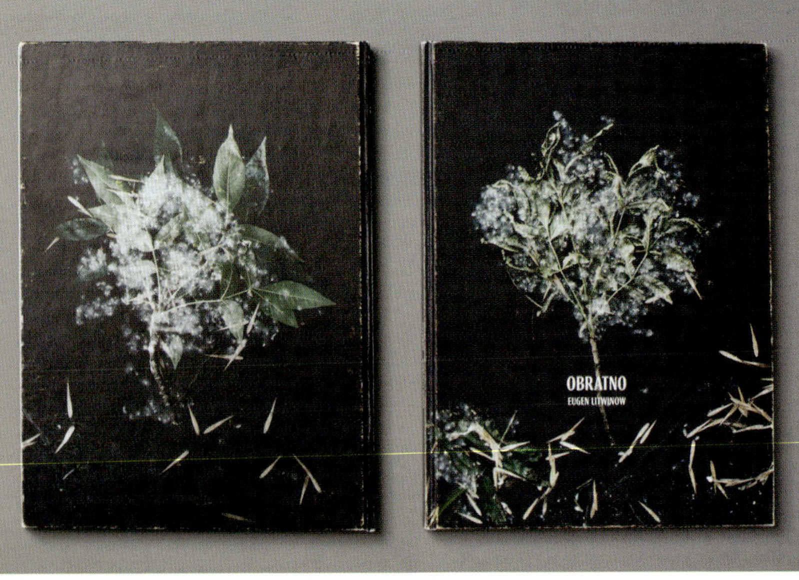

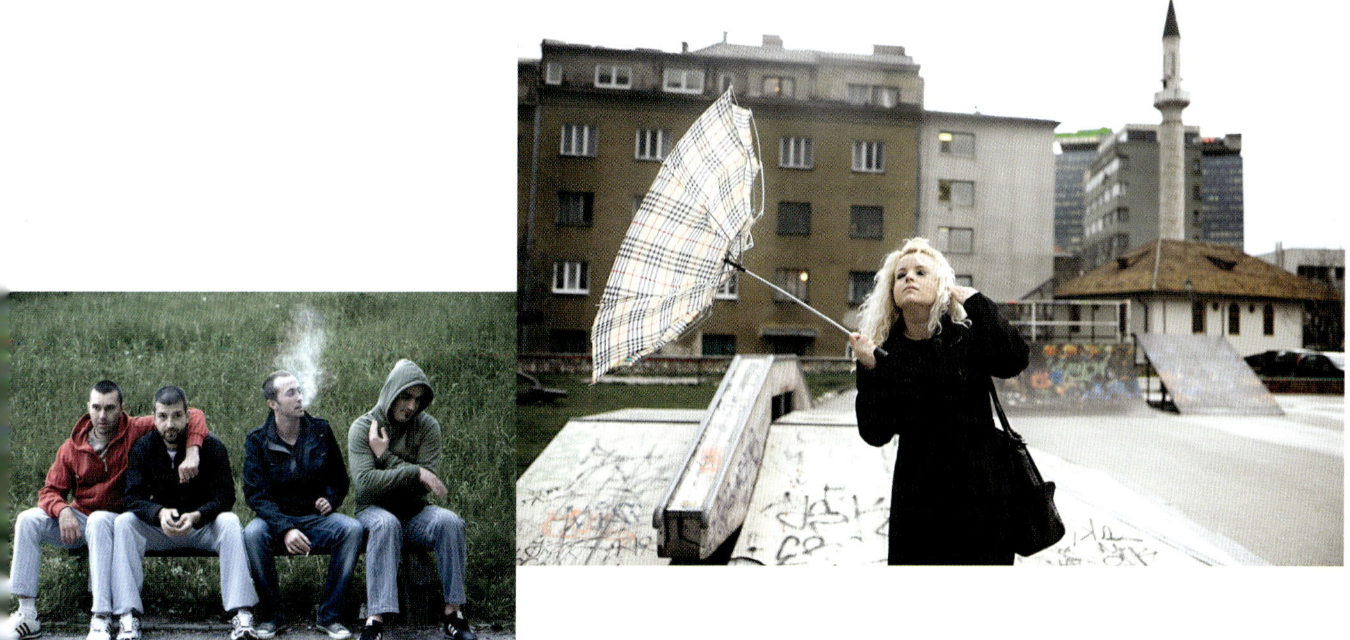

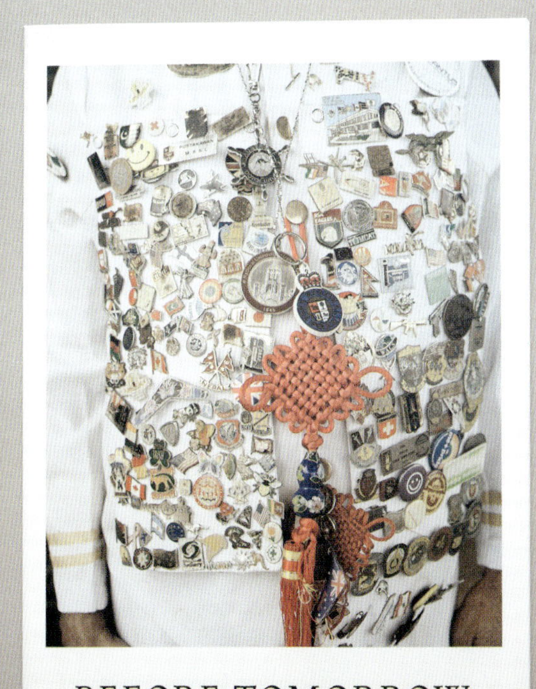

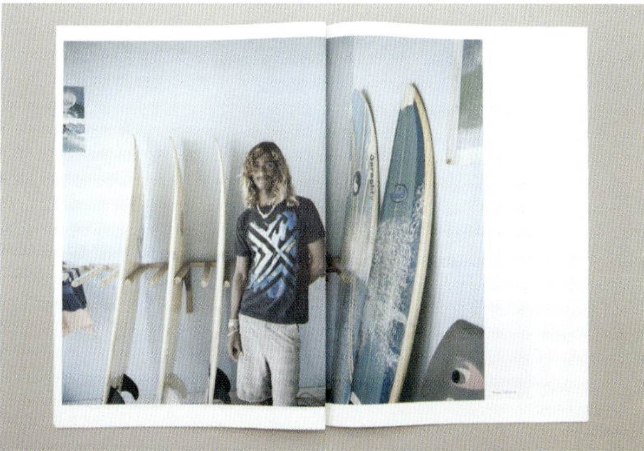

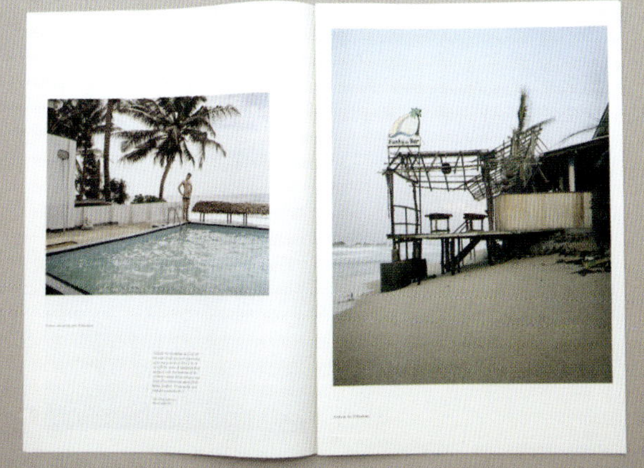

❸

PROUST QUESTIONNAIRE

BY MISS ROSEN

ROGER BALLEN

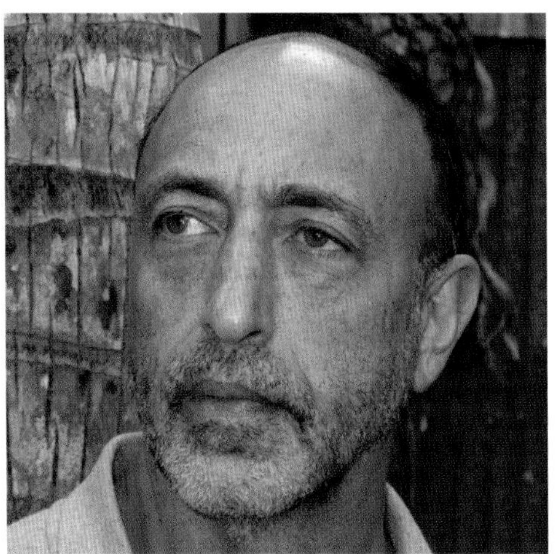
Photo: Marguerite Rossouw

WHAT I APPRECIATE MOST ABOUT PHOTOGRAPHY IS...
It is like a fragment from the past. You create your own fossils. It is separate from other art forms because it is the only one that freezes time and you can reflect on time that way, which is the most difficult thing to do.

THE MOST UNDERRATED THING ABOUT PHOTOGRAPHY IS...
How difficult and complex it is.

THE ONE THING A PHOTOGRAPHIC ARTIST MUST ALWAYS DO IS...
Follow your own intuition.

THE BEST WAY TO VIEW A PHOTOGRAPH IS...
You have to use a combination of scientific and artistic evaluations with objectivity and emotionality. Rely on your own intuition and judge whether it has an effect on you or not. Then it doesn't matter what other people think.

AN EXHIBITION I'LL NEVER FORGET IS...
Every day, mini-exhibitions are taking place. It's just a matter of whether they have a narrative as well. I am one of these people who believes you do not have to go to museums to see art. In my head it has more of an effect on you because you see it in the real world.

IF I HAD JUST ONE CHANCE TO GIFT A PHOTOBOOK, IT WOULD BE...
The early ones had an impact on me:
André Kertész: *Distortions*
Paul Strand: *Living Egypt*
Henri Cartier-Bresson: *The Decisive Moment*.

MY MOST CHERISHED PHOTOGRAPH IS...
A picture I took in St. Louis in 1968. I remember I had just got this Nikon camera for high school graduation and it was one of the first times I went out to take an artistic picture and I found two men and photographed them. Afterwards I saw a van Gogh exhibition and I understood what art was about. This happened on the same day and it was the first time I entered that zone one way or another.

WHAT MAKES AN IMAGE EXTRAORDINARY IS...
It has the ability throughout time to span individual and human consciousness, and it has the ability to make a statement of political, social, and psychological consciousness.

THE BEST THING ABOUT WORKING IN PHOTOGRAPHY IS...
I've been doing this for so long that there's been no better way to document my existence through time. It crystallizes my essence through time.

THE BIGGEST INFLUENCE IN MY APPRECIATION OF PHOTOGRAPHY IS...
My mother worked at Magnum and started one of the first photography galleries in the United States. André Kertész, Henri Cartier-Bresson, these people played a huge roll in my development. By the age 18, I had incorporated subconsciously so many ideas and had a fundamental understanding of the possibilities of photography. I had seen endless images in books and on walls and I was filled with images, energy, and knowledge and that laid the foundation for my appreciation. If I had been born to another mother or my mother had never done this, I probably wouldn't be in photography.

MY FAVORITE QUOTE ON PHOTOGRAPHY IS...
"The pictures are always better or worse than you thought." –Diane Arbus

THE FUTURE OF PHOTOGRAPHY IS...
I was a geologist for 30 years, searching for diamonds in

Africa. You have to go through a million pebbles for one diamond. It is the same with photography. It is getting more and more difficult to find the diamonds.

BIO
Born in New York City in 1950, Roger Ballen has lived and worked in Johannesburg, South Africa for almost 30 years. During this period, from 1982 to 2008, he has produced eight books and his style has evolved from photojournalism to a unique artistic vision. His next book (to be published in 2013) will be on birds photographed in a strange surrealistic place. Ballen's work has been shown in important institutions throughout the world and is represented in many museum collections such as Centre Georges Pompidou, Paris, France; Tate, London, England; and The Museum of Modern Art, New York, USA. Roger Ballen recently directed a video with Die Antwoord that was a great success. His career can be viewed on his website www.rogerballen.com.

ENRICO BOSSAN

WHAT I APPRECIATE MOST ABOUT PHOTOGRAPHY IS...
The simplicity.

THE MOST UNDERRATED THING ABOUT PHOTOGRAPHY IS...
That we learn too much knowing how to look.

THE PHOTOGRAPHER I'D WANT TO EAT/DRINK/SLEEP WITH IS...
Often I love to eat alone.

THE ONE THING A PHOTOGRAPHIC ARTIST MUST ALWAYS DO IS...
Be yourself.

THE BEST WAY TO VIEW A PHOTOGRAPH IS...
Alone in a museum.

AN EXHIBITION I'LL NEVER FORGET IS...
The Venice Biennale 1895.

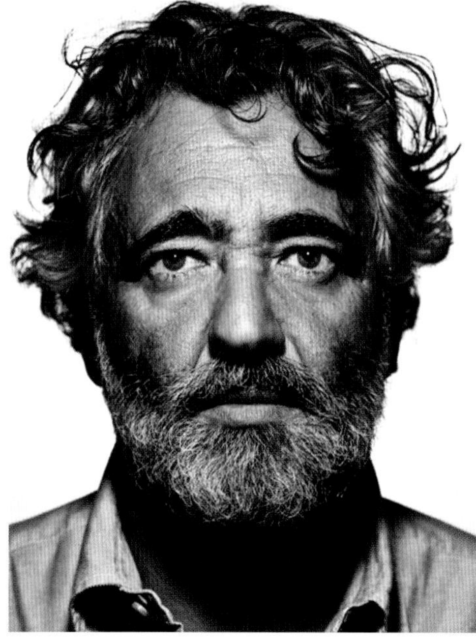

Photo courtesy of Enrico Bossan

WHAT MAKES AN IMAGE EXTRAORDINARY IS...
The capacity to show, to remember, to motivate.

THE BEST THING ABOUT WORKING IN PHOTOGRAPHY IS...
Give us a chance to see beyond.

THE BIGGEST INFLUENCE IN MY APPRECIATION OF PHOTOGRAPHY IS...
The curiosity.

MY FAVORITE QUOTE ON PHOTOGRAPHY IS...
To photograph something that you recognize.

THE FUTURE OF PHOTOGRAPHY IS...
Going in a darkroom.

BIO
Enrico Bossan lives and works in Padua, Italy. A professional photojournalist since 1985, he has published reportage and documentary work in many prominent Italian and international magazines. Bossan has been a member of the Veneto Journalist Order since 1987 and is represented by the Contrasto photo agency. He won the Kodak Gallery Award in 1987. Bossan's work has been exhibited at FotoFest International, Houston; Torino International Photo Biennale; and in Amsterdam, Arles, Milan, Rome, Thessalonica, Tokyo, and Venice. Much of the reporting he did around the world became books, including *Pechino-Parigi* (Fabbri Ediitori, 1986), and *Exit* (Peliti, 1992). He is the editor of *COLORS* magazine and head of the photography department for Fabrica. Bossan is the creator of the FFF prize for Fabrica and Forma and the founder of E-photoreview.com and enricobossanmasterclass.com.

LARRY FINK

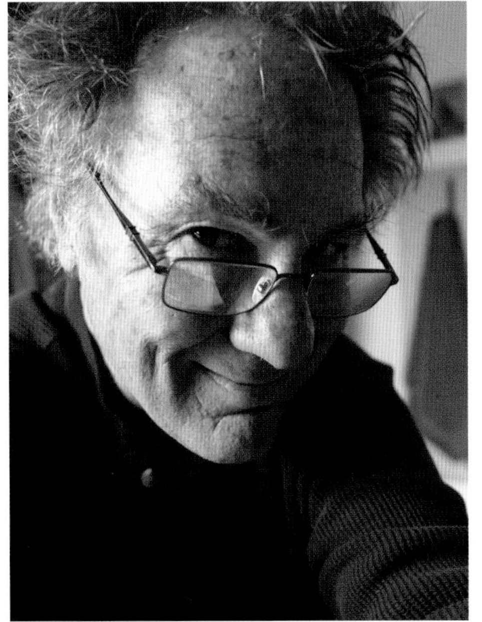
Photo: Larry Fink

WHAT I APPRECIATE MOST ABOUT PHOTOGRAPHY IS...
It takes each increment of reality and crystalizes it so that it stays there as a precise prism within evolutionary time. In other words, it is history.

THE MOST UNDERRATED THING ABOUT PHOTOGRAPHY IS...
There are still certain people in high-end curation who do not trust the veracity and beauty of photography, which is foolish, but such is life. The masses, if you will, underrate the power photography has to tell the deeper stories they point the camera at. Most people don't think about things on a broader spectrum.

THE PHOTOGRAPH I CAN ENVISION WITH MY EYES CLOSED IS...
How many hundreds of thousands of images? I can envision any number of iconic photographs by Bill Brandt, Henri Cartier-Bresson's Spanish village with bright white light, Robert Frank's Valencia, Spain with a band walking across the street. I can envision a photograph I took of my grandson Elijah being kissed profusely by his mother and my wife. Anyone can close their eyes and find pictures like this.

THE PHOTOGRAPHER I'D WANT TO EAT/DRINK/SLEEP WITH IS...
Sleep with is out of the question; I am married, thank you. I would like to eat/drink/meet with Mr. Brassaï. I only met him once, without consequence. I'd like to transport back to a time during his life when he was very active, to a beautiful place in Paris where we could speak at length.

THE ONE THING A PHOTOGRAPHIC ARTIST MUST ALWAYS DO IS...
Eat, sleep, drink, shit, along with other human beings. And be aware.

THE BEST WAY TO VIEW A PHOTOGRAPH IS...
Goodness knows. A book, held in the hand if it is small. On the wall, if it is big. In your mind, as we just did. There is no best way to do anything.

AN EXHIBITION I'LL NEVER FORGET IS...
The Family of Man. I always loved this show even though it was pollyanic propaganda. I thought it had breadth and hope. My retrospective at the Andalusian Centre of Photography, Almeria, Spain, in 2012. My retrospective at Les Rencontres d'Arles. My one man shows at The Museum of Modern Art and The Whitney Museum of American Art. Any exhibition by Diane Arbus; she is unforgettable. The Bill Brandt show, at MoMA recently.

IF I HAD JUST ONE CHANCE TO GIFT A PHOTOBOOK, IT WOULD BE...
I wish that I had a camera in my hand from my inception and made a photo album of my early days as a child. I would gift this to my daughter Molly and my wife Martha.

MY MOST CHERISHED PHOTOGRAPH...
A photograph of Molly when my first wife Joan gave birth 32 years ago. It is full of visceral and physical fluids of the moment—it is not sentimental, but the sentiment of what was going on goes back and forwards. That is unforgettable.

WHAT MAKES AN IMAGE EXTRAORDINARY IS...
The construction and compilation of how the elements are fueled by aesthetics, the power of the moment, and the inner beauty. Does the picture have a soul? Can you ask that of a two-dimensional piece of paper?

THE BEST THING ABOUT WORKING IN PHOTOGRAPHY IS...
From the time I picked up a camera at the age of 12 until now at 72, it has been 60 years that I've had a tool in my hands by which I could record the intensity of my curiosity.

THE BIGGEST INFLUENCE IN MY APPRECIATION OF PHOTOGRAPHY IS...
Lisette Model opened my eyes to the deep humanity of photography's potential.

MY FAVORITE QUOTE ON PHOTOGRAPHY IS...
John Berger and John Szarkowski are people where I would find that quote. Come on a treasure hunt with me for favorite quotes...

THE FUTURE OF PHOTOGRAPHY IS...
I think we have to think about the future of the human race. It is a marriage of glory and doom. Photography will be about how it accords itself to those contradictory particulars.

BIO

Larry Fink is a professional photographer of over 55 years. He has had one-man shows at The Museum of Modern Art, New York; The Whitney Museum of American Art; and The San Francisco Museum of Modern Art, among others. He has been awarded two Guggenheim Fellowships, in 1976 and 1979, and two National Endowment for the Arts, Individual Photography Fellowships, in 1978 and 1986. He has been teaching for the past 41 years. For the last 16 years he has been a professor of photography at Bard College. Fink has had several books published including: *Social Graces* (Aperture, 1984); *Boxing* (powerHouse Books, 1997); *Runway* (powerHouse Books, 2000); *Primal Elegance* (Lodima Press, 2006); *Somewhere There's Music* (Damiani Editore, 2006), *Attraction and Desire: 50 Years in Photography* (The Sheldon Art Galleries, 2011), and most recently, *The Vanities: Hollywood Parties 2000-2009* (Schirmer/Mosel, 2011).

PETER HAY HALPERT

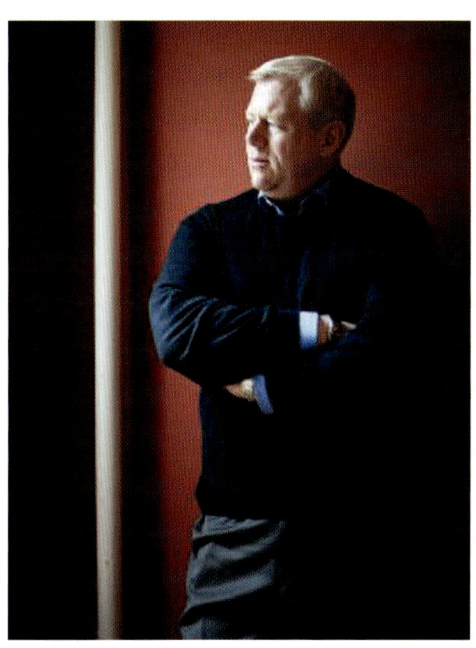

Photo: Stephanie de Rouge

THE MOST UNDERRATED THING ABOUT PHOTOGRAPHY IS...

Everyone focuses on the instantaneous nature of the photograph, but it seems to me what separates the great photograph from the quotidian is when the decisive moment meets the practiced eye. Some people have taught themselves how to look; they have a vision.

THE PHOTOGRAPH I CAN ENVISION WITH MY EYES CLOSED IS...

Chris Bucklow, a self-portrait from the *Guests* series. Ryan McGinely, *Having Sex (Polaroids)*. Bruce Weber, *Marines on Leave*.

THE PHOTOGRAPHER I'D WANT TO EAT/DRINK/ SLEEP WITH IS...

I definitely would not like to sleep with Alfred Stieglitz and Georgia O'Keeffe. Curious about Robert Mapplethorpe, Sam Wagstaff, and Patti Smith.

THE ONE THING A PHOTOGRAPHIC ARTIST MUST ALWAYS DO IS...

Thank the other people who helped them.

THE BEST WAY TO VIEW A PHOTOGRAPH IS...

In person, then in a book.

AN EXHIBITION I'LL NEVER FORGET IS...

The 1987 Whitney Biennial. Bruce Weber had an entire wall hung salon style with portraits. Jonathan Borofsky at the Philadelphia Museum of Art: it included paintings, sculptural figures, mechanical figures, audio, a ping-pong table where you were invited to play, and drawings. I became aware that at a certain point the exhibition would be over and the walls would be whitewashed, and that the table became a work of art if you picked up a paddle and became part of a performance piece. Art could function on several levels, and then it's gone.

IF I HAD JUST ONE CHANCE TO GIFT A PHOTOBOOK, IT WOULD BE...

The Artist's Eye: David Hockney Looking at Pictures in a Book at the National Gallery (The National Gallery, London, England, 1981). *Secret Knowledge* with Henry Geldzahler, the International Center of Photography exhibition catalogue of *Talking Pictures*, curated by Marvin Heiferman.

MY MOST CHERISHED PHOTOGRAPH IS...

Andy Warhol, *Stitched Photograph*. If the place was on fire, I would grab that and the cats. Acquiring that was a whole journey that began in 1986 or '87 at the Robert Miller Gallery. It was the first series intended as a photographic series as the end itself. It ties into the reproduction and factory-like style with being stitched together, and is the perfect apotheosis of the photograph in Warhol's form.

WHAT MAKES AN IMAGE EXTRAORDINARY IS...

The relationship between the artists and subject and viewer. Subconsciously the sitter and artist are acutely aware of a third person in the room, the anonymous viewer. The meaning of the image takes on this dialogue between the three participants.

THE BIGGEST INFLUENCE IN MY APPRECIATION OF PHOTOGRAPHY IS...

Bruce Weber for the spirit he brings to making pictures. David Hockney for the way he looks at pictures and the making of photographs in every form.

MY FAVORITE QUOTE ON PHOTOGRAPHY IS...
"Photography is a foreign language everyone thinks he speaks." –Philip-Lorca diCorcia

THE FUTURE OF PHOTOGRAPHY IS...
Changing. What it is now I don't think it's going to be the same. In less than 200 years, photography has developed from images that appear on daguerreotype plates to the digital world. As every image becomes digitized, information is going to change and evolve.

BIO
Peter Hay Halpert is a private art dealer specialising in contemporary young and emerging artists working with photography and video. The Metropolitan Museum of Art; The Museum of Modern Art; ICP; The Whitney Museum of American Art; Solomon R. Guggenheim Museum; The Getty; the The Museum of Fine Arts, Boston; The San Francisco Museum of Modern Art; The Museum of Fine Arts, Houston; The Canadian Centre for Architecture; Tate; and the Victoria and Albert Museum all collect work by the gallery's artists. He has written as contributing editor of *American Photo*, *The Artnewsletter*, and correspondent for *The Art Newspaper*, as well as for *Aperture*, *Art + Auction*, *ARTnews*, *Art Press International*, *Art & Antiques*, and *The International Herald Tribune*. He authored *Motion Picture*, on the photographs of Hiroshi Sugimoto, contributed an essay to a retrospective catalogue of Sugimoto's work, and a piece on Sugimoto for *Moving Images: Film and Reflection in the Arts*. Halpert was a professor at School of Visual Arts and the International Center of Photography. He has been a regular lecturer at Trinity College and the University of Pennsylvania, and lectured at universities and museums around the world, such as The Whitney Museum of American Art, the High Museum of Art, and the Royal College of Art. He is also an established photography collector and sits on the boards of several organizations and institutions.

DARIUS HIMES

WHAT I APPRECIATE MOST ABOUT PHOTOGRAPHY IS...
The mystery and power.

THE MOST UNDERRATED THING ABOUT PHOTOGRAPHY IS...
The difficulty of making a powerful image.

THE PHOTOGRAPH I CAN ENVISION WITH MY EYES CLOSED IS...
Prom, 1988.

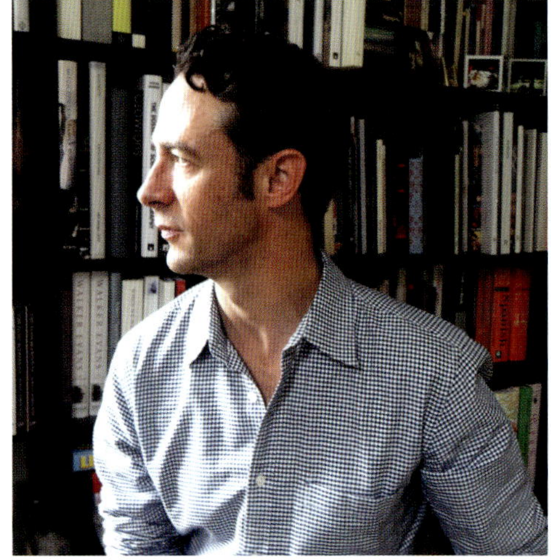

Photo courtesy of Darius Himes

THE PHOTOGRAPHER I'D WANT TO EAT/DRINK/SLEEP WITH IS...
I would love to share a meal at Henry Fox Talbot's table.

THE ONE THING A PHOTOGRAPHIC ARTIST MUST ALWAYS DO IS...
Pay attention to the light.

AN EXHIBITION I'LL NEVER FORGET IS...
Edward Hopper & Company at Fraenkel Gallery, 2009.

IF I HAD JUST ONE CHANCE TO GIFT A PHOTOBOOK, IT WOULD BE...
To someone between the ages of 10 and 14. The world is new and all paths are open at that age.

THE BEST THING ABOUT WORKING IN PHOTOGRAPHY IS...
That my heart and soul are nourished through the medium.

THE BIGGEST INFLUENCE IN MY APPRECIATION OF PHOTOGRAPHY IS...
My undergraduate years at Arizona State University with caring professors, including Bill Jay and William Jenkins.

MY FAVORITE QUOTE ON PHOTOGRAPHY...
"He hastened away, with a delicate photograph of the palm of her hand printed in minute sensations on the palm of his." From *Clayhanger*, by Arnold Bennett

THE FUTURE OF PHOTOGRAPHY IS...
The future, latent within us, is always present.

BIO
Darius Himes is director of Fraenkel Gallery, San Francisco. He is a co-founder of Radius Books, a non-profit publisher of books on photography and the visual arts, where he serves on the board and consults on project acquisitions. He was founding editor of *photo-eye Booklist*, a quarterly magazine devoted to photography books, which ran from 2002–2007. A lecturer, educator, and writer, he has contributed to *Aperture*, *Blind Spot*, *Bookforum*, *BOMB*, *Photo District News*, and *American Photo*. In 2008, he was named by *PDN* as one of the 15 most influential people in photography

book publishing. His most recent title, *Publish Your Photography Book*, co-authored with Mary Virginia Swanson, was released by Princeton Architectural Press in the Spring of 2011. A 2nd edition is planned for Spring, 2014.

W.M. HUNT

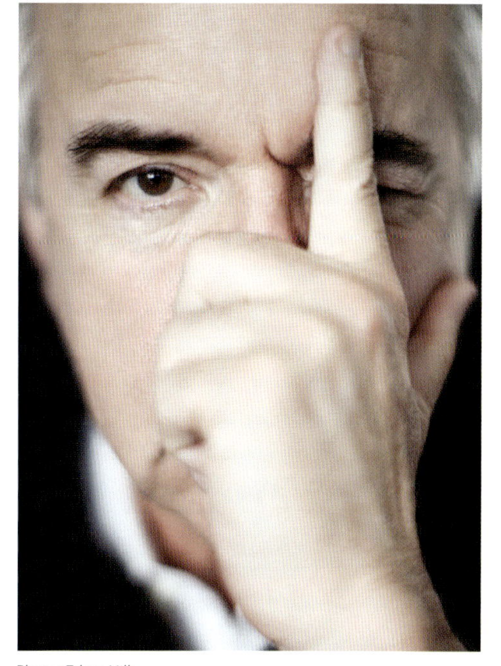

Photo: Ethan Hill

WHAT I APPRECIATE MOST ABOUT PHOTOGRAPHY IS ...
I always look for the delight in photography. Photographs are magical and photography gave me a focus, a life, a network of friends and colleagues. I am eternally grateful.

THE MOST UNDERRATED THING ABOUT PHOTOGRAPHY IS...
The whole, "Do we still question whether or not photography is an art form?" speaks to an ongoing sense of less than full legitimacy. So I would say the most underrated thing about photography is photography itself. It is the language of contemporary culture. Its overall impact is acknowledged but sadly underrated.

THE PHOTOGRAPH I CAN ENVISION WITH MY EYES CLOSED IS...
Irving Penn's *Two Guedras*, 1972, is the greatest photograph ever by the legendary artist, an enigmatic portrait of two inscrutable, veiled shamanic women from North Africa. It is a ravishing platinum palladium print. The image is the cover of his classic *Worlds in a Small Room* published in 1974.

THE PHOTOGRAPHER I'D WANT TO EAT/DRINK/SLEEP WITH IS...
Edward Weston.

THE ONE THING A PHOTOGRAPHIC ARTIST MUST ALWAYS DO IS...
Shut up. Let the pictures talk.

THE BEST WAY TO VIEW A PHOTOGRAPH IS...
By yourself when you're not expecting anything. The downside of this is that you can't turn to someone immediately and say "Look, look. Look at this one!"

AN EXHIBITION I'LL NEVER FORGET IS...
Sans Regard or No Eyes: Highlights from W.M. Hunt/ Collection Dancing Bear in 2005 at Les Rencontres d'Arles in France because that changed my life. Second would be *Artist's Choice: Chuck Close, Head-On / The Modern Portrait* at The Museum of Modern Art in 1991. It was his take on portraiture and encountering art in a museum. It was a thrilling, inspired, fresh show installed astonishingly with nearly 170 portraits and sculptures hung salon-style and on shelves and on wall wedges in a single gallery. Brilliant. I think I saw it 10 times.

IF I HAD JUST ONE CHANCE TO GIFT A PHOTOBOOK, IT WOULD BE...
Henri Cartier-Bresson's *The Decisive Moment*. The book I do give is Bruce Bernard's *One Hundred Photographs* (Phaidon, 2002) a great book about looking.

MY MOST CHERISHED PHOTOGRAPH IS...
Two Guedras. See above. Second: Bill Brandt's *Dubuffet's Eye*, 1960.

WHAT MAKES AN IMAGE EXTRAORDINARY IS...
Combination of inspiration and imagination and a sense of otherness. "It should be," as Goldilocks said, "just right."

THE BEST THING ABOUT WORKING IN PHOTOGRAPHY IS...
The chance that you will stumble upon a great photograph and that can make your day. It will make you dance around the room with it.

THE BIGGEST INFLUENCE IN MY APPRECIATION OF PHOTOGRAPHY IS...
Irving Penn, Duane Michals, Eugenia Parry, Harry Lunn, Richard Avedon, Roger Ricco, and Frank Maresca, gallerists and mentors (and former employers) who taught me to really look.

MY FAVORITE QUOTE ON PHOTOGRAPHY IS...
"I am always looking for the thing I've never seen," which Diana Vreeland apparently never said.

BIO
W.M. Hunt is a photography collector, curator, and consultant who lives and works in New York . Founding partner of the gallery Hasted Hunt, Hunt has been collecting, looking at, and talking about photography for over 40 years. He is the author of *The Unseen Eye: Photographs from the Unconscious* (Aperture). He teaches at the School of Visual Arts and ICP.

lectures, reviews portfolios, judges competitions, and serves on the boards of the W. Eugene Smith Memorial Fund and The Center for Photography at Woodstock.

ADRIANA TERESA LETORNEY

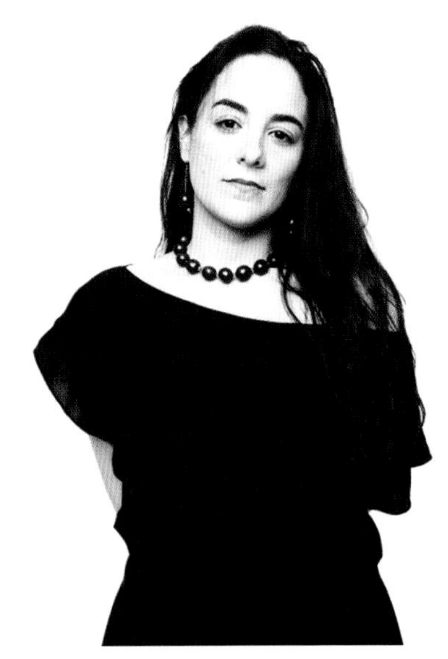

Photo: Robert Leslie/Splashlight for Luice Awards, 2010

WHAT I APPRECIATE MOST ABOUT PHOTOGRAPHY IS...
How it allows me to be exposed to different lives, places, realities, perspectives, approaches, and experiences from a very intimate and personal perspective. It is humbling. As a result I am continuously challenged, both professionally and personally, to such an extent that I have found it a responsibility to dedicate my everyday life to finding ways to support photographers throughout their process, especially students, alumni, and emerging photographers by producing platforms that can serve as resources for them to further their projects and careers.

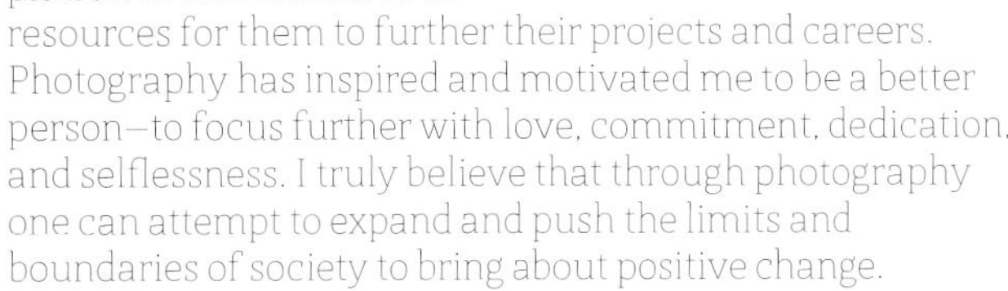

Photography has inspired and motivated me to be a better person—to focus further with love, commitment, dedication, and selflessness. I truly believe that through photography one can attempt to expand and push the limits and boundaries of society to bring about positive change.

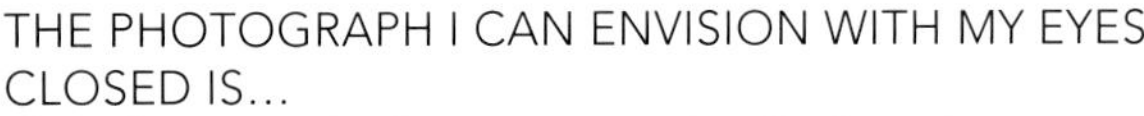

THE PHOTOGRAPH I CAN ENVISION WITH MY EYES CLOSED IS...
The photograph I have yet to take, find, and see.

THE ONE THING A PHOTOGRAPHIC ARTIST MUST ALWAYS DO IS...
Listen to his or her inner voice without ego, take a stand, let go, feel, and photograph. However, if I have to pick one: photograph—hope that acquiring the rest is part of your destiny.

THE BEST WAY TO VIEW A PHOTOGRAPH IS...
In person.

AN EXHIBITION I'LL NEVER FORGET IS...
Song of Myself exhibition featuring Sylvia Plachy, Alex Webb, Rebecca Norris Webb, Jeff Jacobson, Suzanne Opton, Charles Harbutt, Joan Liftin, Naho Kubota, and Lucille Fornasieri-Gold.

IF I HAD JUST ONE CHANCE TO GIFT A PHOTOBOOK, IT WOULD BE...
Travelog by Charles Harbutt.

MY MOST CHERISHED PHOTOGRAPH IS...
One I have not found yet.

THE BEST THING ABOUT WORKING IN PHOTOGRAPHY IS...
Believing in photography as a realm composed of an international community of individuals worldwide with a palpable voice.

MY FAVORITE QUOTE ON PHOTOGRAPHY IS...
"A picture can be an answer as well as a question, but if you cannot answer your question, try to question your question. There are clever questions and stupid answers, as well as stupid questions and clever answers. There can be questions without answers but no answers without questions. To be or not to be—that is a question. To see or not to see—that is an answer."—Ernst Haas.

THE FUTURE OF PHOTOGRAPHY IS...
Unfolding.

BIO
Adriana Teresa Letorney is the cofounder and creative director of FotoVisura Inc.—a publishing, production, design, and online media company. FotoVisura Inc. has produced numerous projects, most notably, *Visura* magazine, FotoVisura.com, The FotoVisura Grant, The FotoVisura Pavilion, and The Photo-Editing and Post Production Workshops at The Visura Lodge in Stowe, Vermont. Amongst her numerous tasks, Adriana is a photo editor, curator, and photographer. She has contributed as a guest writer at the New York Times Lens Blog and Huffington Post and *Le Journal de la Photographie*; she has also participated as a judge and/or reviewer for Photolucida, Center for Photography at Woodstock, International Photography Awards, The New York Photo Awards, Curate NYC, Prix Pictet, Flash Forward Festival, Magnum Foundation Emerging Photographer Award, PDN's 30, The Fence at Photoville, Google Photography Prize at Saatchi Gallery, and New York Portfolio Review, amongst others.

LESLEY A. MARTIN

Photo: Carlo Van de Roer

WHAT I APPRECIATE MOST ABOUT PHOTOGRAPHY IS...
Its elasticity.

THE MOST UNDERRATED THING ABOUT PHOTOGRAPHY IS...
Its mutability.

THE PHOTOGRAPH I CAN ENVISION WITH MY EYES CLOSED IS...
Harry Callahan's *Eleanor, Port Huron*, 1954.

THE PHOTOGRAPHER I'D WANT TO EAT/DRINK/SLEEP WITH IS...
A young Harry Callahan.

THE ONE THING A PHOTOGRAPHIC ARTIST MUST ALWAYS DO IS...
Keep your eyes and mind open.

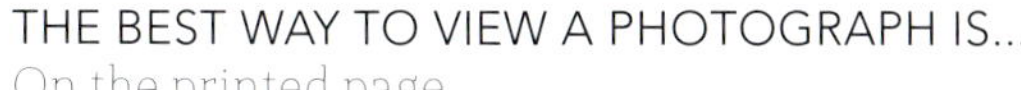

THE BEST WAY TO VIEW A PHOTOGRAPH IS...
On the printed page.

IF I HAD JUST ONE CHANCE TO GIFT A PHOTOBOOK, IT WOULD BE...
Nan Goldin's *The Ballad of Sexual Dependency*.

MY MOST CHERISHED PHOTOGRAPH IS...
A photograph of my mother with her mother and father, who I never met.

WHAT MAKES AN IMAGE EXTRAORDINARY IS...
An image that moves the viewer emotionally or prompts them to think about the world in a different way.

THE BEST THING ABOUT WORKING IN PHOTOGRAPHY IS...
Getting to work with all the creative forces that come together under the wide umbrella of the photographic.

THE BIGGEST INFLUENCE IN MY APPRECIATION OF PHOTOGRAPHY IS...
Books.

MY FAVORITE QUOTE ON PHOTOGRAPHY...
"You don't make a photograph just with a camera. You bring to the act of photography all the pictures you have seen, the books you have read, the music you have heard, the people you have loved." –Ansel Adams

BIO
Lesley A. Martin is publisher of the Aperture Foundation's book program and of the *PhotoBook Review*. Her writing on photography has been published in *Aperture*, *American Photo*, *FOAM* magazine, and *Lay Flat*, among other publications, and she has edited over 80 books of photography, including *Reflex: A Vik Muniz Primer* (Aperture, 2005); *Richard Misrach: On the Beach* (Aperture, 2007); *Rinko Kawauchi: Illuminance* (Aperture, 2011); and *Infra* by Richard Mosse (Aperture/Pulitzer Center on Crisis Reporting, 2012). In 2008, she was named one of the 15 most influential people in photobook publishing by *PDN* and was one of the inaugural curators for the New York Photo Festival along with Martin Parr, Tim Barber, and Kathy Ryan. In 2010, under her leadership, Aperture Foundation received recognition as Publisher of the Year by PHotoEspaña, Madrid. In 2011, she founded the *PhotoBook Review*, a biannual publication dedicated to the consideration of the photobook.

STEPHEN MAYES

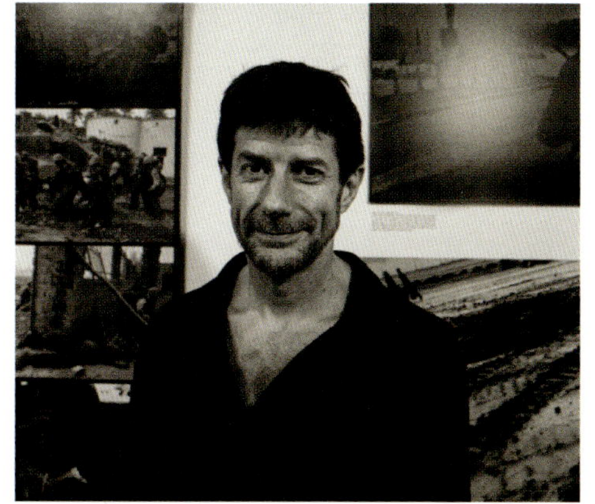

Photo: Jae Shin

WHAT I APPRECIATE MOST ABOUT PHOTOGRAPHY IS...
That it is a window into so many rich experiences, into the world because it is representation; a window into technology, business, art, the art market, and culture, particularly now. Photography is where culture meets technology.

THE MOST UNDERRATED THING ABOUT PHOTOGRAPHY IS...
The complexity. Like language, it appears as easy and natural, yet it is so rich in so many ways with layers, concepts, ideas, information, attitude. It is complex but it reads as completely simple.

THE PHOTOGRAPH I CAN ENVISION WITH MY EYES CLOSED IS...

Jindřich Marco made a photograph in the streets of Warsaw at the end of World War II showing two soldiers getting their portrait taken by a street photographer. I looked at this photo last month and it was not at all what I remembered.

THE PHOTOGRAPHER I'D WANT TO EAT/DRINK/SLEEP WITH IS...
I would like to eat and drink with Martin Parr.

THE ONE THING A PHOTOGRAPHIC ARTIST MUST ALWAYS DO IS...
Be aware.

THE BEST WAY TO VIEW A PHOTOGRAPH IS...
Very quickly, because of the assumed simplicity. If the picture can convey an idea very quickly it becomes a powerful tool.

AN EXHIBITION I'LL NEVER FORGET IS...
The Veronika Dykstra retrospective in Amsterdam. I walked around the gallery with Kathy Ryan and it was wonderful because she deconstructed the work.

MY MOST CHERISHED PHOTOGRAPH...
Is one of my own pictures of me with my former partner who is now dead.

WHAT MAKES AN IMAGE EXTRAORDINARY IS...
The visceral reaction. The emotional reaction.

THE BEST THING ABOUT WORKING IN PHOTOGRAPHY IS...
I find it to be a very privileged position to learn about the world.

THE BIGGEST INFLUENCE IN MY APPRECIATION OF PHOTOGRAPHY IS...
My experience working as a newspaper photographer in the UK where I saw how the photograph was used to tell lies.

MY FAVORITE QUOTE ON PHOTOGRAPHY IS...
"I photograph to see how things look photographed."
—Garry Winogrand

THE FUTURE OF PHOTOGRAPHY IS...
In many ways it is done. What we experience now is not photography because strictly speaking it was a photographic process. Digital photography is fundamentally different.

BIO
Stephen Mayes has worked at the top levels of photography for 25 years in the areas of journalism, art, commerce, and fashion. He was senior vice president at Getty Images developing and implementing content strategies for the world's largest content supplier and later worked as senior vice president at eyestorm.com representing high-end artists in the consumer market. Stephen worked with Art + Commerce as director of image archive representing top fashion and art photographers for commercial licensing. He was CEO of VII Photo Agency for five years, managing the careers of world-leading photojournalists. Stephen has chaired the jury of the World Press Photo competition and also served as secretary for nine years. He is currently working in New York and regularly writes and broadcasts on the ethics and realities of photographic practice in the new digital environment.

MARTIN PARR

WHAT I APPRECIATE MOST ABOUT PHOTOGRAPHY IS...
Democracy, ubiquity, and vernacular nature.

THE MOST UNDERRATED THING ABOUT PHOTOGRAPHY IS...
The unknown photographs and books.

THE PHOTOGRAPH I CAN ENVISION WITH MY EYES CLOSED IS...
Garry Winogrand, *Kid on a Slope*.
Tony Ray-Jones, *Kid on a Slope*.

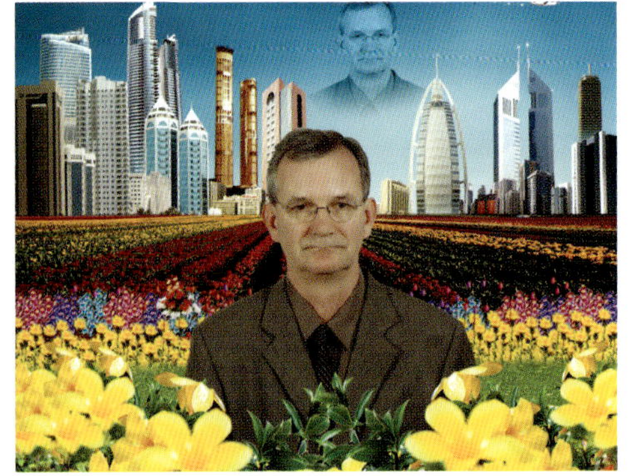

Photo: Martin Parr/Magnum Photos

THE PHOTOGRAPHER I'D WANT TO EAT/DRINK/SLEEP WITH IS...
Garry Winogrand and Tony Ray-Jones.

THE ONE THING A PHOTOGRAPHIC ARTIST MUST ALWAYS DO IS...
Reinvent themselves.

THE BEST WAY TO VIEW A PHOTOGRAPH IS...
In a book.

AN EXHIBITION I'LL NEVER FORGET IS...
Garry Winogrand at The San Francisco Museum of Modern Art.

MY MOST CHERISHED PHOTOGRAPH...
Is a family portrait.

THE BEST THING ABOUT WORKING IN PHOTOGRAPHY IS...
It can take you anywhere.

THE BIGGEST INFLUENCE IN MY APPRECIATION OF PHOTOGRAPHY IS...
My peer group.

THE FUTURE OF PHOTOGRAPHY IS...
Very exciting. The medium is getting bigger and bigger. The future looks bright.

BIO
Martin Parr was born in Epsom, Surrey, UK, in 1952. In 1994 he became a full member of Magnum Photos. In 2002 the Barbican Art Gallery and the National Media Museum initiated a large retrospective that toured Europe for the next five years. Parr was guest artistic director for Les Rencontres D'Arles (2004) and was guest curator at the New York Photo Festival, curating the *New Typologies* exhibition (2008). He also curated the Brighton Photo Biennial (2010). At PHotoEspaña, 2008, Martin Parr won the Baume et Mercier award in recognition of his professional career and contributions to contemporary photography. *Parrworld* opened at Haus de Kunst, Munich, in 2008 and toured for two years. Parr is the author of 58 books including *Life's a Beach*, recently published as a trade edition in fall 2013 with Aperture.

DAVID STRETTELL

WHAT I APPRECIATE MOST ABOUT PHOTOGRAPHY IS...
Its ability to inspire.

THE MOST UNDERRATED THING ABOUT PHOTOGRAPHY IS...
It's still in its infancy.

THE PHOTOGRAPH I CAN ENVISION WITH MY EYES CLOSED IS...
At this precise moment, a photograph by Jin Ohashi of a suicide in a playground... Having a dark morning.

THE PHOTOGRAPHER I'D WANT TO EAT/DRINK/SLEEP WITH IS...
I don't know about the rest, but I wish I could take pictures like Walker Evans.

THE ONE THING A PHOTOGRAPHIC ARTIST MUST ALWAYS DO IS...
Reveal.

THE BEST WAY TO VIEW A PHOTOGRAPH IS...
In silence.

AN EXHIBITION I'LL NEVER FORGET IS...
Robert Mapplethorpe's show at Institute of Contemporary Arts in London, 1983. It had been scandalized in the press and felt genuinely dangerous.

IF I HAD JUST ONE CHANCE TO GIFT A PHOTOBOOK, IT WOULD BE...
Women are Beautiful by Garry Winogrand. Everybody digs Winogrand don't they? And this one is irresistible.

MY MOST CHERISHED PHOTOGRAPH...
One that I possess...Danny Lyon's speckle-faced biker from the track meet.

THE BIGGEST INFLUENCE IN MY APPRECIATION OF PHOTOGRAPHY IS...
All the people I've worked for...Mario Testino, Philip Newton, Pamela Hanson, Magnum.

MY FAVORITE QUOTE ON PHOTOGRAPHY IS...
"Everybody can do it ... that's what makes it so difficult." Paraphrasing Bruce Gilden.

THE FUTURE OF PHOTOGRAPHY IS...
God knows! But bright.

BIO
Dashwood Books is owned and operated by David Strettell, formerly the cultural director of Magnum Photos where, for 12 years, he produced numerous books and exhibitions, advised on countless photographic projects, and developed extensive relationships in publishing and media, as well as with museums, galleries, and with photographers all over the world.

ALBERT WATSON

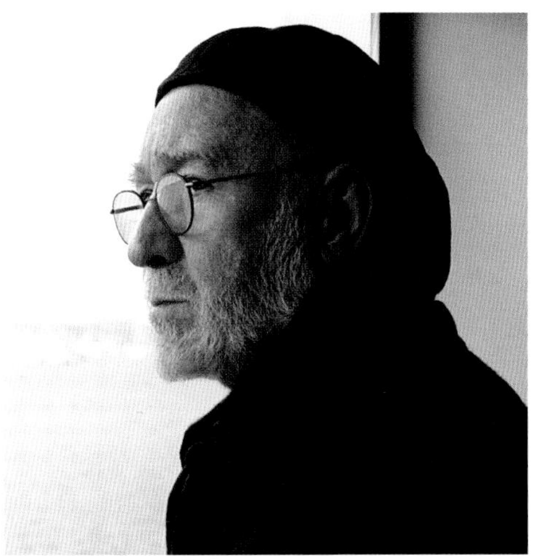
Photo courtesy of Albert Watson

WHAT I APPRECIATE MOST ABOUT PHOTOGRAPHY IS...
That I found it. Sometimes people are looking for things in their life and they don't find them so I consider it lucky that I found photography. It is mysterious and magical, but there is still a degree of control when you click the shutter that I find interesting.

THE MOST UNDERRATED THING ABOUT PHOTOGRAPHY IS...
It used to be underrated but I don't think it is anymore. Photography is more powerful than it ever has been. People can understand photography when they go to an exhibition, whereas art can be very intellectual. Photography communicates with the masses very well.

THE PHOTOGRAPH I CAN ENVISION WITH MY EYES CLOSED IS...
A photograph that I took which is a strong photo, known worldwide, of Steve Jobs, on his book cover.

THE PHOTOGRAPHER I'D WANT TO EAT/DRINK/SLEEP WITH IS...
Edward Weston.

THE ONE THING A PHOTOGRAPHIC ARTIST MUST ALWAYS DO IS...
Plan ahead, have an idea, a concept, and so on.

THE BEST WAY TO VIEW A PHOTOGRAPH IS...
There is not really a single answer. Sometimes it is the intimacy of discovering it in a book. Sometimes it is beautiful on a gallery wall. I do not think it is absolute.

AN EXHIBITION I'LL NEVER FORGET IS...
Albert Watson: Visions, Deichtorhallen, Hamburg, Germany, September 14 - March 3, 2013. It was a massive show. With forty thousand people in attendance.

IF I HAD JUST ONE CHANCE TO GIFT A PHOTOBOOK, IT WOULD BE...
The History of Japanese Photography, Vol 1, 1870–1945 and *Vol 2, 1945–1970*.

MY MOST CHERISHED PHOTOGRAPH...
The Alfred Hitchcock picture. It's not the best, by far, but it was such a confidence booster for me.

WHAT MAKES AN IMAGE EXTRAORDINARY IS...
Memorability, simplicity, and power. These things play together.

THE BEST THING ABOUT WORKING IN PHOTOGRAPHY IS...
Photographing people. I am always meeting people. What I love most, which is more unusual about me, is that I shoot still life, celebrities, fashion, landscape, and portraiture. There is a lot of diversity. This is very enjoyable.

THE BIGGEST INFLUENCE IN MY APPRECIATION OF PHOTOGRAPHY IS...
Art in general. I have a broad acceptance of art and spend time in museums and galleries. I also have a massive library and immersing myself is always very nice.

MY FAVORITE QUOTE ON PHOTOGRAPHY IS...
"There is a magic line that runs straight from the eye of the photographer as he takes a shot to the darkroom where he makes the print. Even if the print is flawed, it is made by his hand, and the decision to accept or reject it belongs to him." –Albert Watson

THE FUTURE OF PHOTOGRAPHY IS...
Limitless. It is absolutely here to stay and won't be superceded by video. One moment can say a lot. Photography has endless possibilities.

BIO
Albert Watson has made his mark as one of the world's most successful fashion and commercial photographers during the last 40 years, while creating his own art along the way. His striking images have appeared on more than 100 covers of *Vogue* and been featured in countless other publications, from *Rolling Stone* to *Time*, many of the photographs iconic portraits of celebrities. Watson has also created the photography for hundreds of successful ad campaigns, for companies such as Prada, Revlon, and Chanel. All the while, Watson has spent much of his time working on personal projects, creating stunning images from his travels and interests, from Marrakech to Las Vegas. His photographs have been featured in gallery and museum shows worldwide, and the photo industry bible, *Photo District News*, named Watson one of the 20 most influential photographers of all time. The Scottish-born photographer's breakthrough came in 1973, with a shot he still considers the most important of his career: Alfred Hitchcock holding a plucked goose.

RICHARD B. WOODWARD

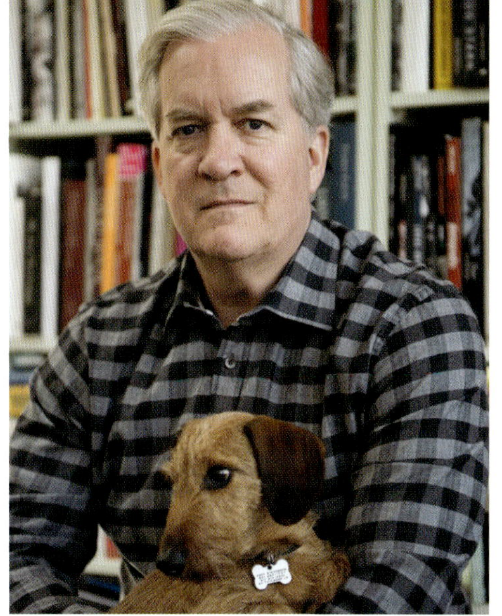

Photo: Jessica Todd Harper

WHAT I APPRECIATE MOST ABOUT PHOTOGRAPHY IS...

Its duality. It can be a telling record of a place and time, evidence that can be used in a physics experiment or a courtroom, with light acting as the means and the substance of its own creation. At the same time a photograph is often partial, deceptive, a fragment of a fragment of reality. I find its ambiguous believability, how it can bring us closer to an understanding of ourselves and the world and yet be something distinct from them, always moving away from us, endlessly fascinating to muse and write about.

THE MOST UNDERRATED THING ABOUT PHOTOGRAPHY IS...

How quickly after its invention people understood the countless applications it might have, transforming everything from warfare to insurance.

THE PHOTOGRAPH I CAN ENVISION WITH MY EYES CLOSED IS...

One of Adam Fuss's ghostly, liminal children. I own one and it's the closet experience I know of to perceiving something faintly on the inside of one's eyelids.

THE PHOTOGRAPHER I'D WANT TO EAT/DRINK/SLEEP WITH IS...

Brassaï/Robert Capa/Halle Berry.

THE ONE THING A PHOTOGRAPHIC ARTIST MUST ALWAYS DO IS...

Edit work ruthlessly.

AN EXHIBITION I'LL NEVER FORGET IS...

Video Skulptur, which I saw in the early fall of 1989 at the Kongresshalle in Berlin, a few months before the Wall came down. Gary Hill's *Crux*, Les Levine's *Chain of Command* and Bruce Nauman's *Live/Taped Video Corridor* left a deep impression on me. I hadn't paid much attention to video in the 1970s. That survey was an immersion course that opened my mind and eyes.

MY MOST CHERISHED PHOTOGRAPH...

Is any old family photograph. I have some wonderful material from my great-grandparents and grandparents who were missionaries in India. But anything from my parents' lives or from my youth is precious, valuable only to me and my sisters, whereas my photographs by artists exist in multiple prints and carry a price tag determined by the marketplace.

WHAT MAKES AN IMAGE EXTRAORDINARY IS...

Its ability to change your relationship to everyday life. Lee Friedlander has permanently altered how I see chain-link fences, the backsides of trucks, car interiors, flowers in vases, and deserts.

THE BEST THING ABOUT WORKING IN PHOTOGRAPHY...

Are the photographers. As a group, they are like jazz musicians: their skills have always been undervalued by the culture at large. As a result, they have a less privileged view of themselves than many who labor to survive in the arts.

THE BIGGEST INFLUENCE IN MY APPRECIATION OF PHOTOGRAPHY...

Was John Szarkowski. Not a week goes by when I don't think about something he wrote or said. Not only was he photography's most graceful critic, he was the wisest.

MY FAVORITE QUOTE ON PHOTOGRAPHY IS...

"The world now contains more photographs than bricks and they are, astonishingly, all different."—Szarkowski

BIO

Richard B. Woodward is an arts critic in New York whose journalism has appeared in *The Atlantic Monthly, The New Yorker, Vanity Fair, Film Comment, The American Scholar, Lingua Franca, Vogue, Bookforum, The Village Voice, The New Criterion*, and many other publications. He has written about photography for more than 25 years and published essays in books and catalogs on Ansel Adams, Robert Adams, Renate Aller, Tina Barney, Corinne Botz, Kevin Bubriski, William Christenberry, Lois Conner, Mike Disfarmer, William Eggleston, Lee Friedlander, Charles Hoff, Justin Kimball, An-My Lê, David Levinthal, Helen Levitt, Ray Metzker, Abelardo Morrell, Irving Penn, Thomas Roma, and Mark Steinmetz. A former editor-at-large for *DoubleTake* magazine, he has taught at Columbia University's Graduate School of the Arts and NYU's Graduate School of Journalism. His documentary films on the curator/photographer John Szarkowski and the poet Billy Collins have been screened at festivals around the US. A regular contributor to the *Wall St. Journal* and *The New York Times*, he is writing a book on photography and violence for Yale University Press.

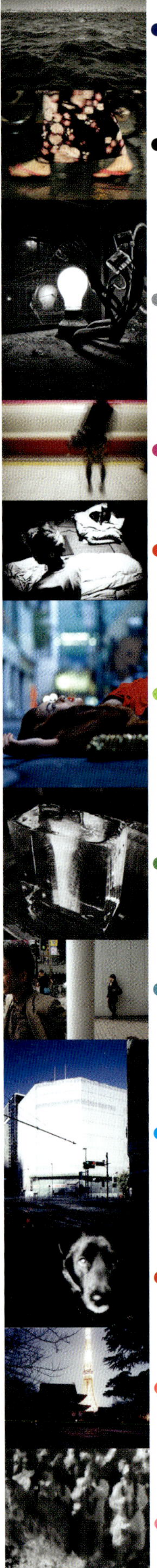

TOKYO-GA

BY NOAKO OHTA AND CORINNE TAPIA

TOKYO-GA created an extensive photographic project by collecting Tokyo-scapes by 100 photographers. TOKYO-GA originated as an internal response to the devastating natural disasters that occurred in Japan in 2011. These events brought an awareness of the global connectedness of not just Japanese people, but of all humanity. Launched in 2011, the TOKYO-GA project aims to assemble a portfolio of photographs of Tokyo by 100 Japanese and international photographers as a sign of commitment to Japan and its future. It is also a presentation of new contemporary photography from Tokyo to the international stage.

The selection, hosted for the first time by New York Photo Festival in 2012, and gathering 56 images from 26 photographers, offered an overview of the architecture of the Japanese capital, its street photography, its contemporary styles, and its mentality, revealing the complexity and the contrast between tradition and modernity in the country. In an act of global solidarity, TOKYO-GA presented for the first time a selection of contemporary Tokyo photographs by Japanese, Asian, American, and European photographers.

Mrs. Naoko Ohta is the commissioner of TOKYO-GA, founder and curator of the project. Mrs. Corinne Tapia, member of the TOKYO-GA commissioner board in Japan and director of Sous Les Etoiles Gallery, edited the work exhibited for the New York Photo Festival.

The exhibition committee of TOKYO-GA is working to bring the exhibition to Europe next year, more precisely, Berlin in spring, 2014 and Paris in the fall.

HTTP://WWW.TOKYO-GA.ORG

- César Ordóñez
- Daido Moriyama
- Hajime Kimura
- Hiroshi Yoda
- Ilse Leenders
- Kaoru Izima
- Manabu Someya
- Munemiysu Komatsu
- Ooki Jingu
- Renato D'Agostin
- Satoshi Asakawa
- Sébastien Lebegue
- Tatsuya Hirabayashi
- Tomoki Hirokawa

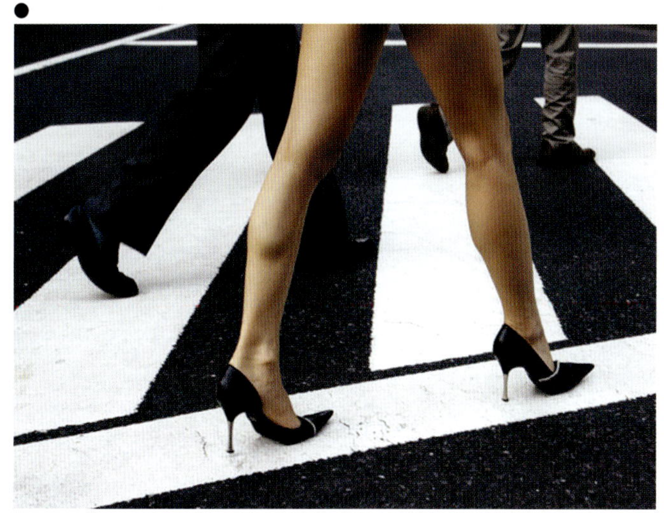

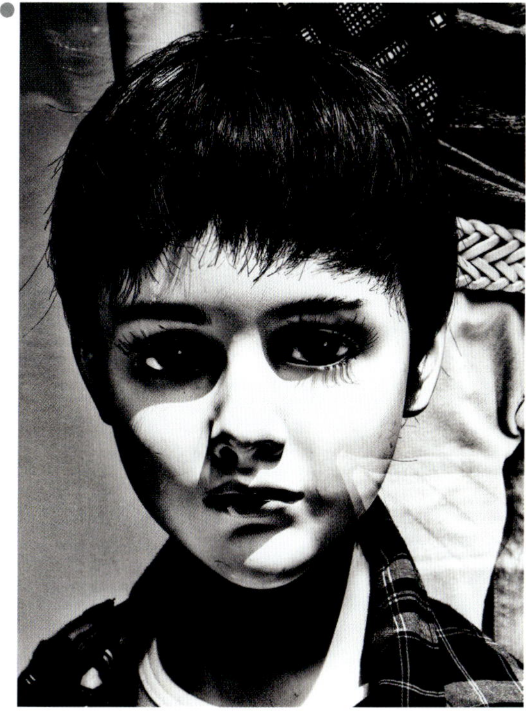

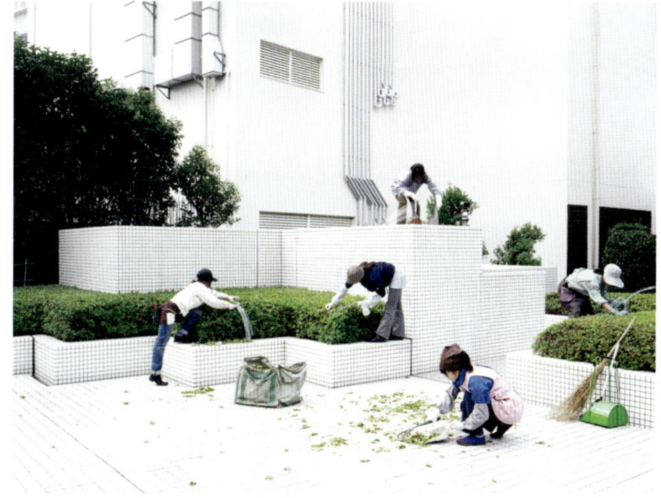

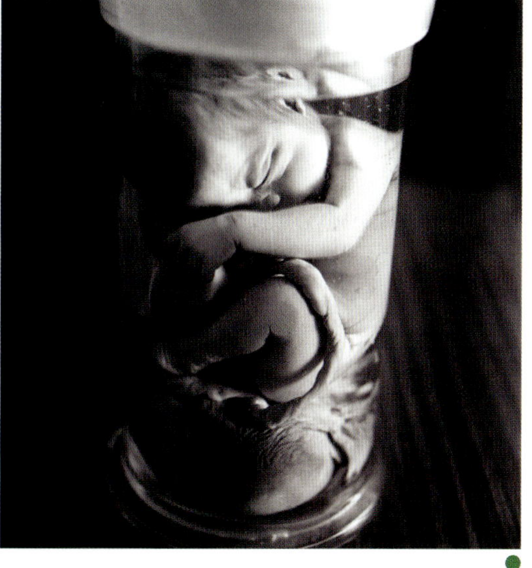

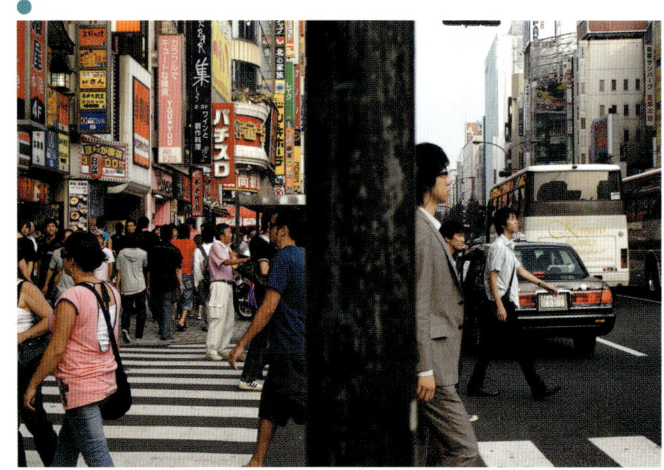

4F
カラフルでキュートな雑貨
集
パチスロ
北の家族
レイク

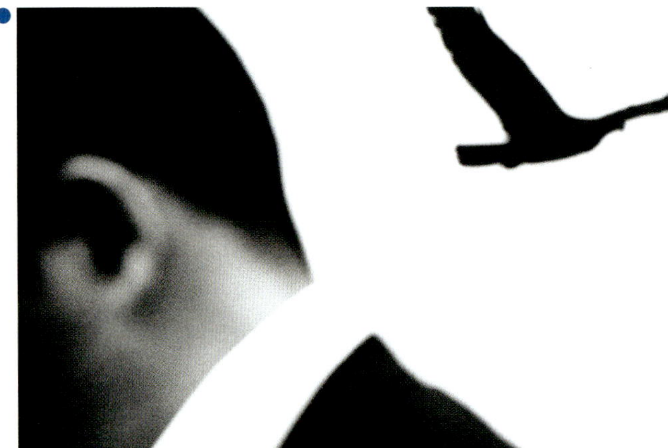

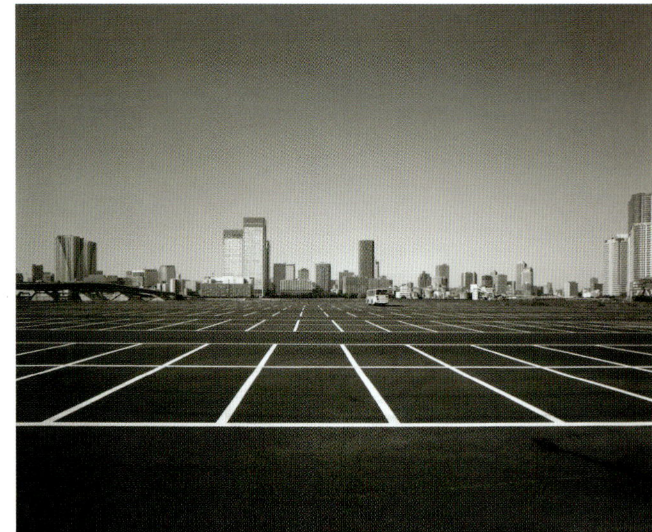

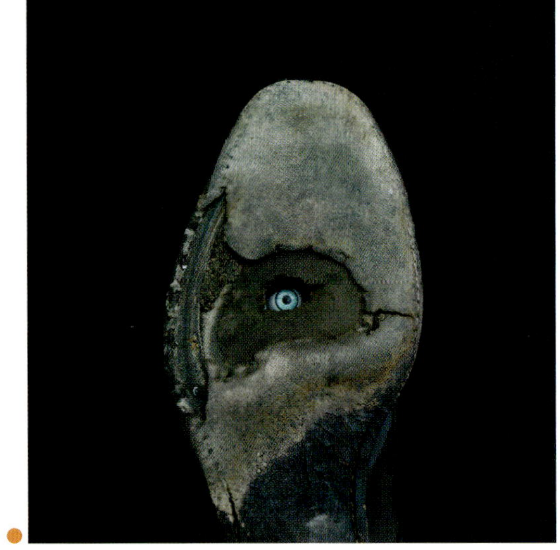

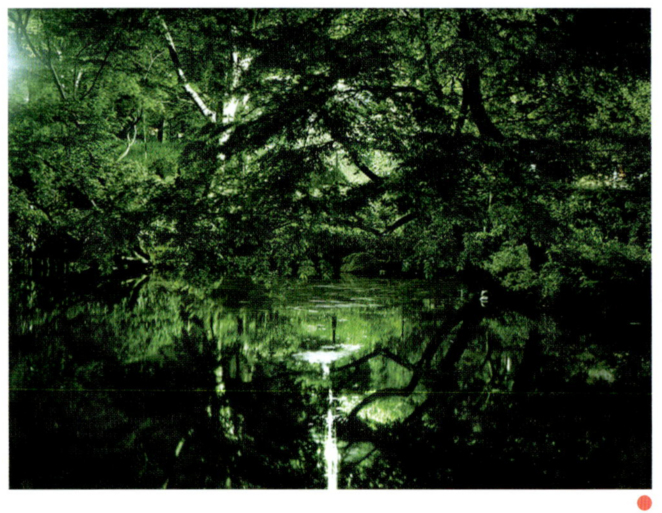

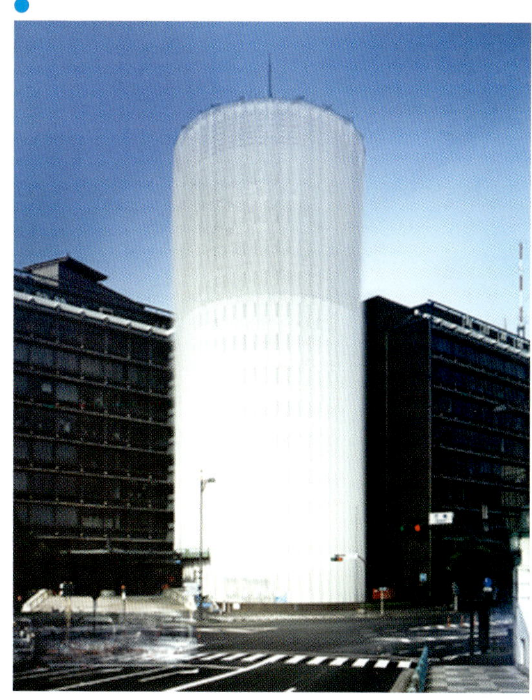

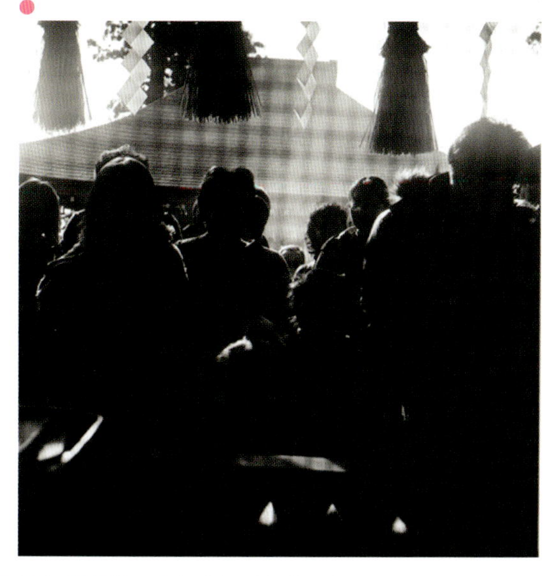

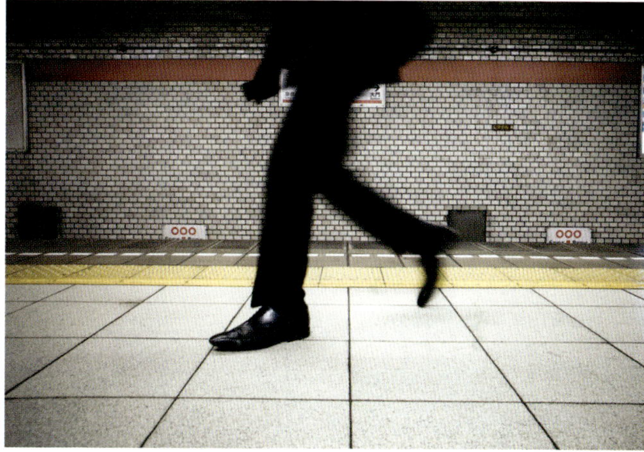

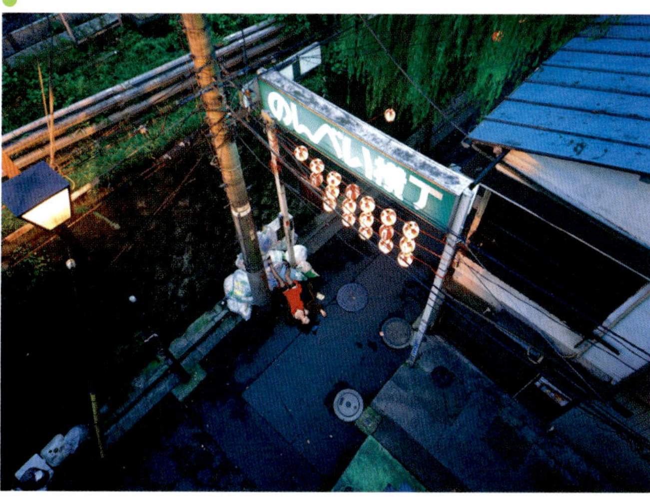
のんべい横丁

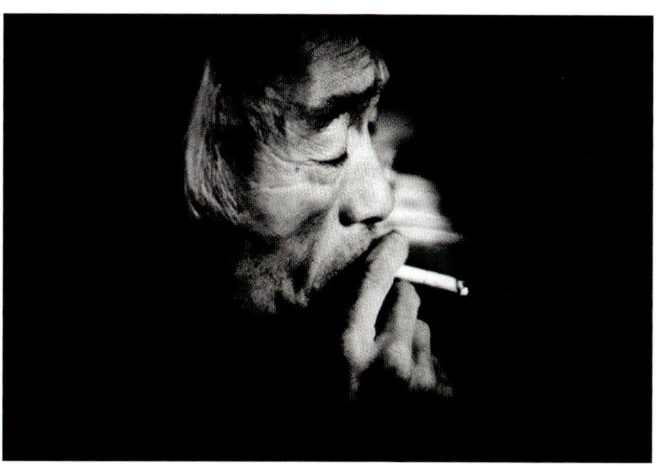

NYPH Journal

Published in the United States by powerHouse Books, a division of powerHouse Cultural Entertainment, Inc.

37 Main Street, Brooklyn, NY 11201-1021
telephone 212.604.9074, fax 212.366.5247
e-mail: info@powerHouseBooks.com
website: www.powerHouseBooks.com

ISBN 978-1-57687-664-0

Printing and binding by Midas Printing, Inc., China

NYPH CEO, Cofounder: Daniel Power
Editor: Jacob Pastrovich
Designer: Krzysztof Poluchowicz
Editorial Assistant: Madison Morales
Cover photo from the series *Nowhere in Taiwan* by I-Hsuen Chen

10 9 8 7 6 5 4 3 2 1

Printed and bound in China